Nutshell Series
Hornbook Series
and
Black Letter Series
of
WEST PUBLISHING COMPANY

P.O. Box 64526
St. Paul, Minnesota 55164–0526

Accounting

FARIS' ACCOUNTING AND LAW IN A NUTSHELL, 377 pages, 1984. Softcover. (Text)

Administrative Law

AMAN AND MAYTON'S HORNBOOK ON ADMINISTRATIVE LAW, Approximately 750 pages, 1992. (Text)

GELLHORN AND LEVIN'S ADMINISTRATIVE LAW AND PROCESS IN A NUTSHELL, Third Edition, 479 pages, 1990. Softcover. (Text)

Admiralty

MARAIST'S ADMIRALTY IN A NUTSHELL, Second Edition, 379 pages, 1988. Softcover. (Text)

SCHOENBAUM'S HORNBOOK ON ADMIRALTY AND MARITIME LAW, Student Edition, 692 pages, 1987 with 1992 pocket part. (Text)

Agency—Partnership

REUSCHLEIN AND GREGORY'S HORNBOOK ON THE LAW OF AGENCY AND PARTNERSHIP, Second Edition, 683 pages, 1990. (Text)

STEFFEN'S AGENCY-PARTNERSHIP IN A NUTSHELL, 364 pages, 1977. Softcover. (Text)

NOLAN–HALEY'S ALTERNATIVE DISPUTE RESOLUTION IN A NUTSHELL, Approximately 300 pages, 1992. Softcover. (Text)

RISKIN'S DISPUTE RESOLUTION FOR LAWYERS VIDEO TAPES, 1992. (Available for purchase by schools and libraries.)

List current as of July, 1992

American Indian Law

CANBY'S AMERICAN INDIAN LAW IN A NUTSHELL, Second Edition, 336 pages, 1988. Softcover. (Text)

Antitrust—see also Regulated Industries, Trade Regulation

GELLHORN'S ANTITRUST LAW AND ECONOMICS IN A NUTSHELL, Third Edition, 472 pages, 1986. Softcover. (Text)

HOVENKAMP'S BLACK LETTER ON ANTITRUST, 323 pages, 1986. Softcover. (Review)

HOVENKAMP'S HORNBOOK ON ECONOMICS AND FEDERAL ANTITRUST LAW, Student Edition, 414 pages, 1985. (Text)

SULLIVAN'S HORNBOOK OF THE LAW OF ANTITRUST, 886 pages, 1977. (Text)

Appellate Advocacy—see Trial and Appellate Advocacy

Art Law

DUBOFF'S ART LAW IN A NUTSHELL, 335 pages, 1984. Softcover. (Text)

Banking Law

LOVETT'S BANKING AND FINANCIAL INSTITUTIONS LAW IN A NUTSHELL, Third Edition, approximately 500 pages, 1992. Softcover. (Text)

Civil Procedure—see also Federal Jurisdiction and Procedure

CLERMONT'S BLACK LETTER ON CIVIL PROCEDURE, Second Edition, 332 pages, 1988. Softcover. (Review)

FRIEDENTHAL, KANE AND MILLER'S HORNBOOK ON CIVIL PROCEDURE, 876 pages, 1985. (Text)

KANE'S CIVIL PROCEDURE IN A NUTSHELL, Third Edition, 303 pages, 1991. Softcover. (Text)

KOFFLER AND REPPY'S HORNBOOK ON COMMON LAW PLEADING, 663 pages, 1969. (Text)

SIEGEL'S HORNBOOK ON NEW YORK PRACTICE, Second Edition, Student Edition, 1068 pages, 1991. Softcover. (Text) 1992 Supplemental Pamphlet.

Commercial Law

BAILEY AND HAGEDORN'S SECURED TRANSACTIONS IN A NUTSHELL, Third Edition, 390 pages, 1988. Softcover. (Text)

HENSON'S HORNBOOK ON SECURED TRANSACTIONS UNDER THE U.C.C., Second Edition, 504 pages, 1979, with 1979 pocket part. (Text)

MEYER AND SPEIDEL'S BLACK LETTER ON SALES AND LEASES OF GOODS, Approximately 400 pages, October 1992 Pub.

Commercial Law—Continued

Softcover. (Review)

NICKLES' BLACK LETTER ON COMMERCIAL PAPER, 450 pages, 1988. Softcover. (Review)

STOCKTON AND MILLER'S SALES AND LEASES OF GOODS IN A NUTSHELL, Third Edition, approximately 425 pages, 1992. Softcover. (Text)

STONE'S UNIFORM COMMERCIAL CODE IN A NUTSHELL, Third Edition, 580 pages, 1989. Softcover. (Text)

WEBER AND SPEIDEL'S COMMERCIAL PAPER IN A NUTSHELL, Third Edition, 404 pages, 1982. Softcover. (Text)

WHITE AND SUMMERS' HORNBOOK ON THE UNIFORM COMMERCIAL CODE, Third Edition, Student Edition, 1386 pages, 1988. (Text)

Community Property

MENNELL AND BOYKOFF'S COMMUNITY PROPERTY IN A NUTSHELL, Second Edition, 432 pages, 1988. Softcover. (Text)

Comparative Law

FOLSOM, MINAN AND OTTO'S LAW AND POLITICS IN THE PEOPLE'S REPUBLIC OF CHINA IN A NUTSHELL, Approximately 450 pages, 1992. Softcover. (Text)

GLENDON, GORDON AND OSAKWE'S COMPARATIVE LEGAL TRADITIONS IN A NUTSHELL. 402 pages, 1982. Softcover. (Text)

Conflict of Laws

HAY'S BLACK LETTER ON CONFLICT OF LAWS, 330 pages, 1989. Softcover. (Review)

SCOLES AND HAY'S HORNBOOK ON CONFLICT OF LAWS, Student Edition, 1160 pages, 1992. (Text)

SIEGEL'S CONFLICTS IN A NUTSHELL, 470 pages, 1982. Softcover. (Text)

Constitutional Law—Civil Rights

BARRON AND DIENES' BLACK LETTER ON CONSTITUTIONAL LAW, Third Edition, 440 pages, 1991. Softcover. (Review)

BARRON AND DIENES' CONSTITUTIONAL LAW IN A NUTSHELL, Second Edition, 483 pages, 1991. Softcover. (Text)

ENGDAHL'S CONSTITUTIONAL FEDERALISM IN A NUTSHELL, Second Edition, 411 pages, 1987. Softcover. (Text)

MARKS AND COOPER'S STATE CONSTITUTIONAL LAW IN A NUTSHELL, 329 pages, 1988. Softcover. (Text)

NOWAK AND ROTUNDA'S HORNBOOK ON CONSTITUTIONAL LAW, Fourth Edition, 1357 pages,

Constitutional Law—Civil Rights—Continued

1991. (Text)

VIEIRA'S CONSTITUTIONAL CIVIL RIGHTS IN A NUTSHELL, Second Edition, 322 pages, 1990. Softcover. (Text)

WILLIAMS' CONSTITUTIONAL ANALYSIS IN A NUTSHELL, 388 pages, 1979. Softcover. (Text)

Consumer Law—see also Commercial Law

EPSTEIN AND NICKLES' CONSUMER LAW IN A NUTSHELL, Second Edition, 418 pages, 1981. Softcover. (Text)

Contracts

CALAMARI AND PERILLO'S BLACK LETTER ON CONTRACTS, Second Edition, 462 pages, 1990. Softcover. (Review)

CALAMARI AND PERILLO'S HORNBOOK ON CONTRACTS, Third Edition, 1049 pages, 1987. (Text)

CORBIN'S TEXT ON CONTRACTS, One Volume Student Edition, 1224 pages, 1952. (Text)

FRIEDMAN'S CONTRACT REMEDIES IN A NUTSHELL, 323 pages, 1981. Softcover. (Text)

KEYES' GOVERNMENT CONTRACTS IN A NUTSHELL, Second Edition, 557 pages, 1990. Softcover. (Text)

SCHABER AND ROHWER'S CONTRACTS IN A NUTSHELL, Third Edition, 457 pages, 1990. Softcover. (Text)

Copyright—see Patent and Copyright Law

Corporations

HAMILTON'S BLACK LETTER ON CORPORATIONS, Third Edition, approximately 550 pages, 1992. Softcover. (Review)

HAMILTON'S THE LAW OF CORPORATIONS IN A NUTSHELL, Third Edition, 518 pages, 1991. Softcover. (Text)

HENN AND ALEXANDER'S HORNBOOK ON LAWS OF CORPORATIONS, Third Edition, Student Edition, 1371 pages, 1983, with 1986 pocket part. (Text)

Corrections

KRANTZ' THE LAW OF CORRECTIONS AND PRISONERS' RIGHTS IN A NUTSHELL, Third Edition, 407 pages, 1988. Softcover. (Text)

Creditors' Rights

EPSTEIN'S DEBTOR-CREDITOR LAW IN A NUTSHELL, Fourth Edition, 401 pages, 1991. Softcover. (Text)

EPSTEIN, NICKLES AND WHITE'S HORNBOOK ON BANKRUPTCY, Approximately 1000 pages, November, 1992 Pub. (Text)

Creditors' Rights—Continued

NICKLES AND EPSTEIN'S BLACK LETTER ON CREDITORS' RIGHTS AND BANKRUPTCY, 576 pages, 1989. (Review)

Criminal Law and Criminal Procedure—see also Corrections, Juvenile Justice

ISRAEL AND LAFAVE'S CRIMINAL PROCEDURE—CONSTITUTIONAL LIMITATIONS IN A NUTSHELL, Fourth Edition, 461 pages, 1988. Softcover. (Text)

LAFAVE AND ISRAEL'S HORNBOOK ON CRIMINAL PROCEDURE, Second Edition, 1309 pages, 1992. (Text)

LAFAVE AND SCOTT'S HORNBOOK ON CRIMINAL LAW, Second Edition, 918 pages, 1986. (Text)

LOEWY'S CRIMINAL LAW IN A NUTSHELL, Second Edition, 321 pages, 1987. Softcover. (Text)

LOW'S BLACK LETTER ON CRIMINAL LAW, Revised First Edition, 443 pages, 1990. Softcover. (Review)

SUBIN, MIRSKY AND WEINSTEIN'S THE CRIMINAL PROCESS: PROSECUTION AND DEFENSE FUNCTIONS, Approximately 450 pages, October, 1992 Pub. Softcover. Teacher's Manual available. (Text)

Domestic Relations

CLARK'S HORNBOOK ON DOMESTIC RELATIONS, Second Edition, Student Edition, 1050 pages, 1988. (Text)

KRAUSE'S BLACK LETTER ON FAMILY LAW, 314 pages, 1988. Softcover. (Review)

KRAUSE'S FAMILY LAW IN A NUTSHELL, Second Edition, 444 pages, 1986. Softcover. (Text)

MALLOY'S LAW AND ECONOMICS: A COMPARATIVE APPROACH TO THEORY AND PRACTICE, 166 pages, 1990. Softcover. (Text)

Education Law

ALEXANDER AND ALEXANDER'S THE LAW OF SCHOOLS, STUDENTS AND TEACHERS IN A NUTSHELL, 409 pages, 1984. Softcover. (Text)

Employment Discrimination—see also Gender Discrimination

PLAYER'S FEDERAL LAW OF EMPLOYMENT DISCRIMINATION IN A NUTSHELL, Third Edition, 338 pages, 1992. Softcover. (Text)

PLAYER'S HORNBOOK ON EMPLOYMENT DISCRIMINATION LAW, Student Edition, 708 pages, 1988. (Text)

Energy and Natural Resources Law—see also Oil and Gas

LAITOS AND TOMAIN'S ENERGY AND NATURAL RESOURCES LAW IN A NUTSHELL, 554 pages, 1992. Softcover. (Text)

Environmental Law—see also Energy and Natural Resources Law; Sea, Law of

FINDLEY AND FARBER'S ENVIRONMENTAL LAW IN A NUTSHELL, Third Edition, 355 pages, 1992. Softcover. (Text)

RODGERS' HORNBOOK ON ENVIRONMENTAL LAW, 956 pages, 1977, with 1984 pocket part. (Text)

Equity—see Remedies

Estate Planning—see also Trusts and Estates; Taxation—Estate and Gift

LYNN'S INTRODUCTION TO ESTATE PLANNING IN A NUTSHELL, Fourth Edition, approximately 350 pages, 1992. Softcover. (Text)

Evidence

BROUN AND BLAKEY'S BLACK LETTER ON EVIDENCE, 269 pages, 1984. Softcover. (Review)

GRAHAM'S FEDERAL RULES OF EVIDENCE IN A NUTSHELL, Third Edition, 486 pages, 1992. Softcover. (Text)

LILLY'S AN INTRODUCTION TO THE LAW OF EVIDENCE, Second Edition, 585 pages, 1987. (Text)

MCCORMICK'S HORNBOOK ON EVIDENCE, Fourth Edition, Student Edition, approximately 1200 pages, 1992. (Text)

ROTHSTEIN'S EVIDENCE IN A NUTSHELL: STATE AND FEDERAL RULES, Second Edition, 514 pages, 1981. Softcover. (Text)

Federal Jurisdiction and Procedure

CURRIE'S FEDERAL JURISDICTION IN A NUTSHELL, Third Edition, 242 pages, 1990. Softcover. (Text)

REDISH'S BLACK LETTER ON FEDERAL JURISDICTION, Second Edition, 234 pages, 1991. Softcover. (Review)

WRIGHT'S HORNBOOK ON FEDERAL COURTS, Fourth Edition, Student Edition, 870 pages, 1983. (Text)

First Amendment

GARVEY AND SCHAUER'S THE FIRST AMENDMENT: A READER, Approximately 530 pages, 1992. Softcover. (Reader)

Future Interests—see Trusts and Estates

Gender Discrimination—see also Employment Discrimination

THOMAS' SEX DISCRIMINATION IN A NUTSHELL, Second Edition, 395 pages, 1991. Softcover. (Text)

Health Law—see Medicine, Law and

Human Rights—see International Law

Immigration Law

WEISSBRODT'S IMMIGRATION LAW AND PROCEDURE IN A NUTSHELL, Third Edition, approximately 350 pages, 1992. Softcover. (Text)

Indian Law—see American Indian Law

Insurance Law

DOBBYN'S INSURANCE LAW IN A NUTSHELL, Second Edition, 316 pages, 1989. Softcover. (Text)

KEETON AND WIDISS' INSURANCE LAW, Student Edition, 1359 pages, 1988. (Text)

International Law—see also Sea, Law of

BUERGENTHAL'S INTERNATIONAL HUMAN RIGHTS IN A NUTSHELL, 283 pages, 1988. Softcover. (Text)

BUERGENTHAL AND MAIER'S PUBLIC INTERNATIONAL LAW IN A NUTSHELL, Second Edition, 275 pages, 1990. Softcover. (Text)

FOLSOM'S EUROPEAN COMMUNITY LAW IN A NUTSHELL, 423 pages, 1992. Softcover. (Text)

FOLSOM, GORDON AND SPANOGLE'S INTERNATIONAL BUSINESS TRANSACTIONS IN A NUTSHELL, Fourth Edition, approximately 540 pages, 1992. Softcover. (Text)

Interviewing and Counseling

SHAFFER AND ELKINS' LEGAL INTERVIEWING AND COUNSELING IN A NUTSHELL, Second Edition, 487 pages, 1987. Softcover. (Text)

Introduction to Law—see Legal Method and Legal System

Introduction to Law Study

HEGLAND'S INTRODUCTION TO THE STUDY AND PRACTICE OF LAW IN A NUTSHELL, 418 pages, 1983. Softcover. (Text)

KINYON'S INTRODUCTION TO LAW STUDY AND LAW EXAMINATIONS IN A NUTSHELL, 389 pages, 1971. Softcover. (Text)

Judicial Process—see Legal Method and Legal System

Juvenile Justice

FOX'S JUVENILE COURTS IN A NUTSHELL, Third Edition, 291

Juvenile Justice—Continued

pages, 1984. Softcover. (Text)

Labor and Employment Law—see also Employment Discrimination, Workers' Compensation

LESLIE'S LABOR LAW IN A NUTSHELL, Third Edition, 388 pages, 1992. Softcover. (Text)

NOLAN'S LABOR ARBITRATION LAW AND PRACTICE IN A NUTSHELL, 358 pages, 1979. Softcover. (Text)

Land Finance—Property Security—see Real Estate Transactions

Land Use

HAGMAN AND JUERGENSMEYER'S HORNBOOK ON URBAN PLANNING AND LAND DEVELOPMENT CONTROL LAW, Second Edition, Student Edition, 680 pages, 1986. (Text)

WRIGHT AND WRIGHT'S LAND USE IN A NUTSHELL, Second Edition, 356 pages, 1985. Softcover. (Text)

Legal Method and Legal System—see also Legal Research, Legal Writing

KEMPIN'S HISTORICAL INTRODUCTION TO ANGLO-AMERICAN LAW IN A NUTSHELL, Third Edition, 323 pages, 1990. Softcover. (Text)

REYNOLDS' JUDICIAL PROCESS IN A NUTSHELL, Second Edition, 308 pages, 1991. Softcover. (Text)

Legal Research

COHEN AND OLSON'S LEGAL RESEARCH IN A NUTSHELL, Fifth Edition, approximately 500 pages, 1992. Softcover. (Text)

COHEN, BERRING AND OLSON'S HOW TO FIND THE LAW, Ninth Edition, 716 pages, 1989. (Text)

Legal Writing and Drafting

MELLINKOFF'S DICTIONARY OF AMERICAN LEGAL USAGE,Approximately 700 pages, 1992. Softcover. (Text)

SQUIRES AND ROMBAUER'S LEGAL WRITING IN A NUTSHELL, 294 pages, 1982. Softcover. (Text)

Legislation—see also Legal Writing and Drafting

DAVIES' LEGISLATIVE LAW AND PROCESS IN A NUTSHELL, Second Edition, 346 pages, 1986. Softcover. (Text)

Local Government

MCCARTHY'S LOCAL GOVERNMENT LAW IN A NUTSHELL, Third Edition, 435 pages, 1990. Softcover. (Text)

REYNOLDS' HORNBOOK ON LOCAL GOVERNMENT LAW, 860 pages,

Local Government—Continued

1982, with 1990 pocket part. (Text)

Mass Communication Law

ZUCKMAN, GAYNES, CARTER AND DEE'S MASS COMMUNICATIONS LAW IN A NUTSHELL, Third Edition, 538 pages, 1988. Softcover. (Text)

Medicine, Law and

HALL AND ELLMAN'S HEALTH CARE LAW AND ETHICS IN A NUTSHELL, 401 pages, 1990. Softcover (Text)

JARVIS, CLOSEN, HERMANN AND LEONARD'S AIDS LAW IN A NUTSHELL, 349 pages, 1991. Softcover. (Text)

KING'S THE LAW OF MEDICAL MALPRACTICE IN A NUTSHELL, Second Edition, 342 pages, 1986. Softcover. (Text)

Military Law

SHANOR AND TERRELL'S MILITARY LAW IN A NUTSHELL, 378 pages, 1980. Softcover. (Text)

Mining Law—see Energy and Natural Resources Law

Mortgages—see Real Estate Transactions

Natural Resources Law—see Energy and Natural Resources Law, Environmental Law

TEPLY'S LEGAL NEGOTIATION IN A NUTSHELL, 282 pages, 1992. Softcover. (Text)

Office Practice—see also Computers and Law, Interviewing and Counseling, Negotiation

HEGLAND'S TRIAL AND PRACTICE SKILLS IN A NUTSHELL, 346 pages, 1978. Softcover (Text)

Oil and Gas—see also Energy and Natural Resources Law

HEMINGWAY'S HORNBOOK ON THE LAW OF OIL AND GAS, Third Edition, Student Edition, 711 pages, 1992. (Text)

LOWE'S OIL AND GAS LAW IN A NUTSHELL, Second Edition, 465 pages, 1988. Softcover. (Text)

Partnership—see Agency—Partnership

Patent and Copyright Law

MILLER AND DAVIS' INTELLECTUAL PROPERTY—PATENTS, TRADEMARKS AND COPYRIGHT IN A NUTSHELL, Second Edition, 437 pages, 1990. Softcover. (Text)

Products Liability

PHILLIPS' PRODUCTS LIABILITY IN A NUTSHELL, Third Edition, 307

Products Liability—Continued

pages, 1988. Softcover. (Text)

Professional Responsibility

ARONSON AND WECKSTEIN'S PROFESSIONAL RESPONSIBILITY IN A NUTSHELL, Second Edition, 514 pages, 1991. Softcover. (Text)

LESNICK'S BEING A LAWYER: INDIVIDUAL CHOICE AND RESPONSIBILITY IN THE PRACTICE OF LAW, Approximately 400 pages, 1992. Softcover. (Coursebook)

ROTUNDA'S BLACK LETTER ON PROFESSIONAL RESPONSIBILITY, Third Edition, 492 pages, 1992. Softcover. (Review)

WOLFRAM'S HORNBOOK ON MODERN LEGAL ETHICS, Student Edition, 1120 pages, 1986. (Text)

WYDICK AND PERSCHBACHER'S CALIFORNIA LEGAL ETHICS, Approximately 430 pages, 1992. Softcover. (Coursebook)

Property—see also Real Estate Transactions, Land Use, Trusts and Estates

BERNHARDT'S BLACK LETTER ON PROPERTY, Second Edition, 388 pages, 1991. Softcover. (Review)

BERNHARDT'S REAL PROPERTY IN A NUTSHELL, Second Edition, 448 pages, 1981. Softcover. (Text)

BOYER, HOVENKAMP AND KURTZ' THE LAW OF PROPERTY, AN INTRODUCTORY SURVEY, Fourth Edition, 696 pages, 1991. (Text)

BURKE'S PERSONAL PROPERTY IN A NUTSHELL, 322 pages, 1983. Softcover. (Text)

CUNNINGHAM, STOEBUCK AND WHITMAN'S HORNBOOK ON THE LAW OF PROPERTY, Student Edition, 916 pages, 1984, with 1987 pocket part. (Text)

HILL'S LANDLORD AND TENANT LAW IN A NUTSHELL, Second Edition, 311 pages, 1986. Softcover. (Text)

Real Estate Transactions

BRUCE'S REAL ESTATE FINANCE IN A NUTSHELL, Third Edition, 287 pages, 1991. Softcover. (Text)

NELSON AND WHITMAN'S BLACK LETTER ON LAND TRANSACTIONS AND FINANCE, Second Edition, 466 pages, 1988. Softcover. (Review)

NELSON AND WHITMAN'S HORNBOOK ON REAL ESTATE FINANCE LAW, Second Edition, 941 pages, 1985 with 1989 pocket part. (Text)

Regulated Industries—see also Mass Communication Law, Banking Law

GELLHORN AND PIERCE'S REGULATED INDUSTRIES IN A NUTSHELL, Second Edition, 389 pages, 1987. Softcover. (Text)

Remedies

DOBBS' HORNBOOK ON REMEDIES, Second Edition, December, 1992 Pub. (Text)

DOBBYN'S INJUNCTIONS IN A NUTSHELL, 264 pages, 1974. Softcover. (Text)

FRIEDMAN'S CONTRACT REMEDIES IN A NUTSHELL, 323 pages, 1981. Softcover. (Text)

O'CONNELL'S REMEDIES IN A NUTSHELL, Second Edition, 320 pages, 1985. Softcover. (Text)

Sea, Law of

SOHN AND GUSTAFSON'S THE LAW OF THE SEA IN A NUTSHELL, 264 pages, 1984. Softcover. (Text)

Securities Regulation

HAZEN'S HORNBOOK ON THE LAW OF SECURITIES REGULATION, Second Edition, Student Edition, 1082 pages, 1990. (Text)

RATNER'S SECURITIES REGULATION IN A NUTSHELL, Fourth Edition, approximately 320 pages, 1992. Softcover. (Text)

Sports Law

SCHUBERT, SMITH AND TRENTADUE'S SPORTS LAW, 395 pages, 1986. (Text)

Tax Practice and Procedure

MORGAN'S TAX PROCEDURE AND TAX FRAUD IN A NUTSHELL, 400 pages, 1990. Softcover. (Text)

Taxation—Corporate

SCHWARZ AND LATHROPE'S BLACK LETTER ON CORPORATE AND PARTNERSHIP TAXATION, 537 pages, 1991. Softcover. (Review)

WEIDENBRUCH AND BURKE'S FEDERAL INCOME TAXATION OF CORPORATIONS AND STOCKHOLDERS IN A NUTSHELL, Third Edition, 309 pages, 1989. Softcover. (Text)

Taxation—Estate & Gift—see also Estate Planning, Trusts and Estates

MCNULTY'S FEDERAL ESTATE AND GIFT TAXATION IN A NUTSHELL, Fourth Edition, 496 pages, 1989. Softcover. (Text)

PEAT AND WILLBANKS' FEDERAL ESTATE AND GIFT TAXATION: AN ANALYSIS AND CRITIQUE, 265 pages, 1991. Softcover. (Text)

Taxation—Individual

DODGE'S THE LOGIC OF TAX, 343 pages, 1989. Softcover. (Text)

HUDSON AND LIND'S BLACK LET-

Taxation—Individual—Continued

TER ON FEDERAL INCOME TAXATION, Fourth Edition, approximately 400 pages, 1992. Softcover. (Review)

MCNULTY'S FEDERAL INCOME TAXATION OF INDIVIDUALS IN A NUTSHELL, Fourth Edition, 503 pages, 1988. Softcover. (Text)

POSIN'S HORNBOOK ON FEDERAL INCOME TAXATION, Student Edition, 491 pages, 1983, with 1989 pocket part. (Text)

ROSE AND CHOMMIE'S HORNBOOK ON FEDERAL INCOME TAXATION, Third Edition, 923 pages, 1988, with 1991 pocket part. (Text)

Taxation—International

DOERNBERG'S INTERNATIONAL TAXATION IN A NUTSHELL, 325 pages, 1989. Softcover. (Text)

BISHOP AND BROOKS' FEDERAL PARTNERSHIP TAXATION: A GUIDE TO THE LEADING CASES, STATUTES, AND REGULATIONS, 545 pages, 1990. Softcover. (Text)

BURKE'S FEDERAL INCOME TAXATION OF PARTNERSHIPS IN A NUTSHELL, 356 pages, 1992. Softcover. (Text)

SCHWARZ AND LATHROPE'S BLACK LETTER ON CORPORATE AND PARTNERSHIP TAXATION, 537 pages, 1991. Softcover. (Review)

Taxation—State & Local

GELFAND AND SALSICH'S STATE AND LOCAL TAXATION AND FINANCE IN A NUTSHELL, 309 pages, 1986. Softcover. (Text)

Torts—see also Products Liability

KIONKA'S BLACK LETTER ON TORTS, 339 pages, 1988. Softcover. (Review)

KIONKA'S TORTS IN A NUTSHELL, Second Edition, 449 pages, 1992. Softcover. (Text)

PROSSER AND KEETON'S HORNBOOK ON TORTS, Fifth Edition, Student Edition, 1286 pages, 1984 with 1988 pocket part. (Text)

Trade Regulation—see also Antitrust, Regulated Industries

MCMANIS' UNFAIR TRADE PRACTICES IN A NUTSHELL, Third Edition, approximately 475 pages, December, 1992 Pub. Softcover. (Text)

SCHECHTER'S BLACK LETTER ON UNFAIR TRADE PRACTICES, 272 pages, 1986. Softcover. (Review)

Trial and Appellate Advocacy—see also Civil Procedure

BERGMAN'S TRIAL ADVOCACY IN A NUTSHELL, Second Edition, 354 pages, 1989. Softcover. (Text)

CLARY'S PRIMER ON THE ANALYSIS AND PRESENTATION OF LEGAL ARGUMENT, 106 pages, 1992. Softcover. (Text)

DESSEM'S PRETRIAL LITIGATION IN A NUTSHELL, Approximately 375 pages, 1992. Softcover. (Text)

GOLDBERG'S THE FIRST TRIAL (WHERE DO I SIT? WHAT DO I SAY?) IN A NUTSHELL, 396 pages, 1982. Softcover. (Text)

HEGLAND'S TRIAL AND PRACTICE SKILLS IN A NUTSHELL, 346 pages, 1978. Softcover. (Text)

HORNSTEIN'S APPELLATE ADVOCACY IN A NUTSHELL, 325 pages, 1984. Softcover. (Text)

JEANS' HANDBOOK ON TRIAL ADVOCACY, Student Edition, 473 pages, 1975. Softcover. (Text)

Trusts and Estates

ATKINSON'S HORNBOOK ON WILLS, Second Edition, 975 pages, 1953. (Text)

AVERILL'S UNIFORM PROBATE CODE IN A NUTSHELL, Second Edition, 454 pages, 1987. Softcover. (Text)

BOGERT'S HORNBOOK ON TRUSTS, Sixth Edition, Student Edition, 794 pages, 1987. (Text)

MCGOVERN, KURTZ AND REIN'S HORNBOOK ON WILLS, TRUSTS AND ESTATES–INCLUDING TAXATION AND FUTURE INTERESTS, 996 pages, 1988. (Text)

MENNELL'S WILLS AND TRUSTS IN A NUTSHELL, 392 pages, 1979. Softcover. (Text)

SIMES' HORNBOOK ON FUTURE INTERESTS, Second Edition, 355 pages, 1966. (Text)

TURANO AND RADIGAN'S HORNBOOK ON NEW YORK ESTATE ADMINISTRATION, 676 pages, 1986 with 1992 pocket part. (Text)

WAGGONER'S FUTURE INTERESTS IN A NUTSHELL, 361 pages, 1981. Softcover. (Text)

Water Law—see also Environmental Law

GETCHES' WATER LAW IN A NUTSHELL, Second Edition, 459 pages, 1990. Softcover. (Text)

Wills—see Trusts and Estates

Workers' Compensation

HOOD, HARDY AND LEWIS' WORKERS' COMPENSATION AND EMPLOYEE PROTECTION LAWS IN A NUTSHELL, Second Edition, 361 pages, 1990. Softcover. (Text)

Advisory Board

LAW AND POLITICS IN THE PEOPLE'S REPUBLIC OF CHINA

IN A NUTSHELL

By

RALPH H. FOLSOM
Professor of Law
University of San Diego

JOHN H. MINAN
Professor of Law
University of San Diego

LEE ANN OTTO
Chair, Department of Political Science
University of San Diego

ST. PAUL, MINN.
WEST PUBLISHING CO.
1992

610 Opperman Drive
P.O. Box 64526
St. Paul, MN 55164–0526

Printed in the United States of America

Library of Congress Cataloging-in-Publication Data

Folsom, Ralph Haughwout.
Law and politics in the People's Republic of China in a nutshell / Ralph H. Folsom, John H. Minan, Lee Ann Otto.
p. cm. — (Nutshell series)
Includes index.
ISBN 0–314–00999–X
1. Law—China. 2. Justice, Administration of—China. 3. Law and politics. 4. China—Politics and Government—1949– I. Minan, John H. II. Otto, Lee Ann. III. Title. IV. Series.
KNQ70.F65 1992
349.51—dc20
[345.1] 92–18871
CIP

ISBN 0–314–00999–X

(F., M. & O.) Law & Pol. in China NS

PREFACE

This Nutshell is an interdisciplinary effort. To our knowledge, *Law and Politics in the People's Republic of China* is the first readily available treatment of modern Chinese law and politics. It is primarily intended for students of political science, law, international business, and Asian or Chinese studies. We hope it will also be enjoyed by those who simply have an interest in the People's Republic of China.

Our survey of the seamless web of law and politics in the People's Republic has necessarily been selective. While the opening chapter reviews China's political and legal traditions, the book's focus is largely on postrevolutionary developments. Each of the succeeding chapters surveys major themes in Chinese law and politics: Power, Governance and Human Rights; The Legal Profession and the Courts; Criminal Justice; Civil Justice; People and Property; Business and Labor; Contract and Tort; Foreign Trade, Investment and Technology; and Hong Kong. Of necessity, there is some repetition of key ideas and themes in the various chapters. We welcome comments on this first edition and suggestions for the second.

RALPH H. FOLSOM
JOHN H. MINAN
LEE ANN OTTO

San Diego
June, 1992

ACKNOWLEDGEMENTS

The authors have read hundreds of articles and books in preparation for the writing of this Nutshell. We are grateful to all the specialists in Chinese law and politics for their ability to bring insights to a field difficult to research. It is always difficult to know where your thoughts begin and those of others end. While we hesitate to list names for fear of overlooking someone, portions of this text undoubtedly reflect the influence of particular specialists, including: Hungdah Chiu, A. Dicks, D. Donovan, T. Epp, T. Gelatt, B. Ingraham, Chin Kim, Shao-chuan Leng, R. Lin, M. Silk, D. Townsend, M. Woo and Yang Xiaobing on criminal justice; A. Dicks, W. Jones, D. Lewis, Ye Lin, T. Manoharan, H. Scogin, Guiguo Wang, Gao Yongfu, and H. Zheng on contracts and torts; P. Allen, T. Baranski, J. Cohen, E. Epstein, Tang Houzi, S. Lubman, S. Ogden, M. Palay, L. Ross, J. A. Spanogle and J.C.F. Wang on dispute settlement; J. Cohen, H. Depei, H. Koguchi, V. Li, S. Ogden, H. Pitney, K. Haun, S. Kanter, Tao–Tai Hsia and Tung–Pi Chen on the Chinese legal profession; S. Austin, D. Brotman, J. Feinerman, D. Fleshler, H. Josephs, B. Kellman, J. Lewis, B. Ottley, N. Stamos and H. Zheng on business and labor; An Chen, J. Cohen, A. Fenwick, T. Gelatt, J. Horsley, Jia Zhao, K. Maher, M. Moser,

J. Nafziger, D. Pierce, P. Torbert, R. Watkins, and Zhao Xiuying on international trade, investment and licensing; A. Chen, D. Jones, S. Karamanian and P. Wesley–Smith on Hong Kong; W. Alford, D. Bodde, D. Forte, D. Funk, R. Grant, Tao–Tai Hsia, A. Jordan, P. Luney, M. Meisner, C. Morris, A. Nathan, W. Rodzinski, H. Scogin, J. Spence, D. Townsend, J. Triska, D. Waller, and W. Zeldin on Chinese legal and political history; D. Bachman, J. Burns, Hungdah Chiu, J. Cohen, R. Edwards, L. Henkin, Tao–Tai Hsia, C. Johnson, S. Ogden, W. Jones, P. Keller, A. Nathan, J.C.F. Wang, Yuan-li Wu and Pu Zengyan on constitutional law, the Chinese Communist Party and human rights; and P. Chang, E. Epstein, M. Hager, M. Palmer, E. Platte, M. Savage, L. Schwartz, H. Scogin and D. Zweig on family and property. Special thanks are due Professors Hugh T. Scogin, Jr. and Margaret Y. K. Woo. We regret any failure to mention other specialists whose works have specifically assisted us in developing this Nutshell. Users are also referred to an extensive collection of readings and materials edited by Profs. Folsom and Minan entitled *Law in the People's Republic of China: Commentary, Readings and Materials* (Kluwer, 1989).

U. S. S. R.
Ulaanbaatar
Mongolia
HEILONGJIANG
Harbin
JILIN
Vla-divos-tok
XINJIANG
NEI MONGGOL
LIAONING
North Korea
BEIJING
Pyongyang
GANSU
Lüda
TIANJIN
Seoul
HEBEI
Yellow Sea
NING XIA
SHANXI
SHANDONG
Qingdao
QINGHAI
South Korea
Xi'an
SHAANXI
HENAN
JIANGSU
XIZANG
SHANGHAI
HUBEI
ANHUI
Hangzhou
Wuhan
East China Sea
Delhi
SICHUAN
ZHEJIANG
Lhasa
Chongning
Nepal
Changsha
HUNAN
JIANGXI
Bhutan
FUJIAN
Fuzhou
GUIZHOU
TAIWAN
India
Bangladesh
YUNNAN
GUANXI
GUANGDONG
Hong Kong
Macao
Hanoi
Burma
Laos
Philippines
Bay of Bengal
Vietnam
South China Sea
Thailand
Bangkok
0
500 Miles

*

CHRONOLOGY

Imperial China

221–207 B.C.	Qin
206 B.C.–9 A.D.	Western or Former Han
9–23 A.D.	Xin
25–220 A.D.	Eastern or Later Han
220–265 A.D.	Three Kingdoms (Shu, Wei, Wu)
265–589 A.D.	Southern and Northern Empires
590–618 A.D.	Sui
618–906 A.D.	Tang
906–960 A.D.	Five Dynasties (Later Liang, Later Tang, Later Jin, Later Han, Later Zhou)
960–1126 A.D.	Northern Song
1127–1279 A.D.	Southern Song
1279–1368 A.D.	Yuan or Mongol
1368–1644 A.D.	Ming
1644–1911 A.D.	Qing or Manchu

Republic of China

1911–1949 A.D.

People's Republic of China

1949–Present

*

OUTLINE

*

LAW AND POLITICS IN THE PEOPLE'S REPUBLIC OF CHINA

IN A NUTSHELL

*

CHAPTER I

POLITICAL AND LEGAL TRADITIONS

"What is the source of the statutes in the books? Whatever previous rulers thought appropriate, they had written down as laws. Whatever subsequent rulers thought to be right, they added as ordinances. Whatever suits the moment is correct; what do the laws of the past matter?"

Du Zhou, Commandant of Justice (c. 100 B.C.)

REFORM AND CONFLICT

The People's Republic of China (PRC) experienced a period of significant economic reform and legal development during the late 1970s and the 1980s. Although political reforms were less dramatic during this period, the leadership of the People's Republic of China generally was viewed as intent on establishing those basic legal institutions and principles that are essential components of a civilized society. China was firmly on the path to modernization. During this period, the PRC seemed to link its future to the rule of law and adopted many Western concepts, especially in the structuring of its legal system. Understanding these developments, as well as more recent events, is aided by appreciating China's legal traditions, political dynamics, and history.

Deng Xiaoping became China's preeminent leader in the late 1970s. His elevation to this position was accompanied by a change in the Communist Party's program: The economic modernization of China was now the key task facing the Party and the people, and mass movements, particularly those promoting class struggle, were declared to be invalid mechanisms of Party rule. Although Deng argued that economic reform necessitated political reform, his views on political reform constituted only a marginal change in the political system. Deng and other members of the "old guard" leadership were not prepared to consider fundamental changes in the political structure that would allow broad participation and influence by the Chinese people in the affairs of the country. Nevertheless, the general idea that political reform was a necessary adjunct to economic reform led students and intellectuals to demonstrate in 1986 and 1987 in favor of greater democracy. In January 1987, Hu Yaobang, who was sympathetic to these demands, was forced by Deng to resign as the Party's General Secretary. When Hu died on April 15, 1989 students took to the streets in Beijing demanding political change and an end to official corruption. Their demands captured the world stage because of Mikhail Gorbachev's visit to China for the Sino–Soviet Summit. When Gorbachev arrived in Beijing on May 15th, the student demonstrations had increased in intensity. By the time Gorbachev left China more than a million people were demonstrating in favor of political and economic reform.

China's leaders did not yield to these demands. Rather, they suppressed the demonstrators with force. Deng's refusal to change the nature of Party rule in the PRC played a key role in the events that led to Tiananmen in the spring of 1989.

The bloody suppression of the Democracy Movement in June of 1989, the subsequent official attempt to portray this suppression in a fictitious manner as necessary to smash a counterrevolutionary rebellion, and the massive sweep of protesters and summary executions of some of those seized, shocked the world. These events contradicted the depiction of China's leadership as valuing law as anything other than a mechanism for control. They also highlighted the discrepancy between the promulgation of law and its actual implementation.

These events are a serious assault on the credibility of the reforms of the Chinese legal system since the Cultural Revolution. They raise a fundamental question. To what degree, if at all, is there a political commitment within the PRC to a viable legal system? The answer to this question is that there is, and will continue to be, the political commitment. But the role the legal system plays in Chinese society will be different from its role in Western society. The legal system will not be the vanguard of change in the PRC. Rather, the driving force of change will be the political response by the leadership to domestic and international concerns.

Although they will rarely make headlines, disputes in the civil and nonpolitical criminal arenas will continue to be resolved in the PRC with procedural and substantive justice. Contracts will be breached, divorces will occur, and nonpolitical crimes will be dealt with by the authorities. Foreigners will continue to do business in China, will enter into agreements, and will have their contract disputes resolved. China also will increasingly play a role as a trading partner in the global economy.

It is important to study these areas, as well as others, since they validate the conceptual importance of the role of law. Domestic economic development and international economic cooperation necessitate a functioning legal system. Moreover, increased international trade can provide a framework of trust within which other issues of concern can be discussed. These are the foundations on which future progress will be built. It would be as misleading to conclude that law has no role in Chinese society as it would be to ignore the failures of the current leadership to protect the civil rights and human liberties of its citizens.

Before long, the present generation of old revolutionaries who continue to exercise power will pass from the scene. The events in the coming months and years will reveal whether the legal reforms introduced following the Cultural Revolution will survive and be a moderating influence on the next generation of China's leaders, or whether they will atrophy as China's leaders continue to rely on the repressive policies associated with Tiananmen Square.

IMPERIAL CHINA

Civilization in China stretches back in history some four thousand years. The Chinese have the oldest centralized state which has survived with certain interruptions since 221 B.C. Two centuries before the beginning of the Christian Era, China had established its basic political structure. This structure, along with its underlying Confucian philosophy, remained essentially unchanged for the next two millennia. For most of this history, China developed its own culture and institutions, including approaches to the solution of legal problems, that were different in many respects from those developed by Western civilizations.

The origins of law in China are ancient. Some historians believe that Chinese law began in the Xia Dynasty (21st–16th century B.C.). The noted archaeologist, Chang Kwang-chih, has argued that the elements of a legal system may have existed as early as the Shang Dynasty (16th–11th century B.C.). Although scholars differ as to when written law first came into existence in China, *The Analects of Confucius* suggest that a formal written legal structure and system were in place by at least the sixth century B.C. Excavations in the 1980s uncovered fragments of laws promulgated in the Qin Dynasty (221–207 B.C.). It is also known that the Han Dynasty (206 B.C.–220 A.D.) had an extensive legal code. By the 5th and 6th centuries A.D., the core values, principles, and rules that were central to classical Chinese law existed. A completely preserved code influential on the development of modern Chinese law dates from the Tang Dynasty (618–906 A.D.). The legal codes of the Song (960–1279 A.D.), Ming (1368–1644 A.D.), and Qing (1644–1911 A.D.) dynasties were based on the seventh century Tang code.

Classical Chinese law is one of the world's great legal traditions, and covers both the preimperial (prior to 221 B.C.) and imperial periods (221 B.C. to 1911 A.D.). It includes both the formal codes and procedures administered by the state and the shared informal values and customs that complemented the formal system. Through two millennia of imperial dynasties, a variety of different legal codes were promulgated by the emperors. Obviously, caution must be exercised in attempting to generalize about law and the legal processes during such a vast period of time. Imperial Chinese legal history should not be viewed as if it were a single unified whole. It was not. There are important distinctions among periods and between substance and procedure during this history. The task of making useful generalizations is further complicated by the fact that the official imperial documents were written in classical Chinese, which is a difficult and complex allusion-filled language.

Traditionally, leading authorities on Chinese law, eminent general historians of China, and influential nonsinologists portray the formal law during the imperial period as an instrument of control and as a mechanism to insure adequate revenue for the state. As a general matter, the Imperial Codes focused on criminal law and obligations owed to the state, and China was ruled primarily through a bureaucratic regime.

Several important features of law and politics during the imperial period are notable. First, administrative, adjudicatory and other authority was aggregated, particularly in the hands of the district magistrates. This integration of authority within one local official, who represented the emperor, was not based on the idea of a separation of powers. It was the direct opposite. The district magistrate was responsible for all aspects of civil governance, including such seemingly diverse matters as the collection of taxes, the maintenance of public order, and the investigation, prosecution, and adjudication of criminal matters. The absence of any independent judicial or administrative official at the district level from whom the populace could seek recourse carried with it enormous potential for the assertion of state power. Moreover, no independent legal profession existed. The absence of professional lawyers meant that there was no institutionalized system of criminal defense.

The formal criminal justice process in imperial China envisioned a different relationship between the state and its citizens than found in Anglo–American law. It was not one defined by the model of citizens granting powers to the state, while retaining certain fundamental, inalienable rights. Rather, the theoretical relationship between the state and its citizens was far more one of trust, modeled after the traditional family. In the Chinese family, those in positions of power owed a moral or fiduciary-like obligation to the other family relations. Similarly, the emperor and his representatives were conceived of more as senior relations than as public figures. The district magistrate, for example, was popularly known as the *fumu guan* or the father-mother official. Within this context, it was far less important to distinguish public and private concerns, or to guard individual prerogatives against the state. In practice, this conceptualization of the relationship between individuals and the state undoubtedly failed on occasion. Nevertheless, it is the theory of the relationship that is important to understanding the imperial Chinese system.

Second, the manner in which trials were conducted emphasized social order and control, not individual rights. The magistrate had the obligation and the authority to ferret out whatever was important about a case, and thus legal counsel at trial was deemed unnecessary. The laws and rules that guided district magistrates in discharging their responsibilities prescribed an inquisitorial mode of adjudication that encompassed little of what would be seen today as embodying fundamental "due process." For example, persons accused of crimes were not presumed to be innocent nor were they entitled to notice, either of the law or of their alleged crimes. Accused persons were not protected by any privilege against self-incrimination, and thus they could not refuse to answer a magistrate's inquiries. Indeed, magistrates were permitted to apply torture long after the practice had been abandoned in Europe in order to secure confessions or simply to obtain evidence from witnesses. Although current research suggests that, at least during the important pretrial stages, more of a legal profession may have existed in late imperial China than conventionally believed, the absence of legal counsel and the inability of the accused to make a defense also suggest the subordination of individual rights to the principle of state control.

Although district magistrates did not receive formal legal training, they were required to master the Confucian classics, which stressed the moral responsibility those in positions of authority had to those in their charge. Magistrates were expected to exercise authority in the same way that we might expect of trustees. In addition, Imperial Codes and rules also established standards. Failure to meet these standards theoretically subjected the magistrate to administrative or, in serious cases, criminal punishment. To ensure compliance, higher authorities reviewed all criminal sentences involving more than the infliction of a light bambooing. The system also provided the presence of an official, known as a censor, who independently evaluated the performance of magistrates and reported to the Emperor.

Evaluating China's legal system based on the presence or absence of contemporary values and forms of due process carries with it the risk of failing to understand the Chinese on their own terms. It also assumes that the content of a "due process" standard can be articulated with sufficient precision. More fundamental, however, is the fact that due process concerns are simply less important when power relations are conceived of in terms of trust.

Third, the substantive laws of the imperial era were administered through a bureaucratic process. Editions of imperial laws and regulations published by the state were generally for official use only. Although some private editions existed, they do not appear to have been readily available to ordinary citizens. The fact that the Imperial Codes were addressed to the civil and military officials, not to the general public, is not particularly surprising. Throughout the imperial period the vast majority of the population was illiterate. Internalized "rules" of proper behavior complemented positive law. Citizens generally stayed within the bounds of the law by conforming to the social roles ordained by the Confucian philosophy and accompanying moral norms, not by knowing and following the content of law codes.

Some of the detail of classical Chinese law indicates significant sophistication, even by modern

Western standards. In the area of criminal law, the actor's state of mind was relevant. Knowledge that an act was criminal was required. For example, the Chinese took pains prior to the Opium War (1839–42) to give notice of Chinese laws to foreigners on the belief that such persons otherwise could not be familiar with them. State of mind was also relevant to the idea of punishment. Someone who voluntarily surrendered prior to the issuance of an arrest warrant could escape punishment or have it reduced on the theory that the individual had already achieved moral reform. The rules of legal procedure included an automatic trial *de novo* when a convicted criminal refused to make a written acknowledgement that the judgment was valid both as to the law and to the facts. Automatic reviews were conducted in cases involving any type of serious punishment, and individuals in the late imperial period could initiate independent appeals. As early as the 7th century A.D., the Tang Dynasty Code made mandatory at least three automatic reviews of a death sentence before it could be carried out.

China also relied on informal systems for dealing with a wide variety of societal problems. These small-group, informal processes were used to communicate behavioral norms for resolving disputes that are essential to understanding the Chinese legal tradition. One of the important distinctive features of these informal systems was the reliance on self-regulation. A preference existed for mediation or arbitration within the community, in lieu of litigation, to resolve most civil matters. As a result, informal processes and institutions generally were developed to resolve disputes, to maintain harmony, and to establish rules of appropriate conduct.

Despite the unlimited power of the emperor in Chinese political and legal theory, which suggests the potential for arbitrariness, classical Chinese law exhibited a high degree of consistency and predictability. These values derived from the general adherence to a number of legal principles, rules of governance and procedures. This legal model has been described as "ruled by law." It is different from the model of "rule of law," which contemplates a legal system that is independent of political authority.

No brief overview can deal adequately with the influential philosophies of law reflected in the various schools of thought in traditional China, such as the Taoists, Yin Yang School, Logicians, Chinese Buddhists, Neo–Confucianists, and so on. Nevertheless, some basic understanding of the philosophy of law is necessary. Traditional legal philosophy, for all practical purposes, begins with Confucius (551–479 B.C.).

For most of its history, the Chinese approach to government and jurisprudence was most significantly influenced by Confucian philosophy, which stressed personal morality as the central factor in the attainment of human satisfaction and political stability. Individuals were regarded as basically good, but they were susceptible to moral corruption. As a general principle, justice and harmony could be achieved only when everyone, including the ruler, conformed to the rules of moral behavior.

The power of the emperors was over "everything under heaven," *tian xia.* An emperor ruled with the Mandate of Heaven, and when an emperor departed from "The Way"—the true path of a good ruler who governed in accordance with Heaven's will—it was up to loyal subjects to replace him. Success in ousting an emperor was seen as evidence that Heaven had transferred its mandate. On more than one occasion, emperors emerged from among the ranks of popular insurgents.

Traditional Chinese jurisprudence employs the concepts of *li* and *fa.* These terms have overlapping meanings, the nuances of which are affected by their context. In a simplified sense, the Confucian philosophy of law involves two polarities, *li* and *fa. Li* has been translated by various scholars as "moral code," "customary law," or "rules of conduct governing relations between men." In its broad sense, *li* includes rules governing administrative, inter-state and civil matters as well as moral propriety. When *fa* is used as a dichotomy with *li,* it customarily means criminal law only.

The essence of *li* is the belief that desirable behavior and societal harmony can be obtained through moral force rather than physical coercion.

Confucius philosophized that if the people are guided by *fa,* formal criminal codes, and order among them is enforced by means of punishment, they will try to evade punishment, but have no sense of shame. But, if they are guided by virtue, and order among them is enforced by *li,* they will have a sense of shame and also be reformed. In a general sense, the idea of the existence of a moral code independent of the laws of the state is similar to the Western concept of natural law. Confucian moral norms were derived from human social practice over the ages, they were not God-given.

The noted scholar, Benjamin Schwartz, described a society guided by *li* as one where "unbridled self interest is placed under effective control from within ... (I)n a society governed by *li,* conflicts of interest can be easily resolved. Both sides will ... make concessions and the necessity for litigation avoided." Townsend, "The Concept of Law in Post–Mao China: A Case Study of Economic Crime," 24 *Stanford Journal of International Law* 227, 230 (1988). Conciliation and compromise were the keys to resolving disputes, not the reliance on technical legal principles. Strict insistence on one's rights violated the basic concepts of harmony and mutual accommodation. As a consequence, laws and courts were viewed as being outside the internalized norms of appropriate moral behavior. Thus, the general preference to avoid litigation as a method of resolving disputes finds its philosophical basis in Confucianism.

Society was ordered according to inegalitarian group hierarchies that emphasized conformity to group interests over individual rights. Justice and social harmony could be achieved by conforming to the rules of behavior contained in Confucian philosophy. The five traditional Confucian principles that governed social relations contained reciprocal rights and duties: 1) Emperor-subject: the ideal ruler is benevolent; the ideal subordinate, loyal; 2) Father-son: the ideal father is compassionate, the ideal son filial; 3) Older brother-younger brother: the ideal elder brother is kind, the ideal younger brother respectful; 4) Husband-wife: the ideal husband is righteous, the ideal wife submissive; and, 5) Friend-friend: the ideal friend is faithful. Although this philosophy was humanistic, it obviously was not egalitarian. Only in the relationship between friends is there evidence of equality. All other relationships involved subordination and service to a superior, counterbalanced by the superior showing compassion and care to the subordinate.

According to the Confucian rule of reason, laws were to reflect custom and public opinion. Thus, the law accorded vastly different treatment to persons depending upon their relative status, with the most crucial distinctions being those of Emperor-subject, Husband-wife, and Father-son. A father striking a son, for example, would receive a far less severe punishment than would a son striking a father. This result was a reflection of the idea that in order to be effective the law must be consistent with the moral order.

The Confucian philosophy prefers virtuous example and morality, but it also recognizes that not all elements of society can be effectively controlled by *li.* It is at this point that the polarity *fa,* which has been variously translated as "positive law," "criminal law" or "punishment," becomes relevant. *Fa* is a standard imposed from above to which people must conform. In ancient China, the rulers did not consider themselves subject to the positive laws which they themselves issued. *Li* was the guiding code of honor for the ruling groups, and *fa* the laws to which the common people were subject.

Formal legal codes that control societal behavior and maintain social harmony through fear of punishment or sanctions illustrate *fa.* This view of law, which relies on positive law, insists that society can achieve harmony only where transgressions are met with firm and swift punishment. *Fa* emphasizes state power and control, rather than the Confucian values of morality and governance by virtuous example. It stresses the idea that only clear and forceful written law vigorously enforced may curb social disruption and crime. According to this view, which is premised on the view that most people are selfish, a mediocre ruler can effectively govern by using positive law. The object of law is to prevent conflict, disorder and crime through deterrence and intimidation.

This view of law can be traced back to the Emperor Qin Shihuang (221–210 B.C.) who founded the first dynasty to unify the country and give

China its name in Western languages. This dynasty was characterized by a strong penal code and the reliance on state coercion, factors that historically are linked with *fa.* The Legalist Tradition, which has become associated with *fa,* viewed the ruler's right to make law as absolute. The Qin Dynasty produced a powerful and wealthy state. Nevertheless, it lasted only about 15 years. Generations of succeeding scholars, many of whom subscribe to the Confucian philosophy, argue that its downfall was based on the ruthless exploitation of people and its disregard of prevailing moral norms.

The source of law for the Legalist Tradition and the Confucian Tradition was different. The former emphasized governance through strict enforcement of state edicts, whereas the latter stressed promoting social order through shared moral principles. Notwithstanding the fundamental difference in approach, the model behavior (*li*) central to Confucian legality and the written positive law (*fa*) have existed side by side throughout Chinese history, although not with equal influence. In a conflict between the two, *li* was preferred by traditional Chinese society. As time passed, the standards of *li* slowly became incorporated in successive dynastic penal codes. This process led to the Confucianization of law, and caused the two concepts to become intertwined. Thus, with the passage of time, the essence of the law contained in the Imperial Codes largely reflected the content of the Confucian moral norms.

In *The Heart of the Dragon* (1985), a book examining the ancient religions and philosophies of the Chinese, Alasdair Clayre provides a useful general historical perspective of the role of law in China. This perspective provides an apt foundation for understanding the present.

> In general the purpose of law in China is and has always been twofold. On the one hand the authorities have tried to make the enforcement of law flexible and adaptable to circumstances. Education, mediation and the reform of offenders have always played a great role and do still today. This view can be seen as a continuation of Confucian ideas. On the other hand, law is and has always been also regarded as a deterrent. This is in conformity with Legalist thinking. The fundamental ideal which lies behind all law and order in socialist China, just as in the Confucian imperial order, is harmony in a world where ideally no infractions of rules should occur.

CHINA IN TRANSITION (1911–1949)

Western legal concepts, which entered China in the late 1800s, were a blend of Anglo–American and European–Continental constitutional, legal and political models, and unlike the Bolsheviks, the Chinese Communists had a relatively longer period in which to experiment with legal forms before taking power. Within one year of the fall of the Qing (Manchu) Dynasty in 1911, China became a nationalist republic with a constitution containing an American-style Bill of Rights. China also adopted the Six Codes of the Guomindang (Organic Law of the Courts, Commercial Law, Civil Code, Criminal Code, Civil Code of Procedure, and Criminal Code of Procedure) that were based on the European–Continental model of the civil law. The specific Chinese codes drew on the laws then in effect in various world states. Thus, for example, the French model generally was used to organize the courts, but this model was combined with the Anglo–American principle of separating the judiciary from the executive. For the most part, these codes were used to govern business transactions and relations with foreigners. Thus, they had little effect on most Chinese. Nevertheless, the adoption of this blend of Western law was significant since China, for the first time, formally moved away from traditionalist Chinese society and the underpinnings of the Confucian philosophy. China's approach to law was in transition.

The period 1911–49 was a period of unrelenting internal conflict, complicated and made more humiliating by the Japanese occupation and invasion of China. In 1919, the Versailles Peace Conference ceded the German territories in Shandong to Japan and the Japanese established an armed presence there. On May 4, 1919, students enraged by Japanese imperialism that infringed on Chinese sovereignty protested the Versailles Peace Conference. These demonstrations in favor of "democracy and science" and against the government and traditional Chinese culture became a turning point in Chinese history, leading to the overthrow of the warlord government. These events also marked the beginning of a self-conscious Chinese nationalism. Since then, the May 4th Movement has become a code word in China for the struggle for democracy. Thus, the history of student protest in recent times in favor of democracy finds it roots in the May 4th Movement.

Sun Yatsen, leader of the Guomindang or Chinese Nationalist Party, planned to restore Chinese unity after the death of Yuan Shikai in 1916. He received assistance from Russia in the form of money, arms, and expert advisors in furtherance of this goal. This was the period when regional military chiefs or warlords raised armies, collected taxes, and fought each other for power. When Sun died in 1925, a power struggle developed within the Nationalist Party between Wang Jingwei, a left-wing Nationalist leader, and Chiang Kaishek, the more right wing Commandant of the Whampoa Military Academy. By 1927, Chiang headed the Nationalist Party.

The small Chinese Communist Party (CCP) joined the Guomindang, and from 1924 until 1927, the Party followed the Comintern-sponsored policy of a united front with the Guomindang to rid China of the warlords. The Northern Expedition to reunify China began in the summer of 1926. By 1927, the Expedition had successfully defeated the warlords in much of the south and central areas of

China between Guangzhou (Canton) and Shanghai. Chiang Kaishek, concerned about the CCP's increasing support among the people and seeking to consolidate his control over the Nationalist Party, attacked CCP members and sympathizers in April 1927 in Shanghai. This event led to the end of the First United Front between the Communists and the Nationalists.

The CCP initially focused its efforts on organizing the urban proletariat. However, following the Shanghai attack, the Communist Party began to more actively organize the peasants in Hunan, Guangdong, Jiangxi, Fujian, and other provinces. Much of this mobilization was now under the direction of Mao Zedong. In the inaccessible area between Jiangxi and Hunan, Mao began to weld groups of rebellious and displaced peasants into the Red Army that ultimately drove the Guomindang from China. In addition, Communist soviets or councils were set up in rural areas for the purposes of acting as local rebel governments, introducing social and economic reforms, and suppressing landlords and counterrevolutionaries. To these councils, as to members of the CCP generally, law was what it was to Lenin—"the program of the Party uttered in the language of power," the will of the new ruling class.

Legal developments at this time have been described as a combination of Leninist ideology, militant Bolshevism, *fa* styles of punishments, and a desire to smash Confucianism and to construct a new *li* among the people. Policies such as land reform and equal status for women were promulgated and enforced by special *ad hoc* revolutionary tribunals. To the extent that legal rules existed, they were direct applications of substantive revolutionary goals.

The social transformation of rural China was backed by physical sanctions and propaganda. Between 1927 and 1931, the Communist soviets were establishing and enforcing their own system of "revolutionary justice," combining simple decrees with popular terror. In 1931, the Communists declared the areas of Jiangxi and Fujian under their control to be an independent Chinese Soviet Republic. The governing regime inaugurated a legal superstructure that copied many of the non-Romanist aspects of the Soviet Union's system: Substantive legislation was passed dealing with land reform, labor conditions, marriage, and activities of counterrevolutionaries.

In 1934, during his fifth campaign against the CCP, Chiang Kaishek succeeded in driving the Communists from their base in the south. This began the Communists' 6000 mile "Long March" ending in north-west China near Yanan in 1935. By 1936, Mao Zedong emerged as the unquestioned leader of the Communists. The "Yanan Period" of Chinese communism from 1935 to 1945 remained, in essence, a period of grass-roots revolutionary activity.

During the Yanan Period, Mao studied the writings of Marx, Lenin, and Stalin. He and his fellow Communists also extended their power over northwest China. Unlike the Soviet Union's experience, Mao's communist revolution was forged in the countryside, not in the industrial cities. The characteristic attributes of much subsequent Chinese communist legal administration—the melding together of political, administrative, and judicial interests through committees operating at all levels of the court hierarchy and associating Party and government personnel, including the procurators, with court problems and decisions; the use of trials as forms of propaganda; the involvement of the masses in judicial decisions through elected assessors and mass on-the-spot trials; the fostering of conciliation under Party guidance; the emphasis on repentance and reform—combined an interesting blend of revolutionary Marxist and popular traditional Chinese attitudes and concerns.

The Japanese presence in Manchuria was a continuing source of contention between China and Japan. After 1919, the Japanese established an armed presence in Manchuria. In 1932, they created a Manchurian state, Manchukuo, ruled by the puppet Qing ex-emperor Puyi. From this base, the Japanese occupied much of north China. In 1937, Japan unleashed its military forces and within a year occupied most of north and east China. The Nationalists withdrew to Chonqqing in Sichuan, but continued to fight the Japanese. More than two million Chinese soldiers were killed or wounded in fighting the Japanese in central China. For a few years after 1937, the CCP and the Nationalists formed a nominal alliance against the Japanese. By early 1941, the alliance collapsed and the parties were in armed conflict.

The Nationalists gained military support in their war effort against Japan from the West after the United States entered World War II. When the Second World War ended in 1945, the Nationalists were unable to restore their prewar control. Mao and his army, in a series of well-organized military actions, occupied north-east China and then swept into central China. The Chinese Nationalist Party forces were defeated in China's civil war of 1945–49, and retreated to Taiwan in 1949 where they continued to govern a *de facto* state known as the Republic of China. Many scholars attribute the Communists' victory to their ability to mobilize the peasantry, especially during the Sino–Japanese War. This mobilizing organization was then used against the Chinese Nationalist Party. Historian Maurice Meisner argues that the Nationalists' defeat can be traced largely to the Japanese invasion. The Japanese undermined the foundations of the Guomindang regime by driving the Nationalists from the major cities from which they derived their main sources of financial and political support. In addition, the ravages of war resulted in incredible economic chaos and bureaucratic corruption—and, eventually, in almost total demoralization within the Guomindang.

THE PEOPLE'S REPUBLIC OF CHINA (1949–1965)

The Communists came to power in 1949 and established the People's Republic of China. Their struggle for power had given them experience with a variety of legal practices: direct revolutionary rule; *fa*-style punishments; *li*-style adjudications; Soviet models; imperial judicial structures; and Romanist forms. In February of 1949, the Central Committee of the CCP declared that the work of the people's judiciary should not be based on the Guomindang's Six Codes but should be based on the people's laws. In September 1949, this Party directive was incorporated into the Common Program of the Chinese People's Consultive Conference, which became the temporary basic law of the PRC until a constitution was adopted 1954. This Common Program states: "All laws, decrees, and judicial systems of the Guomindang Reactionary Government which oppress the people shall be abolished. Laws and decrees protecting the people shall be enacted and the people's judicial system shall be set up." Thus, the former legal system of the Nationalists was repudiated, and in the process the private practice of law banned.

The period 1949–56 is officially regarded by the Chinese government as a "period of transition." From 1949–52, the new leadership of the PRC focused on consolidating its control and establishing a foundation for future political and economic development. China's First Five Year Plan, initiated in 1953, was based on the Soviet model of economic development emphasizing the construction of a heavy industrial base at the expense of light industry and agriculture.

Soviet-style judicial institutions, such as the People's Courts, People's Procuracies and Legal Advisory Offices, were introduced. Local courts were politically controlled and had jurisdiction over both civil and criminal matters. During the first few years of this period, many of the judges and other legally trained personnel who had served the Nationalists continued to hold office because there were insufficient numbers of trained Communist personnel. In 1952, the Legal Reform Campaign resulted in the removal of those experienced officials. Western legal concepts were also rooted out. For example, legal concepts such as the separation of law from politics, the equality of all persons before the law, the independence of the judiciary, and statutes of limitations were seen as aiding landlords and counterrevolutionaries at the expense of the people.

During the 1949–56 period, *ad hoc* revolutionary tribunals flourished and were effectively used to suppress counterrevolutionary activities. A series of political movements, based on the political education of the people but often backed by terror and violence, were conducted. These included the Land Reform Movement, the Movement to Suppress Counterrevolutionaries, the Movement for the Ideological Remolding of the Intellectuals, the

Three–Anti Movement (against corruption, waste, and bureaucracy within the Party, government, army, and mass organizations), and the Five–Anti Movement (against bribery, tax evasion, theft of state property, cheating on government contracts, and stealing of economic information by private industrial and commercial enterprises). Each of these movements had its own political and social target group. Thus, for example, the Five–Anti Movement was aimed at the urban bourgeoisie in private industry and business. Its basic objective was to pressure, if not terrorize, private business into accepting a subsequent government takeover. Within these various movements, special people's tribunals existed that possessed unrestricted jurisdiction. They could impose any penalty, and had the power to try cases on the spot. No provision for defense lawyers and no right of appeal to higher courts existed, although death sentences were required to be submitted to courts at a higher level for approval. Substantive legislation was limited to land reform, marriage, labor conditions, corrective labor camps, and counterrevolutionary laws. In general, the Chinese leadership used legal instruments to accomplish political objectives.

The general legal framework for the PRC was established with the adoption of the 1954 Constitution, and it was supplemented by various laws for judicial, administrative and legislative organs. Soviet lawyers regularly visited China, and Chinese students visited the USSR. Judicial procedures were unified and regularized. Organic laws for the courts and the procuracy were enacted. Economic restructuring also took place. Nationalization of private industrial and commercial activities occurred and rural collectivization was implemented. The socialist transformation was being implemented at a rapid pace. By the end of 1956, 94 percent of private industry and 82 percent of private commercial activities were nationalized, and by the end of 1957, 96 percent of all rural families had become members of higher-stage cooperatives (collectives).

The next major period of development occurred between 1957 and 1965. It began with the disintegration of the Soviet–Chinese alliance in the late 1950s. A criminal code and a criminal procedure code that drew heavily on Soviet legal models were about to be promulgated when the Chinese–Soviet split occurred. The willingness to consider adopting Soviet models ended—rejected as not suitable for Chinese conditions, which needed less rigidity and a greater emphasis on Chinese tradition. Since the Soviet–Chinese split, Chinese communism has developed numerous positions contrary to the communism then practiced in the Soviet Union.

After the split with the Soviet Union, the Chinese leadership, led by Mao, turned its attention toward producing uniquely Chinese codes. This effort was not successful, however. Some Chinese reformers urged the adoption of Western legal concepts, such as judicial independence, equality before the law and due process. This legal reform movement ended abruptly when the Party launched a wave of extra-judicial persecution and "liquidation of class enemies."

Law was cast by Mao as an obstacle to achieving socialist ideology. Law schools were closed, legal research ended, and the legal profession disappeared. Legal reformers were condemned as "rightist intellectuals with antisocial views." They were accused of using law against the Party when the Anti-Rightist Campaign was launched in 1957. Mao proclaimed the "mass line," requiring the judge or court to "rely on the masses" in determining punishment. During this period, the legal system was weakened, some judicial and law enforcement institutions were dismantled, serious failures to follow the law and violations of the legal system existed, and few laws were enacted.

In 1958, Mao launched a new economic policy, known as the "Great Leap Forward," that proposed to overtake Great Britain within 15 years in terms of industrial production. In an attempt to consolidate power and to bring China forward in the communist world as a genuine rival to the Soviet Union, Mao directed a breakneck pace in industrial and agricultural production as well as a more highly intensified organization of communal life. Agricultural production was directed by Party fiat. Intense mobilization, which ran directly against the needs and wishes of the people, occurred. Hundreds of millions of farmers were forced into people's communes, revolutionizing their lives. In retrospect, the Great Leap Forward has been seen by the Chinese leadership as a time involving disastrous economic programs and empty boasting of economic achievements. Appalling famine resulted and millions perished. The Great Leap stands as a dramatic illustration of Mao's disregard for social and economic reality in search of radical political and economic goals. The early 1960s were years of economic and political retrenchment in an attempt to deal with the devastation and corruption of the late 1950s.

During the late 1950s and early 1960s, the Party took effective control of the judiciary. Chao Yuan, President of the Higher Provincial People's Court of Fujian, said in a speech to the Fujian People's Congress published in early 1959:

> The people's courts must not only observe the policy and directives of the Party, but also obey the direction and supervision of the Party over adjudication of actual cases. They must voluntarily seek instructions from and report their work to the Party committees. When an official of a court goes to the countryside, he must do his work under the unified leadership of the local Party committee, no matter where he happens to be. Forte, "Western Law and Communist Dictatorship," 32 *Emory Law Journal* 135, 190 (1983).

The systematic replacement by the Party of judicial procedures and judicial organs occurred. The Ministry of Justice was eliminated, and courts were prohibited from hearing economic disputes between state enterprises in favor of "mediated" solutions within appropriate ministries. Just prior to the Cultural Revolution, an American law professor asked a former Chinese official from Shanghai about the legal profession there. The official answered, "Lawyers in Shanghai? What do you think China is—the Soviet Union?"

THE CULTURAL REVOLUTION (1966–1976)

The economic devastation of the Great Leap Forward was followed by increased factionalism within the CCP. The intraparty struggle over the pace and direction of economic and political change festered and finally burst forth into the Great Proletarian Cultural Revolution. The ten years of the Cultural Revolution, which began in May 1966 and ended in October 1976, one month after Mao's death, disrupted all aspects of life within the PRC. It was launched by Mao, his wife, Jiang Qing, and Lin Biao, the Minister of Defense who controlled the military. It was the culmination of Mao's continued struggle to achieve his radical policies. The Cultural Revolution affected all aspects of Chinese life during this period, and its impact still reverberates through China today.

A number of factors lay at the heart of the Cultural Revolution. Mao envisioned China as a country based on revolutionary exuberance. He favored massive social action rather than slow bureaucratic construction. He also preferred political enthusiasm to educated technical competence, and objected to the separation of intellectuals and cadres from the hardships of peasant work. Mao believed that men and women, in great numbers, would spontaneously create a new social order that would surpass the accomplishments of mere machines and technology. In this effort, the army would constitute a new center of political power and would guide the Red Guards in creating a new party and a new society. Tradition would be rejected in a wholesale manner as being reactionary and not an appropriate source for the creation of the new order.

The war in Vietnam was a second factor that fueled the Cultural Revolution. U.S. involvement in Vietnam was viewed by the Chinese leadership as a threat to China's national security. Mao used this perceived threat as a propaganda tool for further imposing his radical views on the hierarchy of the Communist Party.

A third factor was Mao's intent to change the Party by silencing some of his rivals and ridding himself of others. Mao bolstered his campaign to radically transform the Party by actively supporting the mass propaganda surrounding the fanatical cult of himself. Fueled by an expanded cult of his own person, Mao set out to dismantle the Communist Party hierarchy. In this effort, an entirely new and unprecedented organization, the Red Guards, was invented and then set loose upon

Chinese society. The Red Guards were squads of university and middle-school students who were to be vanguards of the new revolutionary upheaval. They constituted a notable exception to the political hegemony universally exercised by the Party in communist states at the time. Though officially guided by the army, the Red Guard cadres roamed free and outside the law. They exercised unchallenged and arbitrary authority over all institutions except the army. They attacked the offices and sometimes the persons of middle and high ranking Communist Party members accused of losing revolutionary diligence and of being soft bourgeois "capitalist roaders." During the height of the Cultural Revolution, Mao's writings were required reading. Any deviation from his *Little Red Book* could bring accusations of reactionary views, denunciation and possibly public trial.

The Cultural Revolution became a reign of terror—"smash the security bureau, procuratorial system and judicial system." Implementation of this dictate resulted in the collapse of what remained of the judicial and legal systems. Along with other professions and disciplines, the law, the courts and attorneys suffered tremendously during the Cultural Revolution. This suffering was compounded by the traditional Chinese resistance to legal rules, attorneys and formal legal proceedings. Law was perceived as an impediment to modern China's future. Mao and his followers thought that justice should not be separated from the masses by the barriers of lawyers, laws and law courts.

They believed the people in their masses could judge and decide questions of policy as well as everyday concrete disputes. Almost no laws were enacted during the ten years of the Cultural Revolution.

Beginning in 1966, all law schools were closed. Attorneys, judges, courtroom personnel and law teachers were removed from their positions and sent to farms for forced "reeducation." This proved emotionally and physically debilitating and large numbers of people perished. Many legal specialists went years before they were allowed to return to their homes, and many others were never able to return to their professions. The positions of those who were sent for reeducation were occupied by new revolutionaries. The Red Guards, with Mao's blessing, freely searched houses without legal process, arrested anyone, investigated anything, sentenced, imprisoned, and frequently executed. There were no legal procedures to constrain the Red Guards, no time limits, and no prohibitions on torture. Rape to humiliate was a common occurrence. In the end, Mao failed to appreciate that a rational structure of law, which orders relations in a society in a predictable way, is a vital mechanism for the exercise of state power.

POST–CULTURAL REVOLUTION (1977–1989)

The end of the Cultural Revolution marked a new beginning in the history of the PRC—one that emphasized economic development and political stability. It was the beginning of the Four Modernizations Program, which focused on modernizing industry, agriculture, science and technology, and national defense. The campaign against the "Gang of Four" (Yao Wenyuan, Zhang Chunqiao, Wang Hongwen, and Jiang Qing) in 1976 signalled the beginning of the ascendancy of the legal reformers. After almost four years of detention, Yao, Zhang, Wang and Jiang were placed on trial, together with six other figures active during the Cultural Revolution, for allegedly committing a variety of counterrevolutionary acts. On January 23, 1981, each defendant was found guilty of the principal charges of which he or she stood accused, although some were acquitted of certain of the lesser charges. Jiang and Zhang were each given a sentence of "death with a two-year reprieve" which, after the two years expired, was converted to life imprisonment. This unusual sentence, which has antecedents in Chinese legal history back to the Han Dynasty (206 B.C.–220 A.D.), provided that the death sentence be suspended for a two-year period in order to give the convicted the opportunity to reform sufficiently to merit a lesser penalty than death. The other defendants received sentences of imprisonment ranging from 17 to 20 years.

The new legalists marked their ascent to power by promulgating the 1978 Constitution. The swing toward a highly organized legal system following the Cultural Revolution may be seen as an attempt to achieve economic and political goals. Establishing a legal system became important as a means of encouraging international trade, expanding foreign investment in China, and promoting general international economic cooperation. It was also seen as a mechanism to provide protection against the types of arbitrary behavior by Party and government officials that occurred during the Cultural Revolution. Thus, the new emphasis on law was also a reaction to the excesses of Mao's intense efforts to uproot all bourgeois traditional institutions and the accompanying disruptions.

Domestic economic reforms were an important force behind the effort to restore the legal system following the Cultural Revolution. China faced significant economic challenges. China's per capita gross national product in 1980, for example, was only the equivalent of $250. As the post-Mao era began, the Chinese economy was "directed" by ideological bureaucrats who were committed to orthodox Marxist principles.

By 1980, Deng Xiaoping had emerged from a leadership struggle with Hua Guofeng as China's paramount leader. Deng confronted China's economic problems by launching a series of reforms calculated to provide productivity incentives in both the urban and rural sectors of the economy. His broad strategy was to move away from Party control of all economic decisions through centralized planning, and toward greater use of decentralized economic decision making. During most of the 1980s, there were experiments with enterprise autonomy, securitization of state enterprises through stock offerings, denationalization of small state enterprises to collective or private operations, and the introduction of individual enterprise. Although the Chinese did not adopt Western style capitalism, a dramatic move away from the historical Soviet-style Marxist economy occurred. The development in the 1980s was toward an economic system with unique Chinese characteristics.

Deng started the reform effort in the rural sector of the economy by introducing the household or production responsibility system. Under this system, the farm family became the basic unit of production. Long-term leases to the production unit, and the ability to market that part of the family's crop that exceeded obligatory state quotas, were the predominant characteristics of this system. The results of this improved incentive system were dramatic between 1978 and 1986. Encouraged by the successes in agriculture, Deng launched a counterpart management responsibility system for urban enterprises based on the same concepts of leasing or contracts. Although the assets of the state-owned enterprises were still owned by the state, the managers developed increased control over the management of those assets. The managers of some state-owned enterprises took responsibility for the enterprises' productivity, wages, and profits and losses. These enterprises agreed to deliver a quota of goods to the state at a predetermined price, and when that quota was met, the managers were then allowed to sell the excess on the free market and to use the proceeds to improve their facilities or to distribute to employees as bonuses. As a result, enterprises developed greater independence and responsibility in deciding from whom to buy, what to produce, to whom to sell, and at what prices.

In the mid–1980s, collective enterprises began to issue stock, and the government even introduced some experimental programs that allowed state-owned enterprises to sell a portion of their ownership to their workers through stock issuances. This securitization was designed to stimulate productivity by giving workers a stake in their own company.

Deng's reforms also led to the resurgence of the individual enterprise in both the rural and urban sectors of the economy. Originally limited in size to ten workers, this particular reform proved so dynamic that the limit on the number of workers was subsequently removed. More than 15 million licensed individuals were working in this sector in 1985. Stone Enterprises, for example, started in 1983 as a small computer manufacturing firm with only a few workers. By 1988 it had grown, without state funding, to the point that it was producing the highest quality computer in the PRC and was paying wages several times that paid by state-run computer factories.

By 1988, the Chinese economy was a mixed centrally-planned and market-determined economy.

While the state still owned all the land and controlled the means of industrial production, the general tendency through most of the 1980s was to reduce central planning and to tolerate a less equal distribution in wealth among citizens. Greater sway was also given to the creative contribution made by intellectuals, a class that includes lawyers. Significant problems started to appear during the late 1980s, however. Rampant corruption, especially predominant in the special economic zones, and serious inflation—estimated by World Bank Officials at 30 percent in urban areas in mid-1988—stalled China's economic progress. Deng described the economic dilemma posed by this economic admixture when he used the metaphor that we are in the middle of the river and must choose whether to go forward or backward.

Political developments since the end of the Cultural Revolution have been filled with contradictions. On the one hand, political participation expanded significantly during most of the 1980s, although not to the point of being pluralistic. The role of official ideology in political affairs decreased in favor of pragmatism. The development of regular bureaucratic procedures and institutional processes were stressed to promote economic growth. On the other hand, strict limits existed on both the form and content of political expression. Periodic campaigns, such as the 1983 campaign against spiritual contamination, were conducted against ideas officially branded as heterodox and counterrevolutionary. The Communist Party continued to demonstrate its commitment to maintaining power and to opposing popularly supported democratic reforms.

There are other political implications to the post-Cultural Revolution period. On the one hand, a generation of young people exists whose confidence in any code of belief was destroyed and whose chance for a meaningful education was lost. Thus, one unfortunate legacy of the Cultural Revolution is a "missing generation" of professionals and specialists. On the other hand, the Cultural Revolution also led many former Red Guards not only to question the Party leadership but also to question Marxist ideology. Instead of the revolutionary utopia promised by Mao, the Cultural Revolution became a nationally alienating experience. After responding to the 1966 call of the "Great Helmsman," the Red Guards soon found themselves embroiled in bitter, often violent internecine conflicts, manipulated by feuding Party factions. As the Party attempted to restore order in the wake of the Cultural Revolution, many Red Guards were sent to remote countryside regions to "serve the people." For many, particularly for those from elite families connected to the Party, this experience exposed them, for the first time, to the harsh realities of socialist life as lived by hundreds of millions of China's rural masses. As a result, many former Red Guards lost much of their faith in Mao and the Communist system. The legacy of the Cultural Revolution has been, to some extent, the reduction of the unquestioned authority of the

CCP, its ideology, and organization. The Cultural Revolution also created a generation of young people with a rebellious spirit. Ironically, these individuals, who were organized to promote Mao's ideal of pure communism, may ultimately emerge as a powerful political force for continued reform and moderation within China.

Values centered around the importance of the family have traditionally been important, especially in rural China. Although those values were attacked during the Cultural Revolution, the family and the virtues related to the family are once again publicly honored and observed. Unfilial conduct is considered morally objectionable in both rural and urban China.

The winds of change for legal reform began to blow in the late 1970s. The Standing Committee of the National People's Congress (NPC) adopted a resolution in 1979 that declared that all laws enacted during the 1950s and 1960s were to remain in effect, as long as they did not conflict with the Constitution or more recently enacted legislation. The government also reviewed over 50,000 regulations that had been adopted since the founding of the PRC and abolished or revised those that were contrary to the Constitution or newly enacted legislation. The legal profession was restored. In 1979, law schools were reopened, legal personnel who had been sent to the countryside during the Cultural Revolution were rehabilitated, and the Ministry of Justice was reestablished. The 1980

Provisional Regulations for Lawyers of the People's Republic of China declared: "Lawyers are legal workers of the state whose duties are to give legal advice to government agencies, enterprises, institutions, public organizations, people's communes, and citizens, in order to promote the proper enforcement of the law and safeguard the interests of the state and the collectives as well as the legitimate rights and interests of citizens." By 1982, there were 5,500 full-time and 1,300 part-time lawyers working in China. These were the nascent beginnings of a post-Cultural Revolution movement to construct a new socialist legal system, one that contained a blend of the Soviet model, German model and other civil law traditions.

Enhancing the role of law in China involves more than just enacting laws, publishing regulations and establishing legal institutions. Nevertheless, these actions are an important first step. Since 1979, the State Council has issued more than four hundred regulations, and the provincial people's congresses and their committees have passed over eight hundred decrees. A sense of the remarkable attempt at legal reform is conveyed by noting some of the more important laws that were enacted since then. Among the 1979 enactments were a Forestry Law, a revised Act on Arrest and Detention, and an Environmental Protection Law. In July 1979, the long-awaited Criminal Law and Criminal Procedure Law were adopted along with five other laws: an Organic Law of the Local People's Congresses and Local People's Governments, an Electoral Law for the NPC and the Local People's Congresses, an Organic Law of the People's Courts, an Organic Law of the People's Procuratorates, and a Law on Joint Ventures Using Chinese and Foreign Investment. In 1980, a Nationality Law, a revised Marriage Law, a Joint Venture Income Tax Law, and an Individual Income Tax Law were enacted by the NPC. Other laws adopted in 1980 included the Act on Academic Degrees and the Provisional Act on Lawyers. Important enactments affecting economic matters included the Economic Contract Law (1981), the Act on Land Requisition for National Construction (1982), the Trademark Law (1982), the Law on Marine Environmental Protection (1982), and the Law on Statistics (1983). In 1982 the following four new or revised laws were enacted: the Organic Law of the National People's Congress, the Organic Law of the State Council, the Organic Law of the Local People's Congresses and Governments, and the Electoral Law for the National People's Congress and the Local People's Congresses. The 1982 Constitution and a new charter for the Chinese Communist Party were also adopted; the Civil Procedure Law was adopted in March 1982. In 1983, the Law on the Safety of Maritime Traffic was enacted, and the Organic Law of the People's Courts and the Organic Law of the People's Procuratorates revised. In 1984, China adopted a Patent Law that became effective as of April 1, 1985. The Law of the People's Republic of China on Economic Contracts Involving Foreign Interest and the Law of Succession of the People's Republic of China also became effective in 1985. The Civil Law was adopted in 1986. A new PRC Customs Law and Bankruptcy Law were adopted in 1987 and 1988 respectively. They were followed by the State Enterprise Law and Administrative Litigation Law in 1989. The adoption of significant, new laws continued as China entered the 1990s.

An extensive formal legal system emerged from the ashes of the Cultural Revolution. An examination of its general structure reveals that Chinese legal procedures represent a modified version of the civil law traditions of Western Europe. Similarities to the former Soviet legal system are also evident. In the criminal area, for example, a trial is conducted by a judge and two lay assessors. The procurator prepares the case, and it is then reviewed and independently investigated by the judge. The role of the defense attorney is to present evidence pertaining to the guilt of the defendant and to argue for the mitigation of any sentence imposed. The judicial administration of the law is tied closely to the policies of the Chinese Communist Party, especially in trials with political implications. True judicial independence is more chimerical than real. Another feature of the Chinese judicial system worthy of note is that cases, at least theoretically, do not have precedential value. Judges in applying law to a specific case do not create binding authority. Notwithstanding this general principle, the Supreme People's Court and the Supreme People's Procuratorate may make binding interpretations on trial and procuratorial work, respectively, as long as the interpretations are separate from any particular case decision. Unfortunately, the absence of the principle of precedent leads to inconsistent decisions and inconsistent sentencing for similar crimes.

The ties to the distant past are evident. Evidence of Confucian philosophy generally exists in a diffused form, not as established and formally recognized doctrine. The concept of *li,* which underlies the preference for mediation as a means of resolving disputes, can be found in the 1982 constitutional provision establishing neighborhood and municipal people's mediation committees. The suppression of the 1989 Democracy Movement after the declaration of martial law and the severe punishment of demonstrators are consistent with the tradition of *fa.* Other links to the past can also be identified. The internalized Confucian striving for a harmonious and highly structured society are reflected in modern Chinese judicial proceedings. The criminal system, for example, endeavors to change the attitude of those accused of deviant behavior by teaching them socially appropriate norms. The focus is on reeducation. Thus, the first step in the criminal process is the attempt to get a confession from the accused. This is important because a confession not only affirms the court and prosecution's pretrial investigation and decision making, but it also indicates that the accused disavows the deviant behavior and has set out on a path to restoring societal harmony. Self-criticism and rehabilitation, not for the individual's well-being but for the sake of the social order, make the confession of prime importance in criminal proceedings. A criminal trial in China, whether under emperor, warlord or communist leader, is primarily ritualistic, not adversarial. Confessions often lead to reduced sentences, whereas vigorous defenses often result in harsher punishment. An individual's willingness to submit to societal harmony has always been respected in China. The historical Confucian ideal remains: ultimate social harmony, with China as the center of a harmonious world order.

THE PRESENT

Can China escape from its age-old authoritarian tradition? On May 20, 1989, the Premier of the PRC, Li Peng, announced that he was sending the People's Liberation Army to Beijing "to restore order and discipline." This announcement followed weeks of peaceful demonstrations in Beijing. Hundreds of thousands of citizens of Beijing prevented the soldiers from entering Tiananmen Square, the symbolic center of China, for more than two weeks. All hopes for a peaceful resolution to the impasse ended on the morning of June 4, 1989 when Chinese soldiers attacked the demonstrators, killing and injuring many people. Television and news reports provided verifiable evidence of these tragic events.

The massive demonstrations in May and June of 1989 are in large measure a replay of events in the late 1970s and 1985/86. Although some of the actors are different, the core problems and resentments are remarkably the same. There are still no official channels for the expression of dissent in China. The unchecked power of selected Party officials and their families persists. The media is still both tightly controlled and in many instances censored. The lack of social mobility and of job advancement is a serious problem. The exercise of authority is in many instances arbitrary.

The hard-line resistance to the demands for political reforms in 1989 is ironic. Only a little more than a decade ago Deng rode to power on the crest of a similar wave of popular discontent. Following Premier Zhou Enlai's death, the Gang of Four banned all public mourning ceremonies out of fear that such popular displays of grief for him might undercut their own political power. Denied legitimate channels of expression for their sorrow, resentment which had been fueled by the ten years of turmoil of the Cultural Revolution welled up in the Chinese people. In April of 1976, tens of thousands of people gathered in Beijing to express their feelings of powerlessness and sorrow by placing commemorative wreaths, poems, and essays honoring Zhou and critical of the "Gang of Four" at the foot of the monument to the Heroes of the Chinese Revolution.

Fearing a stronger wave of popular unrest, the Gang of Four sought to suppress the public's expression of restiveness. They ordered the offending wreaths and writings removed under the cover of darkness. The next day, more than 100,000 people gathered demanding to know who was responsible. The People's Liberation Army and security police restored order, and the demonstration was labeled "counterrevolutionary" by the authorities. Deng became the scapegoat for the incident. He was stripped of his official posts and titles, and was vilified in the mass media.

Deng's fall from power was short-lived, however. Following the death of Mao in September of 1976, a popular crisis of confidence swept through China which led to the arrest of the Gang of Four on charges of conspiring to usurp party leadership. Deng was rehabilitated in 1977, and began his reemergence as the power to be reckoned with in China. The events surrounding the suppression of the 1989 Democracy Movement have unfolded in a tragically ironic manner, for it was Deng who played the role of autocratic antihero, a role previously played by the Gang of Four. He was the engineer of the clamp-down on the perceived sources of dissent and disorder, and like countless emperors and warlords before him, he opted for order over freedom.

The articulated themes of the 1989 demonstrations were the promotion of greater democracy, including free speech and press, and the elimination of corruption and nepotism. In a broader sense, the demonstrations represent a deep-seated moral disaffection with current Chinese society and a demand for government accountability. Although only a few individuals have, at this point, directly challenged the legitimacy and authority of the Communist Party, these demonstrations indirectly included such a challenge. In 1987, Fang Lizhi put the following explanation on the demand for greater democracy: "If the democracy we are striving for remains one that is granted only from the top, then the democracy that is practiced in our society is not the true democracy.... We should not place our hope on grants from the top leadership. Democracy granted from above is not democracy in a real sense. It is the relaxation of control." *The Washington Post,* January 18, 1987, at C 1.

Following the brutal suppression of the 1989 Democracy Movement, there was increased political support to reassert centralized control over major segments of the Chinese economy. The development of a "true" market economy was explicitly rejected, and experiments with the issuance of new stocks suspended. New restrictions were imposed on collectives and individual enterprises. As a result, many enterprises in the market-oriented sector collapsed for lack of loans, raw materials or markets, or were ended by administrative direction. The application of centralized control principles also affected the number of domestic companies engaged in foreign trade. Predictably, there will be fewer specialized state-owned trading companies that handle China's trade. Some fear the current leadership, which includes Premier Li Peng, and Communist Party General Secretary Jiang Zemin, has as its goal the reestablishment of a 1950s type Stalinist command economy. China's economic future hangs in the balance.

China's economic future is also clouded by the expanding size of its population. Today, the People's Republic of China is the world's most populous nation. It is the home of nearly one out of every four persons, with a population of over a billion people. Based on the reproduction rate reflected in the 1982 census, the population of the PRC in the year 2002 will be approximately 1.33 billion, which is considerably above the planned population targets. Meeting the demands and needs of its expanding population is perhaps the greatest challenge of the government.

Fundamental problems also exist in rural China. Throughout its history, China has always been an agricultural nation. This fact will also affect China's economic future. China's land area is about 9.6 million square kilometers, which makes it one of the world's largest nations. Although 80 per cent of China's people are tied to the land today, less than 30 per cent of the land is suitable for agriculture uses. Most of the land is either too dry or too mountainous for cost-effective agricultural exploitation. Mountains cover about two-thirds of China's land mass. Agricultural yields can be increased, but only with massive investments of capital, technology, and the effective exploitation of marginal lands. Realizing China's economic potential will require a stable political environment. Such an environment will need legal institutions committed to the rule of law.

The democratic changes that occurred in Eastern Europe in 1989–90 and in the Soviet Union in 1991–92 are not likely to be a significant stimulus to promoting democratic change in China. There are a number of reasons for this prediction. First, there are fundamental differences between the communist leadership which was replaced in Eastern Europe and the Soviet Union and existing communist leadership in China. The octogenarian "old guard" who carried out the Chinese revolution still have power. Because they accumulated power through the use of force, they are quite willing to defend it through the same method. In Eastern Europe and the Soviet Union, there was no comparable group of old guard leaders who were either prepared or able to defend their leadership with the use of force. Second, and perhaps more importantly, is the fact that the events in Eastern Europe were directly affected by the hands-off approach taken by the former Soviet Union. The communist governments of Eastern Europe were, in effect, colonial regimes of the Soviet Union that were linked to Soviet support. At the time, President Gorbachev made it clear that Soviet troops would not intervene in Eastern Europe to support the existing communist leadership. This political decision played a critical role in encouraging change. Neither the Soviet Union nor any other country has ever had this sort of influence in China. Finally, Eastern Europe has a history and tradition of democratic institutions and values. In addition, Eastern Europe has had a greater exposure to Western democratic ideas and institutional forms than the Chinese, including a pluralistic structure which allowed the Catholic Church and labor unions to operate. In China, the exercise of political power has not been subjected historically to influence or constraint by other centers of political or economic power. The PRC has an authoritarian political tradition. Thus, the soil for the roots of democratic movement was far richer in Eastern Europe than it is in China.

The toppling of the communist governments in Eastern Europe and the Soviet Union are not likely to presage the same result in China. Nevertheless, the Chinese leadership will have to deal with the effects of increased relations with the West. Ever since China first experienced significant contacts with the Western world in the late 18th and early 19th centuries, Chinese leaders have been both concerned and apprehensive about the domestic consequences of an extensive relationship with the outside world. There has been the fear that cultural and economic ties with the West would subject the economy to exploitation, introduce disruptive ideas and values, and thereby undermine the security of the state. Determining the appropriate balance between increased economic interdependence with the West and dealing with the disrupting Western ideas and values that accompany increased economic interdependence is a fundamental challenge for the current and future Chinese leadership. As the leadership meets this challenge, it is useful to recall that 1789 marked the beginning—not the end—of the French revolution. The same ultimately may be said for 1989 in the history of the People's Republic of China.

CHAPTER II

POWER, GOVERNANCE AND HUMAN RIGHTS: CONSTITUTIONAL LAW AND THE CHINESE COMMUNIST PARTY

"Law has to serve politics. What should be included in a constitution depends on whether or not it is advantageous to the present political objectives."

Zhang Youyu, Beijing Review, 1980

In order to properly understand Chinese constitutional law and politics, it is important to avoid transferring assumptions about the underlying foundations of the United States system of government. This is particularly important because surface similarities in form and structure exist between the Chinese and the U.S. Constitutions. Notwithstanding surface similarities, fundamental differences exist in the political, economic and cultural arrangements of the two countries. The United States has adopted an economic system based on private ownership and market forces while China still relies heavily on a planned economy with public ownership playing a dominant role. The U.S. system of government incorporates a separation of powers among the branches of government, control over which is regularly contested by two major political parties. China uses a governmental system focused on people's congresses under the singular influence of the Chinese Communist Party. Yet, there is a more fundamental difference—one that relates to the state's role and relationship to society and the individual. Unlike the U.S. Constitution that provides an institutional framework for adjusting the relations between the political forces governing society, the Chinese Constitution is a statement that formalizes the existing power structure.

The Chinese Constitution is a source of law, but not in the same sense as the U.S. Constitution is a source of law. In *Constitutions of Communist Party-States* (1968), Professor Jan Triska observed of all Marxist socialist constitutions that:

> Communist party-state constitutions do not limit the respective governments; instead, they are themselves limited by the ruling party's decision-makers, whether in government or not. Men are supreme, not law; hence, the communist party-state constitutions are not the symbols of freedom they are in Western democracies.... And because they serve the rulers rather than limiting them, the norms which they contain are interpreted from the sole point of view of the interests of the state as determined by the rulers.

Notwithstanding the importance of this observation as it relates to constitutional theory, socialist constitutions should not be considered empty vessels. They serve as barometers of the state's policies and values, and are often the best available guide to a state's social and political norms and institutions.

CONSTITUTIONAL HISTORY IN THE PEOPLE'S REPUBLIC OF CHINA

American constitutional law has developed gradually over a two hundred year period and it has had an important role in the evolution of the American social and political system. The development of constitutional law has been most directly influenced by the existence of an independent judiciary whose function has been to interpret the broad strokes and grand generalities of the U.S. Constitution.

The constitutional history of the PRC has not been the same. Since its founding in 1949, China has had five constitutions: The Provisional Constitution of 1949 (the Common Program); 1954; 1975; 1978; and 1982. Each of these constitutions has signaled a change in power or a change in the economic or political objectives of the Chinese leadership. Thus, each constitution has simply confirmed a change, rather than being a stimulus for the change. The judiciary had virtually no significant role in this constitutional evolution.

Certain generalizations about the constitutional history of the PRC are possible. First, the Chinese constitutional tradition since the founding of the PRC recognizes the dominant position of a single party, the Communist Party. Although factions have existed within the Party, competing political parties have not. The levers of political power have not been available to those outside of the Party. Second, each constitution has been premised on the belief that rights are granted to citizens by the state. Rights are not derived from human personhood, nor are they enshrined or fixed within the constitution itself. This premise or belief allows the state to change both the quality and quantity of a citizen's rights whenever it is believed necessary because the existence of such rights does not limit the power of the state. Consequently, each constitution has either implicitly or explicitly permitted the state to define the nature of a citizen's rights by legislation. This view of law and the nature of rights finds its taproots in the Chinese historical tradition that recognized the ruler's prerogative to adopt those laws necessary to strengthen the state. Third, the U.S. constitutional principle of checks and balances between the traditional branches of government (executive, judicial, and legislative) is absent. The legislature in China has the formal sovereign power to determine constitutional questions, not the judiciary. Fourth, although the national legislature has been elected either indirectly or directly by a limited electorate, the executive has not been directly elected. Moreover, the electoral process has been effectively controlled by the Communist Party, whose membership is a small percentage of the total population. Fifth, each constitution has reflected certain political programs or goals. Professor Andrew Nathan recognized the programmatic nature of Chinese constitutions: "Chinese constitutions assume a harmony of interests between state and citizen. They did not encourage or even recognize the possibility of conflict between the two. For them the purpose of citizen participation was to mobilize popular energies to serve the state." A. Nathan, *Chinese Democracy,* 113 (1986). This programmatic feature of the Chinese constitutional tradition is significant because the constitution can declare a right without it being actually available on the theory that it is a goal.

The 1949 Provisional Constitution declared victory by the Communists in their civil war against the Nationalists. The former laws of the Nationalist government were repealed, and the PRC established. Between 1949 and 1953, a group of emergency laws and decrees were enacted to formally establish a socialist economy governed by the central government. In 1953, a constitutional drafting committee was established under the chairmanship of Mao Zedong. A year later, the First National People's Congress (NPC) adopted the PRC's second constitution and the central government declared its commitment to socialism. The new government was in complete military and political control of China.

The period 1966–76 was marked by a disruption of the legal system caused by the Cultural Revolution. In 1975, the PRC adopted its third constitution. It was significantly influenced by the Cultural Revolution and the belief that Mao Zedong and the "Gang of Four" had won the struggle to solidify political control. In general, the 1975 Constitution reflected the strengthening of the CCP's centralized leadership over the state government. Many of the existing political principles and institutions established by the 1954 Constitution were repudiated, including the basic principle that all citizens were equal before the law, the regulation providing those persons whose rights were violated by government bureaucrats with compensation, the right to inherit private property, and the principle that trials must be independent and serve the law. Institutions such as the Chairperson of the Republic (the most powerful position in the government), the public assessor, public trials, legal defense, the procuracy and the many self-governing rights of minority groups were also abolished. These actions resulted in the elimination of cooperation and balance between the institutions of public security, the procuracy, and the courts.

In addition to abolishing established principles, certain political beliefs or practices underlying the Cultural Revolution were incorporated into the 1975 Constitution. Among these were the belief that "the proletariat must exercise all-around dictatorship over the bourgeoisie in the superstructure, including all spheres of culture"; and that "speaking out freely, airing views fully, holding great debates and writing big character posters are new forms of carrying on socialist revolution created by the masses of the people."

The NPC substantially revised the 1975 Constitution in 1978. The 1978 Constitution repudiated many of the leftist tenets held by the CCP faction that led the Cultural Revolution, including the dictatorship of the proletariat. In order to accelerate the development of China's economy, the constitution declared the programmatic goals of modernizing agriculture, industry, defense, and science and technology. It proposed that the people undertake the planned, proportionate and high-speed development of the national economy to improve their material and cultural life. Finally, the constitution stressed the role of law, reestablished the procuracy, and restored the political rights of the province, county and commune. In general, the 1978 constitutional changes reflected the leadership's desire to return China to a more orderly state of affairs after the turmoil of the Cultural Revolution.

In 1979, the NPC adopted Regulations Concerning the Revision of the Constitution of the People's Republic of China. These regulations expanded the scope of direct elections and provided for the universal use of the secret ballot. The regulations were designed to expand the people's democracy and to strengthen their right of supervision and control over every level of government. A committee was created by the NPC in 1980 to revise the 1978 Constitution. The revisions were necessitated by the change in the CCP leadership from Hua Guofeng to Deng Xiaoping and Hu Yaobang. The 1978 Constitution was seen as obsolete and needed to be updated to reflect the thinking of the new leadership. The Committee for Revision of the Constitution deliberated for two years on the changes. During this time, the revised draft of the constitution was circulated and discussed within Party and government circles. According to the Chinese, 7.3 million speakers commented on the draft in meetings across the country. The final version was adopted by the NPC on December 4, 1982.

The 1982 Constitution of the PRC is at the apex of the legal hierarchy. It provides: "No laws or administrative or local rules and regulations may contravene the Constitution." Taken literally, this provision may be misleading because the Standing Committee of the NPC is given the power to "interpret" the Constitution. The Standing Committee has the formal power to interpret as "constitutional" a law that otherwise might be considered "unconstitutional." The Constitution also gives the Standing Committee the power to partially supplement and amend laws enacted by the NPC, provided the basic principles of these laws are not contravened. Given these general grants of power, an obvious problem exists in viewing the Constitution as the preeminent source of law in the PRC. Moreover, no legal mechanism exists to assure that the NPC or Standing Committee will neither interpret laws nor enact laws in violation of the letter or spirit of the Constitution.

CHANGES IMPLEMENTED BY THE 1982 CONSTITUTION

The 1982 Constitution consists of a Preamble and four chapters. Chapter I contains basic General Principles. Chapter II outlines the Fundamental Rights and Duties of Citizens, and Chapter III sets out the Structure of the State. The final chapter, Chapter IV, is dedicated to the National Flag, National Emblem and the Capital.

The preamble states the four principles to which the People's Republic of China is committed: socialism, the people's democratic dictatorship, Marxism–Leninism and Mao Zedong Thought, and the leadership of the Chinese Communist Party (CCP). The CCP, which in 1992 has approximately 46 million members, is referred to as having under its leadership the "broad patriotic united front that is composed of democratic parties and the people's organizations and embraces all socialist working people. . . ."

The 1982 Constitution contains some significant changes from the 1978 Constitution. The preamble no longer includes lavish praise of Mao Zedong or references the Cultural Revolution. In addition, especially notable changes were made in the areas of citizen rights and obligations, government structure, economic policy, and the stated relationship of the CCP to the process of governance. The increased role and importance of law reflected in the 1982 Constitution is also notable.

The official commentary to the 1982 Constitution identified several changes considered particularly significant for the functioning of the government. First, the power of the National People's Congress was increased since more power was given to its Standing Committee. Because the Standing Committee can meet frequently and is much smaller than the Congress as a whole, it can exercise power effectively. Second, the position of President of the Republic which had been deleted from the 1975 and 1978 constitutions was restored. Third, a Central Military Commission was established whereas formerly the armed forces had been solely under the Party's control. Fourth, the Premier was made responsible to National People's Congress for the actions of the government. In addition, each government ministry operates under a system whereby the minister is responsible for the action of the ministry to the Premier. Fifth, a system of auditing was instituted both at the national and local levels in order to strengthen the supervision of fiscal matters. Finally, the President and members of the Standing Committee of the National People's Congress may not serve more than two terms.

The 1982 Constitution also implemented some important changes in economic policy. The absolute predominance of the commune's collective economy was superseded. The lawful rights and interests of the individual economy, which were declared to be a complement to the socialist sector of the economy, were constitutionally protected. The right to inherit private property was recognized. The constitution also provided for "the proportionate and coordinated growth of the national economy through overall balancing by economic planning and the supplemental role of regulation by the market." Finally, the principle of economic self-reliance was to some extent subordinated to the goal of economic modernization and development. Foreign enterprises and other foreign economic organizations received express protection.

Additional changes in economic policy have been adopted more recently. The 1982 Constitution was amended in 1988 to expressly allow the right to transfer the use of land. The strict prohibition of the 1982 Constitution was softened by adding: "The usufructus of a land-lot may be transferred within the legal framework." In ordinary language, this means that though the land will remain state or collective property, it can be leased to individuals or enterprises. Leases may be inherited, transferred and mortgaged.

The 1982 Constitution recognized the socialist public economy. There was a constitutional provision protecting the "economy of individual urban and suburban laborers" as a supplement to socialist public ownership, but this referred only to small holdings which all communist systems allow, primarily for the satisfaction of personal and family needs, with an occasional surplus for the market. No provision existed in the 1982 Constitution for what might be called "private economy." The 1982 Constitution was amended in 1988 to permit and protect the private economy: "The state permits the private economy to exist and grow within the legal framework as a supplement to socialist public ownership and protects the legitimate rights and interests of the private economy by guiding, controlling and supervising it." This amendment constitutionally recognized the legal status of Chinese/foreign joint ventures and of other forms of economic cooperation with foreigners. It means that foreign investors may rest even more assured that any prejudicial policy change has become most unlikely, short of a further constitutional amendment outlawing private economy. Equally significant, it also expanded the possibility of private enterprise where no foreign investors participate.

The 1982 Constitution also eliminated the 1975 provision that "speaking out freely, airing views fully, holding great debates and writing big character posters are new forms of carrying on socialist revolution created by the masses of the people." This was done on the theory that this provision promoted political instability. In fact, these "four key freedoms" had been abolished in 1980 by an NPC resolution after the CCP leaders complained about their being abused by dissidents during the 1978–79 Democracy Wall Movement.

Finally, Article 31 of the 1982 Constitution authorized the NPC to establish "special administrative regions." This provision was seen as opening the way for the return of Hong Kong, Macao, and possibly Taiwan as special administrative regions under the Party's "one country, two systems" policy.

THE GOVERNMENT STRUCTURE AND THE LEGISLATIVE PROCESS

The 1982 Constitution outlines the basic structure of the branches of government: the National People's Congress (legislature), the State Council (executive) and the Supreme People's Court (judiciary). See Figure 1: Governmental Structure of the People's Republic of China. Under the formal provisions of the Constitution, the legislature dominates the system of government and legislative process. The principle of the checks and balance of powers between the legislative, executive and judicial branches of government contained in the U.S. Constitution is not followed.

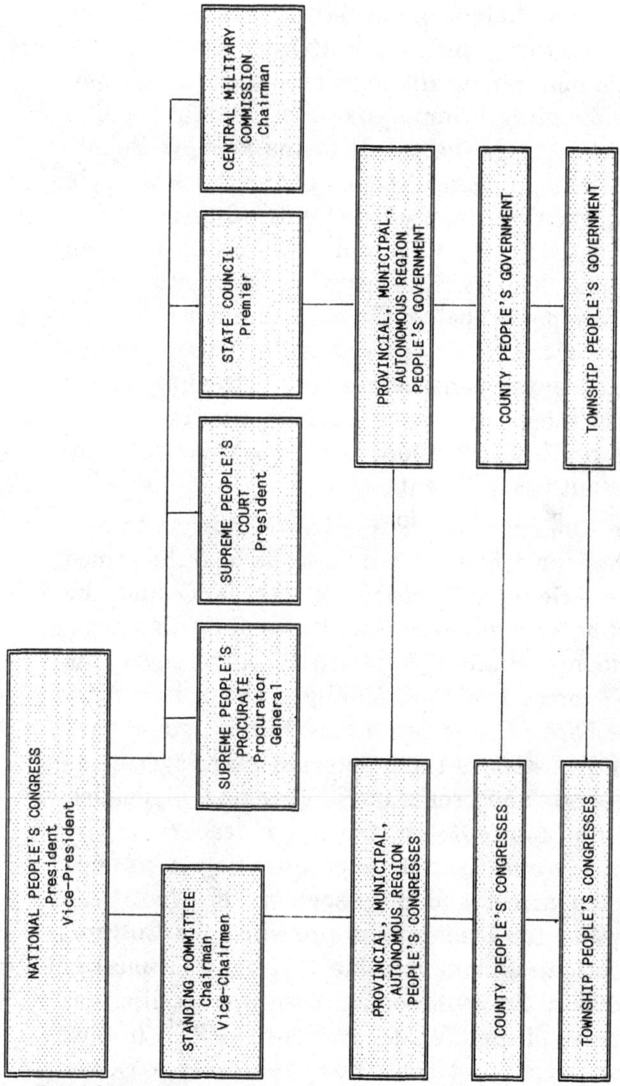

FIGURE 1: GOVERNMENTAL STRUCTURE OF THE PEOPLE'S REPUBLIC OF CHINA [G10241]

More than half of the Constitution deals with the state structure. An examination of this structure reveals four important leaders: (1) the Chairman of the Standing Committee of the National People's Congress; (2) the President of the People's Republic of China; (3) the Premier of the State Council; and (4) the Chairman of the Central Military Commission (CMC). The actual relationship between these four leaders in terms of rank, prestige, stature, and power will only become clear with the passage of time. However, it is likely to depend as much on the personal power base of the individuals holding these titles as the official positions themselves and the provisions outlining their constitutional authority.

The Chairman of the Central Military Commission has the constitutional power to lead the armed forces. He is responsible to the NPC and the Standing Committee. Notwithstanding this organizational relationship, formal control over the armed forces has traditionally been an important power base. China has a long history, going back many dynasties, of the praetorian guard overseeing succession and sometimes changing dynasties. Following Mao's death, the senior leaders in China's army and security apparatus helped to engineer the arrest and imprisonment of Mao's wife and other top leaders who propelled the Cultural Revolution. During the late 1970s and for most of the 1980s, Deng Xiaoping used his position as Chairman of the CMC to control the PRC. In fact, one of Deng's first goals upon returning to power after the Cultural Revolution was to consolidate his control over the armed forces. Although Deng gave up the Chairmanship of the CMC in 1990, the occupant of this position plays an important role in maintaining political stability. In addition, the military undoubtedly will play an important role in determining the future line of leadership succession in China.

National legislative power is exercised through the National People's Congress. The NPC is the highest of four levels of congresses, which correspond to the three-level structure of Chinese administration (townships; counties; and provinces, autonomous regions, and major cities with provincial-level administrative status). The lawmaking powers of the NPC include constitutional amendments, enactments and amendments of basic laws in areas such as criminal or civil law, and laws on state institutions. Although the NPC has supreme legislative power, the Constitution provides that it meet only once a year or on request of the Standing Committee or one-fifth of the NPC. Consequently, it is not a parliamentary body in the usual sense of the word since it is too large (approximately 3,000 members) and meets too infrequently. Moreover, no parliamentary responsibility is available through votes of confidence in the government. As a practical matter, the NPC has been more of a rubber-stamp than an effective law making body.

Legislative immunity is granted members of the NPC. A deputy of the NPC may not be arrested or subjected to criminal prosecution for actions taken in connection with legislative activities without consent of the Presidium of the NPC (composed of the Chairman and Vice–Chairmen of the Standing Committee of the NPC) or, when the NPC is not in session, the Standing Committee.

The Standing Committee of the NPC acts on behalf of the NPC when it is not in session. It has a membership of approximately 150. While their members are elected by the NPC, it is the Standing Committee that has the power to conduct elections for the NPC delegates and to convene the NPC sessions. Since the NPC meets only annually, the Standing Committee controls a great deal of the NPC's power.

The Chairman of the NPC Standing Committee, who works through a small Chairmanship Conference, has a key position in the central government. Although the Standing Committee has the power to interpret and supervise the enforcement of the Constitution, it has rarely exercised these powers. In large measure, the Standing Committee has not done so because it has been occupied with the volume of new legislation. As a result, the Supreme People's Court has emerged as the leading authority on the interpretation of national laws. Its judicial interpretations have been issued either as replies to specific requests for instructions from lower courts or as general interpretative statements on questions of law.

The Standing Committee is also authorized to enact statutes in certain areas not specifically reserved to the NPC itself and may issue decrees (*faling*), decisions (*jueyi*), orders (*mingling*), and instructions (*zhishi*) based on existing laws when the NPC is not in session. The NPC and Standing Committee have the power of legislation, judicial review, appointment, supervision, inquiry and investigation. But, the exact legislative jurisdiction of the NPC and Standing Committee is not always clear. The Constitution gives the NPC the power to enact "basic laws," but fails to define this phrase. Article 67 of the Constitution provides the Standing Committee with the power to enact and amend statutes except for those that should be enacted by the NPC. For example, the Economic Contract Law was adopted by the NPC, whereas the Foreign Economic Contract Law was adopted by the Standing Committee. Thus, the jurisdiction of these bodies is not clearly defined.

In part, the Communist Party exercises its leadership role for society by controlling and influencing the legislative process. Initially, the CCP issues a directive outlining a legislative need. While the principal responsibility for legislative work now rests with the NPC or its Standing Committee, the Party Central Committee's approval is critical to the adoption of all legislation. In the case of codifying a substantive or procedural law, the Legal Affairs Commission of the Standing Committee, together with the Legal Research Institute of the Chinese Academy of Social Sciences and the concerned departments and agencies under the State Council, organizes a special group to prepare a draft to respond to the CCP directive. This group often designates a smaller group of prominent experts and jurists as the key members. They typically gather relevant information and data. Once the first draft is complete, it is submitted to the Party's Central Committee for approval. Party participation in the drafting process ensures new legislation is consistent with Party policy and ideology. Sometimes laws are issued jointly by the CCP and the State. For example, the statute prohibiting cadres from engaging in business and running enterprises was promulgated jointly by the CCP Central Committee and the State Council.

The President of the PRC, who is the head of State, represents the country in its domestic affairs and in its relations with foreign countries. The office of President is separate from that of the Chairman of the Standing Committee. The President shares the responsibilities of the Chief Executive Officer with the Premier. The President and Vice President are elected by the NPC for a five year term, and they may not hold those offices for more than two consecutive terms. Although the President ranks first by protocol, this post appears much weaker than Chairman of the Standing Committee. The essential powers of the President of the PRC are delineated in Articles 80 and 81 of the Constitution. Perhaps the most important is the political power to appoint and remove the Premier and other specified persons. However, in practice, the functions of the President are mainly ceremonial.

The State Council is the executive or administrative branch of government with control over the roughly 41 ministries and commissions of the government. Its membership of approximately 100 in 1991 included a premier, vice-premiers, and the ministers and vice-ministers of China's ministeries and commissions. The Premier, who is the head of the State Council, is responsible for running the administrative machinery of the state. The Premier, along with the top officials of the various ministries, is in actual control of the administration of the State bureaucracy. As with other branches of government, there is a close link between the leadership of the State Council and the Communist Party. The Premier and Vice–Premiers usually are members of the Party's Politburo.

The State Council possesses the power to draft and introduce legislation to the NPC. It also has extensive rule making powers. The Constitution grants the State Council the authority to promulgate "administrative laws and regulations," but does not define the scope of this authority. In practice, the administrative authority has been broadly exercised. For example, the State Council and its ministries promulgated numerous regulations in the contract area dealing with such subjects as insurance contracts, loan agreements, and investments. By constitutional mandate, the administrative laws and regulations issued by the State Council are subordinate to the laws enacted by the NPC or Standing Committee. This general principle does not apply when the NPC expressly delegates authority to the State Council to promulgate regulations different from existing law. Thus, for example, the State Council was given the authority by the NPC to promulgate regulations permitting foreigners investing in coastal cities to have preferential tax treatment other than existed under the then applicable tax laws.

Regional law is also an important source of PRC law. The Constitution gives regional governments the power to enact regional laws in their respective jurisdictions. Such laws cannot conflict with national laws and regulations. In general, however, the national laws are considered the supreme law of China except when the central government specifically authorizes a regional government to enact laws that differ from the national laws. Thus, for example, certain provincial governments in special economic zones have enacted separate laws for special economic zones that differ from the national laws.

Some general observations about government and the legislative process are noteworthy. First, the formal rules governing the legislative process evolved slowly during the 1980s. The Standing Committee of the National People's Congress only established in 1987 the procedural guidelines to govern its activities, and the NPC did not adopt rules of procedure until 1989. Second, the President of the NPC, the Standing Committee, the State Council, the Supreme People's Court, the Supreme People's Procuratorate, and a small number of special committees and delegates may introduce legislative bills. In practice, however, most bills that become law are introduced by either the Standing Committee or State Council. Third, although substantial progress has been made in regularizing the legislative process, a large body of laws and interpretations are not available to either the Chinese public or foreigners. Oftentimes laws and regulations are available only to the officials administering them. In reality, this practice likely continues in spite of a 1988 announcement that the State Council would publicly publish all regulations. Fourth, although the CCP is not a constitutionally established organ of government, it plays an important, but often undocumented, role in the legislative process. In addition, although the day-to-day work of the government is managed by the state bureaucracy, this management occurs under the supervision of the CCP. Fifth, the "old guard," including Deng Xiaoping, Chen Yun, Li Xiannian, Peng Zhen, Yang Shangkun, and Wang Zhen, have and continue to exercise important control over the regime's policy priorities despite the fact that most of them are no longer members of the CCP Politburo or Central Committee.

THE COMMUNIST PARTY

The Communist Party has been in power in the PRC for over forty years. During this time it has increasingly alienated larger and larger segments of Chinese society. Nevertheless, the Party is not likely to fall from power in the near term. In the mid–1980s Professor Andrew Nathan observed:

> Most intellectuals appear to accept the party's claim that political order in their country requires leaders with strong authority. They hold to the old view that, because of China's feudal tradition and peasant backwardness, institutional change is useless until the culture is reformed. Many who speak this way seem unaware of how their words echo back through history: to the judgment of Liang Qichao that China was fit only for enlightened despotism; to the political passivity and cultural reformism of dispirited liberals of the 1920s and 1930s; to the tutelage theory of the Guomindang. A. Nathan, *Chinese Democracy* (1986).

The CCP has the central role in China's domestic and foreign policies and also in the forecast of China's future. No consideration of law in the PRC would be complete without considering the relationship between the CCP and the State and legal system. In understanding the role of the Communist Party in China, a distinction should be made between the laws of the state and decisions of the Party. The term state generally is reserved for the sovereign authority, and the word law refers to the rules that the state commands its subjects to obey. Laws are enacted through the formal procedures of the legislative process, not through the policies of the ruling party. But, the practical import of this distinction has been blurred because until recently the CCP has held that it can legitimately restrict rights through its own decisions or policies rather than only through state law. The Chairman of the Standing Committee of the NPC underscored the important historical role of Party policy in 1984 when he said: "We must gradually make the transition from relying on policy in managing affairs, to establishing and strengthening the legal system and relying not only on policy but also on law to manage affairs." It is clear, at least historically, that Party policy could have the same effect as law. This is still likely to be the case when the law is either unclear or absent. Another dimension to Party policy exists in the fact that it is also the guiding force behind law enacted by the state. In this situation, Chinese laws conform to Party policies.

The governing structure of the PRC consists of two systems: the Communist Party and the state government. These systems do not have equal power, however. The Communist Party's power effectively overrides the government's power either by requiring that its policies have the effect of law or by controlling the formal processes of government, including the legislative process. The Constitution obliquely provides the legal basis for the Party's pervasive authority. The Preamble to the

Constitution states that each citizen is obligated to uphold the four basic principles of party leadership, socialism, dictatorship of the proletariat, and Marxism–Leninism–Mao Zedong Thought.

The Party exercises its authority through a national party structure, based on the Central Committee at the national level and on leading Party committees at the regional and local levels. See Figure 2: Structure of the Chinese Communist Party. Organizationally, the CCP operates on the basis of a Leninist model reflecting hierarchical and elitist principles. The lowest level of the CCP organization consists of the primary party units or "cells." These Party branches can be found in factories, farms, city neighborhoods, or wherever there are three or more full party members. It is at this level that organizational activities such as membership recruitment, political and ideological education about the current party line, the maintenance of close ties with the non-CCP masses, and party discipline are carried out. The primary units are combined into larger groups at the city, town, and county (district) levels. These local party organizations report on their work and get instructions from higher party officials at the provincial level.

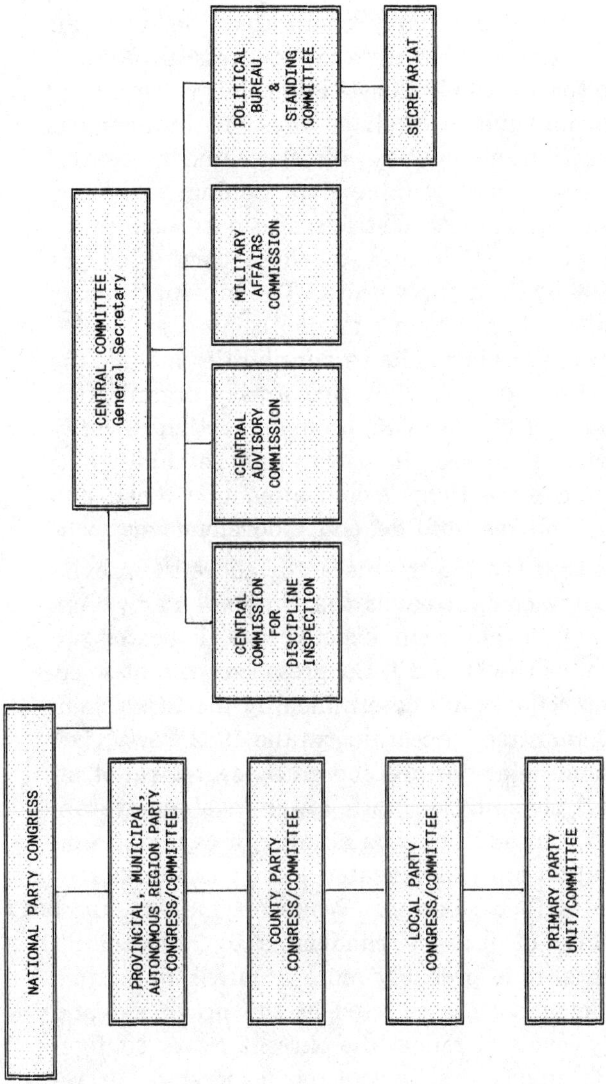

[G10240]

FIGURE 2: STRUCTURE OF THE CHINESE COMMUNIST PARTY

The provincial party committees derive their power from provincial party congresses. According to the 1982 CCP Constitution, congresses at the provincial level as well as those in autonomous regions, municipalities directly under central government control (Shanghai, Beijing, and Tianjin), and cities with districts are to be held every three years. Delegates to these congresses are selected by local party units. The provincial party committee is run by a standing committee headed by a first secretary. Its responsibilities include the supervision of policy in five areas: organization and control of the CCP; economic activities relating to agriculture, industry, finance and trade; capital construction; mobilization of women and youth; and research for policy development.

The next level in the hierarchy above the provincial party committees is the National Party Congress. It is not clear exactly how delegates are chosen for the National Congress except that selection procedures are determined by the CCP's Central Committee. According to the 1982 Party Constitution, delegates are chosen by secret ballot after full consultation with lower level party congresses. In addition, the number of candidates on the ballot must be greater than the number of delegates to be elected. While one might expect the slate of possible candidates to reflect local concerns, it is probably more accurate to assume that delegates are selected at the provincial and county levels to reflect the current power configurations among the Party's top leadership. It remains possible for central Party officials to pack the slate of candidates with their supporters.

The National Party Congress is a very large body. The Thirteenth Party Congress held in 1987 was attended by close to two thousand delegates. According to the 1982 CCP Constitution, the National Party Congress must meet every five years. In spite of meeting infrequently, National Party Congress sessions are usually very short. The 1987 meeting lasted only six days. Given its large size and its infrequent and short meeting schedule, the National Party Congress while theoretically the supreme authority within the CCP, in reality it is not a truly deliberative body. It serves primarily as a forum for top party officials to report on CCP policies. These meetings also serve as opportunities for party members to renew their commitment and participation in Party affairs. One major task the National Party Congress carries out is the election of members to the next higher CCP body, the Central Committee. In actuality, it ratifies a membership slate prepared by the top Party leadership.

While the exact number varies over time, the Central Committee of the CCP elected in 1987 included 175 regular and 110 alternate members. This membership reflected the replacement of some older cadre with younger individuals (average age fifty-five), who were better educated and more professionally competent. According to the CCP Constitution, the Central Committee must meet at least once a year. It has the supreme authority to govern party affairs and enact party policies when the National Party Congress is not in session. However, like the Party Congress, due to its large size and infrequent meetings, the Central Committee rarely initiates policy. However, at its meetings, it does officially approve policies and changes in the membership of leading Party organs.

When the Central Committee is not in session, the CCP Constitution stipulates that the Political Bureau (Politburo) will act on its behalf. In February of 1992 there were fourteen members of the Politburo. The members of the Politburo and its smaller Standing Committee actually exercise the supreme authority within the Communist Party. The Standing Committee carries out the day-to-day work of the Politburo. It is at the apex of the hierarchical structure of the CCP. The Politburo and its Standing Committee possess essentially unlimited power over the general policies of the CCP and all important governmental matters. For example, the Politburo selects the top personnel to direct the vast apparatus of the Party, State, and military.

The Politburo is elected by the Central Committee from a slate prepared by the Party's top leaders. Between 1935 and 1975 Mao Zedong generally performed this function. Beginning in the early 1980s, Deng Xiaoping has dominated the creation of the candidate slate. The Politburo meets frequently and generally makes decisions based on a consensus. The General Secretary of the Central Committee (who must be a member of the Standing Committee of the Politburo) is responsible for calling meetings of the Politburo and its Standing Committee and presides over the operation of the Party's Secretariat.

The Secretariat is the administrative agency that supervises the CCP's functional departments that parallel the ministries of the central state government. Under a 1987 revision to the 1982 Party Constitution, the Secretariat is appointed by the Politburo, subject to the approval of the Central Committee. It is specifically designed as a working body of the Standing Committee and the Politburo. It meets regularly (probably twice a week) and frequently invites leaders in industry, agriculture, science, and education to brief it on current developments and problems in their areas. The Secretariat and its departments interact on a regular basis with the relevant members of the State Council and governmental ministries and agencies in policy formulation.

The central party organization also includes a Military Affairs Commission (MAC), a Central Commission for Discipline Inspection, and a Central Advisory Commission. The MAC is institutionally responsible to the Central Committee; however, it reports directly to the Politburo and its Standing Committee. It makes policies on national defense, and supervises the administration of China's armed forces including the establishment of criteria for selection and promotion within the ranks of the military. The Central Commission for Discipline Inspection also reports to the Central Committee. Its specific functions are not spelled out in any public document. However, it appears to be responsible for maintaining party morality and discipline, controlling the performance of party organizations, and investigating breaches of party discipline. The Central Advisory Commission, established in 1982, was created primarily as a device to encourage aging party leaders to give up their other official positions in order to provide opportunities for upward mobility for younger party leaders. Membership on this commission is restricted to individuals with at least forty years of service to the CCP. It was designed to serve as a consulting body to the Central Committee and was not intended to have any real political power. However, since the late 1980s members of this body have begun to play key roles in speaking out on party matters, including the resignation of Hu Yaobang as General Secretary in 1987.

The Central Committee of the CCP reaffirmed the Party's preeminent role at its meeting in March of 1990: "The session holds that our Party is the vanguard of the working class armed with Marxism–Leninism and Mao Zedong Thought. . . ." Although the Party is the repository of power, the personal power exercised by one or a small number of individual party members can be extensive. The extent to which the CCP can be dominated by one individual was seen most dramatically in the power exerted by Mao Zedong until his death in 1976. However, the pervasive influence of one individual, in this case Deng Xiaoping, was seen again in the suppression of the 1989 Democracy Movement. The enduring quality of China's patrimonalism has not diminished. From an examination of the backgrounds of CCP leaders, it appears that factors such as class origin and political credentials, revolutionary experiences such as participation in the Long March (1934–35), loyalty, experience and expertise, and success in implementing policies have been instrumental in an individual's ability to seize and retain power. Support from a powerful mentor and family relations do not hurt either.

The CCP is not monolithic. Even before the establishment of the PRC in 1949, the Party experienced fissures usually based more on differences over the means to achieve CCP goals rather than the goals themselves. However, since the early 1980s, factions within the leadership have also developed around differences on basic CCP objectives. Membership in factions is generally based on personal relationships and associations. While the influence of individual leaders within the CCP has been extraordinary at times, in order to wield this influence effectively, individuals have had to rely frequently on the support of various Party groups or factions.

Scholars have differed on their categorization of factions in China since the Cultural Revolution.

Professor Paris Chang focuses on the post–1976 emergence of two factions: a group consisting of Mao loyalists including Hua Guofeng, and the pragmatists led by Deng Xiaoping. The pragmatist group includes many Politburo members who were Party leaders victimized by the Cultural Revolution. Professor Dorothy Fontana developed a factional model based on a radical-left (Gang of Four and loyal Maoists), left-of-center (Long March military leaders and veteran economists and technocrats who are central state administrators) and political-right (purged Party victims of the Cultural Revolution including Deng Xiaoping) spectrum. Finally focusing specifically on China after 1989, Professor James Wang notes the growing power struggle between three leadership factions: (1) Younger leaders sponsored by Deng Xiaoping who are more reform and open-door oriented; (2) more conservative party leaders led by Li Peng who advocate increased centralized control over the economy; and (3) a military faction led by Yang Shangkun.

Regardless of the exact nature of the divisions within the CCP, their significance lies primarily in their mere existence. Officials with factional ties favor those with similar views. Through the years, CCP leaders have learned that personal ties and mutual help, more than holding a correct ideological position and institutional loyalty, are the best means to protect one's career and enhance personal political power. In the 1990s, factional infighting within the CCP has become more intense as leaders jockey for political domination. It has also become more visible to outside observers thus destroying whatever facade may have existed of a unified Chinese leadership.

No set pattern for the succession of top Party leaders exists. This does not mean that the current leadership under Deng Xiaoping does not appreciate the need for an orderly leadership transition to continue current reform programs. Deng has planned for his replacement by building a second and third echelon of leaders to follow him. The first echelon includes those individuals, like Deng, who are old CCP veterans usually in their late 70s or 80s. The second echelon encompasses reform oriented leaders, mostly in their 60s, who came to power with Deng in 1978. Finally, the third echelon is made up of younger reform-minded leaders in their 40s and 50s.

Since 1982, in fact, Deng Xiaoping has attempted to ensure the continuation of his reformist policies through the placement of his followers in key Party bodies. In the mid–1980s, he tried and failed to convince the Long March generation of CCP leaders to follow his example and retire from office. By 1987, Deng felt he had achieved his goal of a reformist legacy when Zhao Ziyang became Party General Secretary, the Politburo was relatively balanced between reformers and conservatives, and many older generation leaders finally retired from office. However, Deng's plans began to unravel first with the implementation of an economic austerity program in September of 1988 and later with the Tiananmen Square crackdown in June 1989. Following these events, Zhao Ziyang was ousted from office while the conservatives within the CCP gained power. Deng will try, once again, at the Fourteenth Party Congress in the fall of 1992 to get a majority of his reformist supporters on the Central Committee and Politburo.

While Deng's general plan is for the second and, more likely due to age, the third echelon of leaders to take over from the first, indications within China suggest that the transfer of power will not be an easy one. Many Chinese, especially young people, were angered by the current leadership's recruitment of a third echelon in the mid–1980s. They see this selection as merely perpetuating the nepotism of earlier Chinese leaders. Many in the third echelon are, in fact, the children or grandchildren of aging leaders who refused to retire until their offspring were guaranteed posts in the second or third echelons. The creation of a third echelon also effectively means that individuals not currently designated as part of the future leadership will not have the opportunity for leadership positions in the next thirty to forty years.

Regardless of who the current CCP leaders have chosen as their successors, the ability of China's leaders to maintain their positions and hence continue their policies will depend greatly on the success of their political and economic programs to bring visible improvements and sustained economic growth to China. As noted by Professor Suzanne Ogden, a strong economy would create an excellent foundation that a politically powerful leadership could use to resist destabilizing forces. A weak economy does not bode well for the CCP or China's people.

The CCP is not a party in the Western sense of political parties. It is not a vote-getting mechanism nor is it a part of a pluralistic whole. The CCP claims to represent the whole of Chinese society. It asserts the right to determine the general perspectives for the development of society and the course of domestic and foreign policy. The CCP maintains its domination through three mechanisms. First, under the direction of the Politburo it establishes China's basic policies. Second, Party representatives occupy the highest offices of the State. Finally, the Party apparatus is intertwined into the State's system of administration. The CCP effectively controls and directs the government machinery through the interlocking nature of Party and top state personnel as well as bureaucratic structures.

As previously noted, the Communist Party plays an important role in implementing its policy through the legislative process. There are indications that the Party has been ostensibly trying to reduce its control over the legal system. A number of provisions in the 1982 Constitution were designed to elevate and guarantee the rule of law in China. These provisions, at least theoretically, affect the power of the CCP to independently restrict rights through Party decisions. For example, the Constitution provides "all state organs, the armed forces, all political parties and public organizations and all enterprises and undertakings must abide by the Constitution and the law. All acts in violation of the Constitution and the law must be looked into. No organization or individual may enjoy the privilege of being above the Constitution and the law." It also establishes the general duty of every citizen to abide by the Constitution and law. This provision ostensibly applies to all citizens, including Party members. Another constitutional article provides that "the people's courts shall, in accordance with the law, exercise judicial power independently and are not subject to interference by administrative organs, public organizations or individuals."

The judiciary is not independent of the Party's influence, however, because the Party is the guardian of socialist legality. Its relationship to the judicial system has three dimensions. First, the Party conducts education programs to ensure conformity to Party ideology. Second, it is involved in the selection process of judges. Third, it constantly supervises whether the judicial organs strictly execute the law in conformity with Party policy. A judge considered a model jurist wrote in the mid–1950s:

> When cases I have handled required arresting and sentencing, had a relatively strong policy

> nature, or involved village or cooperative cadres, I asked instructions from the Party committee both before and during the process of handling the cases, and afterward I reported to the Party committee.... Whenever the Party committee gave me instructions, I conscientiously studied and thoroughly implemented them. Note, "Concepts of Law in the Chinese Anti-Crime Campaign," 98 *Harvard Law Review* 1890, 1891 (1985).

Although changes have occurred since that time, it is still accurate to say that when a case has a strong policy component, the Political-Legal Committee or *Zhengfa Weiyuanhui* of the CCP will give the court instructions on the handling of the case. Through these mechanisms, the Party becomes the guardian of the law, and politics still influences the Chinese legal system today. In reality, the highest judicial decision-making body, higher than the Supreme People's Court and the Supreme People's Procuratorate, is the Political-Legal Committee of the CCP.

The 1982 Party Constitution states the Communist Party is subject to the laws of the State. But it also provides "[the Party] must see to it that the legislative, judicial and administrative organs of the State and the economic, cultural and people's organizations work actively and with initiative, independently, responsibly and in harmony." These two provisions involve a contradiction. If the Party is subject to the state's laws, it cannot legitimately supervise the State as a lawmaking body. Official Party pronouncements such as these reflect an ambivalent attitude towards the law. When contradictions between Party policy and law exist, it is not clear whether such contradictions will be resolved by following the Party policy, the law, or handling them on a case-by-case basis.

The potential for conflict can be illustrated. The Organic Law of the Local People's Congresses and Local People's Governments of the PRC describes the functions of the people's congresses of local government units. It states that they are to enforce "the Constitution, laws, policies, decrees, and orders of the state ...," thus listing policies together with other legal documents. In another part of this law, the standing committees of the people's congresses of provinces, autonomous regions, and municipalities are given the right to make local statutes, provided they do not contradict "the Constitution, laws, policies, decrees, or administrative orders of the state...."

The relationship between Party policy decisions and state legal norms arguably might be considered in some respects similar to the relationship between equity and the common law. Just as equity provides a gloss on the common law, Party decisions provide a gloss on State legal norms. But just as a rule of common law must give way when it conflicts with a principle of equity, so must any rule of state law give way when it is inconsistent with an ideological principle of the Party. In the final analysis, the overriding idea is that legality is defined as what is in the public's interest, as determined by the Communist Party. This idea was expressed in early 1990 by the President of the Supreme People's Court, Ren Jianxin: "It is a mistake to think that, because there is law, justice can be executed without the guidance of [Party] policies."

The bloody suppression of the 1989 Democracy Movement has weakened the moral authority of the CCP. In addition, many of the economic reforms introduced during the 1980s may have weakened the Party's claim as the leading force. Unfortunately, the Party is likely to attempt to tighten rather than loosen its controls over government administration in response to the direct and indirect challenges to its authority.

INTERNATIONAL STANDARDS ON HUMAN RIGHTS AND CHINA

An issue of growing concern in the development of the Chinese legal system is human rights. Louis Henkin, a specialist in international human rights, has argued that human rights are universal claims which individuals have as members of the society in which they live. See "The Human Rights Idea in Contemporary China: A Comparative Perspective" in R. Randle Edwards, Louis Henkin, and Andrew J. Nathan, *Human Rights in Contemporary China* (1986). The exact nature of these rights has been the subject of frequent debate. In part, the debate has centered around whether human rights are universal or whether, under the concept of state sovereignty, each state determines what human rights are provided and protected within its own territory. Another part of the debate relates to the division of human rights into two general groups: political-civil rights and economic-social-cultural rights. Here the question is the relationship between the categories and whether one category has priority over the other.

With regard to the universality of human rights, a growing consensus appears to exist within the international community that international law sets the standards for all states. The practice of human rights by individual states should be measured by reference to these standards. However, China rejects the concept of universal human rights, despite its adherence to the United Nations Charter. China argues that each nation has the right to define human rights as it pertains to the conditions within its own territory. China also argues that no nation or international organization has the "legal right" to apply its definition of human rights to another country. Consequently, criticism of its human rights record by international organizations is rejected by the Chinese government as an unwarranted interference in its internal affairs.

In general, China views all rights as being collectively based, nonuniversal and subordinate to state sovereignty and state security. This view of rights is based on traditional concepts, traceable to the imperial period, that reflect the relationship between the state and its citizens wherein individual rights are subordinate to collective rights. The PRC leadership also adheres to the socialist view that emphasizes collectively based economic, social and cultural rights. This emphasis is illustrated by the preference for state ownership of the means of production. Similarly, adoption of the political theory of democratic centralism (examined in the next section of this chapter) results in the subordination of civil and political rights.

During most of the 1980s, the PRC appeared to be moving towards a more general acceptance of the concept of universal human rights. A study by the Chinese Social Development Research Center of Beijing University on human rights, which was published in the official Party journal (*Qiushi*) just before the suppression of the 1989 Democracy Movement, used the term as embracing the "common interests of all mankind" and reflecting the view that "no political system in the world, whatever its ideology, could publicly oppose the concept of human rights."

The Chinese reasserted their traditional position regarding human rights in March of 1989 after international criticism of their use of lethal force to put down demonstrations by monks and their supporters calling for the independence of Tibet. They were even more forceful in their response to the international outcry that followed the June 1989 military suppression of the Democracy Movement. With regard to both of these incidents, the Chinese government claimed that its actions were legitimate in that they were necessary to maintain law and order. The Chinese leadership has denounced all criticism of its handling of these situations as unjustified interference in its internal affairs. Thus, the Chinese have reaffirmed their strict interpretation of state sovereignty that rejects any foreign interference, including that aimed at ensuring the protection of citizens' rights.

A compelling argument can be made that China is obliged to ensure that its national practices meet the human rights standards established by international consensus. China has ratified or acceded to several United Nations sponsored multilateral human rights treaties relating to women, racial discrimination, refugees, apartheid, genocide, and torture. By becoming a party to these treaties, China has not only assumed a number of specific obligations to ensure that its citizens can enjoy certain civil and political rights, it has also accepted the legitimacy of international supervision of its treatment of its citizens relating to these issues. In addition, under the UN Charter *all* member states, which since 1971 includes the PRC as the representative of China, have an obligation to promote and protect human rights. As a member of the UN Commission on Human Rights, China has acknowledged that human rights are international and that UN members have a right to investigate human rights violations. China has, in fact, voted to send UN investigatory teams to South Africa, Chile, and Afghanistan.

Human rights are frequently divided into two groups: civil-political and social-economic-cultural. Any discussion of human rights necessitates providing content to subdivisions within each category. The Universal Declaration of Human Rights of 1948, the International Covenant on Civil and Political Rights and the International Covenant on Economic, Social and Cultural Rights, which were both adopted by the United Nations in 1966, provide elaborative detail for each category. "Civil rights," which are not normally dependent on social conditions, include: freedom of thought, conscience and religion, expression and association, residence and movement; every person's right to life, freedom from slavery, arbitrary arrest or detention; freedom from arbitrary killing, torture, or mistreatment; and equality before the law. "Political rights" include an individual's right "to take part in the government of his country, directly or through freely chosen representatives;" the right of access to public service; and the right of election and recall of government on the basis of universal and equal suffrage by secret ballot. "Social rights" include the right of everyone to a standard of living adequate for health and well being. Encompassed within this right is food, clothing, housing, medical care, and necessary social service, and the right to security in the event of unemployment, sickness, disability or the lack of livelihood in circumstances beyond his or her control. "Economic rights" include the right to work, to free choice in employment, to equal pay for equal work, and the right to reasonable limitations of working hours. It also includes the right to strike. "Cultural rights" allow for access to the "cultural life of the community."

CHINESE CONSTITUTIONAL NORMS ON RIGHTS AND DUTIES

The national norms of a state are reflected in its constitution. According to Marxist–Leninist theory, the rights and duties of citizens do not have universally applicable meaning or content. The 1982 Constitution, as have prior constitutions, accepts this theoretical postulate. Chinese law in general and Chinese constitutional law in particular are essentially positive law. Natural law is not considered a source of law nor is the concept of inalienable rights recognized. As a result, a right not specifically granted by the State cannot be presumed.

The 1982 Constitution follows the principle of interconnecting a citizen's rights and duties. Constitutionally granted rights come with attendant duties: "Every citizen enjoys the rights and at the same time must perform the duties prescribed by the Constitution and the law." Thus, constitutional rights and freedoms become conditional. The exercise of granted rights and freedoms "may not infringe upon the interests of the state, of society and of the collective, or upon the lawful freedoms and rights of other citizens." From the standpoint of the theory of rights, the rights contained within the 1982 Constitution may be effectively canceled out by offsetting prescribed duties.

In addition to making rights conditional, the 1982 Constitution seems to recognize two classes of rights: dispositive rights and peremptory rights. Citizens are free to exercise or refrain from exercising dispositive rights, such as freedom of speech. But citizens are not free to accept or reject peremptory rights. Peremptory rights are those that the state deems essential to either society or the individual. Thus, for example, the Constitution provides that citizens "have the duty as well as the right to receive education." Under this regime, a citizen would not have the right to refuse to receive an education, although as a practical matter many people, especially those in the countryside, do not receive the benefit of this constitutional right.

The 1982 Constitution, as did prior Chinese constitutions, contains a comprehensive statement of rights, freedoms, and obligations of Chinese citizens. The comprehensive set of duties imposed on citizens of the PRC by the Constitution include: the duty to receive education; to work; to support one's parents; to safeguard state secrets; to take care of public property, observe labor discipline, and observe public order. The rights and freedoms include: equality before the law; freedom of speech, press, assembly, association, procession and demonstration; freedom of religious belief; personal freedom; personal dignity, and freedom from insult or slander; the right to make criticisms of and proposals, reports, appeals, or complaints to any organ of state or functionary; compensation according to provisions of the law when a citizen's rights have been infringed by an organ of state or functionary; material assistance in old age, illness or disability; and, the protection of both Chinese persons returned from abroad and those who have relatives abroad.

An individual's right to privacy and freedom of correspondence is also provided for in the 1982 Constitution with the limit that censorship may be used "to meet the needs of state security or of investigation into criminal offenses" (Article 40). Additional rights discussed in the Constitution include the protection against arbitrary interference with privacy, the family, one's home or reputation and certain procedural rights such as a public trial for most cases and a right to a defense and to appeal. As with the rights already discussed, these are also limited to varying degrees by other constitutional provisions or the simple inability or more likely the unwillingness of officials to see that they are protected.

Both the existence of the 1989 Democracy Movement demonstrations and the suppression by the government provide a useful opportunity to consider the limits on the right of free speech. As previously noted, the free speech provision does not limit the power of government to legislatively restrict it. One limitation on free speech is found in Article 51 of the Constitution. It provides that "the exercise by citizens of the People's Republic of China of their freedoms and rights may not infringe upon the interests of the state, of society and of the collective, or upon the lawful freedoms and rights of other citizens." Other constitutional provisions, such as those contained in Articles 38 (on libel), 53 (on observing public order), and 54 (on not acting to the detriment of the country) also expressly limit or qualify the free speech guarantee. The right is also restricted by other laws. Various provisions contained in the Criminal Law of 1979, such as Article 102 dealing with the crime of counterrevolution—a provision that was used by the government against those citizens who demonstrated in the 1989 Democracy Movement—may be used by the government to penalize those who exceed the allowable bounds of permissible speech set by the state. The state-secret regulations of 1988 can also be used as a brake on the exercise of "free speech."

In contrast, the limits on free speech under the U.S. constitutional system are not expressed in the U.S. Constitution as they are in the Chinese Constitution. The boundaries of free speech in the United States have been developed over a 200 year history by the judiciary, principally the U.S. Supreme Court. In China the boundaries are determined legislatively. As a result, the right of free speech is likely to be more narrowly drawn in the PRC than it is in the United States for several reasons. First, a legislature is more susceptible to political pressure than an independent judiciary. Second, free speech has and continues to be important in shaping debate on public issues in the United States. This has not been the case in China. The advocacy of ideas which may be contrary to fundamental tenets of the Chinese social and political system is not permitted. In part, the Chinese approach to the role of speech may be accounted for by their concept of "democratic centralism." In general, democratic centralism refers to a process in which lower government or CCP bodies are consulted and asked to express their opinions on specified issues (the democratic component). However, the centralist aspects of democratic centralism demand that the individual is always subordinated to the organization, the minority to the majority, and the lower level to the higher. In practice, centralism far outweighs democracy. The theory of democratic centralism is, however, predicated on *government for the people,* not *by the people,* a view that can be traced back two thousand years to Confucianism. It is government "by good men" for the people. According to this view of the relationship between the government and the people, the Communist Party and the NPC exercise the power of government for the welfare of the people. In the process of exercising this power, free speech has played a minor role in shaping the public debate on important issues.

Other rights and freedoms contained in the Chinese Constitution are also expressly limited. In the area of freedom of religious belief, for example, the 1982 Constitution provides that no one may make use of religion to engage in activities that disrupt public order, impair the health of citizens or interfere with the educational system of the state. The Constitution also provides that "... religious affairs are not subject to any foreign domination." The area of private communications provides another illustration. The Constitution states that the freedom and privacy of correspondence can be infringed upon in accordance with procedures prescribed by law to meet the needs of state security or of investigation into criminal offenses.

HUMAN RIGHTS IN CHINA

In considering human rights in China, it is not sufficient to merely compare the national norms contained in the 1982 Constitution with the international standards on human rights. Actual realities must also be considered. This task is difficult because reliable and comprehensive information on the actual realities, especially as they pertain to the operation of the criminal justice system, is not generally available. The scope of the inquiry is also daunting because the subject of human rights is broad and includes various categories of internationally recognized rights.

From the late 1970s through early 1989, there was movement in China in the direction of greater freedoms. China appeared on the cusp of accepting an international view of human rights. During this period, the government made a serious effort to protect the rights of citizens by instituting a working legal system, to expand access to information, to allow some political dissent, to adopt a more tolerant approach to national minorities and religious groups, to liberalize emigration policies and to involve more citizens in local elections. Thousands of scholars, officials, and religious figures who were purged during the numerous past political campaigns were rehabilitated, and many resumed positions of authority. China became a less oppressive place to live. The press was a livelier forum for debate, differences of opinion were publicly discussed, and contacts and friendships with foreigners were possible. Chinese students and scholars went overseas with the intent to return to the PRC.

The various reforms that produced greater freedom during this period did not break certain entrenched patterns of abuse of authority. For example, a disquieting recent study by Asia Watch offers proof that in Tibet, the authorities continue to engage in "systematic human-rights abuses." With chilling documentation, Asia Watch charges Chinese authorities in Tibet maintain a close surveillance of the entire population, discriminate against Tibetans in housing and education, brutally repress all political dissent, make arbitrary arrests and run prisons where "torture is part of the ... routine." Former prisoners have told Asia Watch that jailers routinely use cattle prods on anyone who resists during "struggle sessions." This is a violation of international law. The use of torture is prohibited by both Article 7 of the International Covenant on Civil and Political Rights and Article 1 of the Convention Against Torture and Other Cruel, Inhuman or Degrading Treatment or Punishment. Although the use of torture is not prohibited by the 1982 Constitution, the PRC Criminal Procedure Law does proscribe extorting confessions by torture.

Since the 1959 Tibetan Rebellion that forced the Dalai Lama to flee to India, China has generally succeeded in shielding what happens in Tibet from the rest of the world. This situation changed in 1987 when Lhasa police officers fired on unarmed Buddhist monks and other demonstrators who chanted independence slogans and attacked a police station to free political prisoners. After these events, the Chinese promptly banned foreign journalists and most tourists from Tibet in an attempt to throw a veil around the region once again. The government was less successful in shielding itself from the events that rocked China in the spring of 1989. The world watched the tragic events unfold.

The Chinese leadership's reaction to the 1989 Democracy Movement and the events following provide an important opportunity to examine human rights in the PRC. China failed to meet its obligation to promote and protect human rights and fundamental freedoms. International norms were systematically and comprehensively ignored. The Chinese government violated the United Nations Charter and the Universal Declaration of Human Rights provision which protects the rights to life, liberty and security of the person. It ignored the International Covenant on Civil and Political Rights' stipulation that the right to life, protected by Article 6, may not be derogated even in times of public emergency which threatens the life of the nation. It failed to follow the Convention against Torture and Other Cruel, Inhuman or Degrading Treatment or Punishment, as well as other international human rights instruments. The Chinese leadership also committed systematic violations of the 1982 Constitution, the Criminal Law and the Criminal Procedure Law. These events and reports demonstrate that the struggle against the arbitrary abuse of power in the PRC continues.

The government's reaction to religious practices is another dimension of human rights in the PRC. The largest group of religious believers in China are Buddhists, who belong to the dominant Han ethnic group. Han Buddhist leaders generally cooperate with the government, and thus they have experienced few reported difficulties. However, the government does not tolerate religious manifestations advocating Tibetan independence. Thus, Tibetan Buddhism is tightly monitored and controlled.

One of the major changes in rights within the PRC since the death of Mao Zedong has been a relaxation in control over religion. The 1982 Constitution states that Chinese citizens have the right to "enjoy freedom of religious belief." The only explicit constraint on religious practice is that the religion cannot be dominated by a foreign country. Nevertheless, the Government severely restricts religious practice outside officially recognized and government-controlled religious institutions. Religious proselytizing is limited to officially sanctioned places of worship or to the homes of persons properly registered with an officially recognized religious institution. While some harassment continues, since the early 1980s there has been an increase in religious practice in China.

Economic and social rights are elaborately set out in the 1982 Constitution. As a practical matter, the state has not been able to provide certain constitutionally guaranteed economic and social rights. In many instances, this ability has been overturned by actual events. The guaranteed right to work, for example, has been undermined by the government's restructuring effort to combine a planned economy and market regulation. Unemployment and inflation have also hampered the state in providing these economic rights. The economic right to material assistance from the state when citizens are old, ill or disabled has been adversely affected by economic restructuring. Structural alterations in the Chinese economy have not been paralleled by actual changes in social security legislation or by the provision of adequate funding for social welfare infrastructure. Thus, the formal extension of social and economic constitutional rights has failed to mesh with reality.

The "right to strike" is a recognized international right. This right was included in both the 1975 and 1978 Constitutions. It was contained in these constitutions not to protect individual expression or to promote the material or economic interests of the workers, but rather to empower the masses to participate in the political struggle of the Cultural Revolution under the direction of the Party leadership. The right simply was considered a political weapon for mobilizing the masses to undermine the power and privilege of the bureaucracy. This right was removed from the 1982 Constitution for several reasons. It was potentially destabilizing from both a political and economic perspective. In addition, the ideological justification for its inclusion in the earlier constitutions was rejected. Notwithstanding these reasons, the fact remains that the right to strike is not an economic right recognized by the state.

Criticism of China's failure to live up to the rights set forth in the Chinese Constitution and various international conventions continues. In the late 1980s and early 1990s, these criticisms have centered on the killings in Lhasa and Beijing in the spring of 1989, the arbitrary arrest and detention of individuals associated with the 1989 demonstrations, reports of the torture of persons detained for what the Chinese government called counterrevolutionary crimes, the Chinese government's highly intrusive family planning program that limits families to one child and frequently results in coerced abortions, limits on freedom of speech, and the use of forced prison labor in the production of goods for export. The general response of the Chinese government to these and other accusations has been to argue that the actions have been taken so as to maintain order and to meet the needs of society as a whole. In all cases, the Chinese stress that these matters are the sole concern of the Chinese government and other states should not infringe on China's sovereignty through interference in Chinese internal affairs.

The approach that the Chinese government has taken towards human rights has emerged out of the interaction of traditional Chinese attitudes, current ideology, and national needs. Four themes can be identified as emerging out of this combination. First, they have combined to produce a system in which the state has the power to restrict rights by law. Thus, the state can define the limits of each right denying the individual the opportunity to challenge state interpretations of the rights. Second, the Chinese condemn selfish individualism and praise action that serves the interests of the state. Thus, the interests of the individual are equated with the interests of the state. Third, the Chinese see the inclusion of individual rights in their Constitution not specifically as a means to protect these rights but to emphasize that the individual should exercise the specified rights so as to strengthen the state. Finally, the political rights that have existed in post–1949 China have been justified by their social utility as a way to achieve a strong state.

Chinese citizens like the citizens of most states are granted certain rights by their government. The extent to which most of the Chinese population (with the exception of individuals seen as antisocialist) actually enjoyed these rights had been improving after the Cultural Revolution, at least until 1989. The actual extent to which these rights will be expanded or even adhered to in the future will depend primarily on the will of a small group of elites within the CCP. This is a reflection of traditional Chinese political and social attitudes as well the PRC's adherence to the former Soviet model of a highly centralized political system.

MARTIAL LAW

The events surrounding the suppression of the pro-democracy movement in 1989 indicate the current leaders' low regard for both the Party's rules and the State's rules of procedure. According to the Constitution, a decision of the Standing Committee of the National People's Congress is required to place Beijing under martial law. Article 67(20) of the Constitution gives it the power "to decide on the enforcement of martial law throughout the country or in particular provinces, autonomous regions or municipalities directly under the Central Government." Under Article 89(16), the State Council has the authority to invoke martial law in only parts of Beijing. The martial law decree that was issued by the State Council in 1989 was narrowly drafted to avoid the necessity of using the Standing Committee, which is a larger and more public body. As a practical matter the decree included all of Beijing. As a technical matter the decree included all of urban Beijing and four of its six suburban districts, but not its rural counties.

The narrow framing of the martial law decree technically gave the State Council the jurisdiction to issue the decree, but it is questionable whether the decree was approved as required by law. The members who form the State Council are defined in the 1982 Constitution. One American scholar of Chinese law, Jerome Cohen, observed that "as far as outside observers can determine, neither the entire State Council nor its Executive Committee" appears "to have voted on the decree ... because of the difficulty of winning agreement from a properly constituted body." This raises the question of whether the decree was legally defective.

Under the Constitution, the Standing Committee of the NPC has the power to override a martial law decree. Yet, it was not allowed to convene until late June by the Party Central Committee because the Party Central Committee had not been allowed to meet itself until its members had been "persuaded" to endorse Deng's decisions, including the ouster of Party General Secretary Zhao Ziyang. When the Standing Committee finally did meet, it was convinced by the account of events in the Chinese media, as well as by the detention of the Party General Secretary and the punishment of other dissenters, that martial law was proper.

Notwithstanding the inability to confirm the legality of the martial law decree, the process leading to martial law is instructive. It is testimony to the fundamental difference between the nature and function of law in China and the West. Law in the West is a mechanism whereby society exercises control over the political leadership. In China, law is essentially a means whereby the political leadership directs and controls society. This is not surprising because it must be remembered that China has never had a deeply rooted tradition of a system of formal law that binds its rulers.

CHAPTER III

THE LEGAL PROFESSION AND THE COURTS

The development of the legal profession in the People's Republic has been constrained by the interplay of three factors: traditional culture; ideology; and the problems associated with modernization. In traditional China, employment of lawyers involved a certain measure of cultural embarrassment, a public acknowledgement of disharmony. Distrust of lawyers was widespread. They often were referred to as "people who write with poisoned pens." Under the Qing Dynasty (1644–1911) it was actually a crime to "manage a lawsuit." Much of the emphasis in imperial China was on the resolution of disputes through mediation relying on local leaders rather than adjudication by formally trained lawyers.

Similarly, the communists were also critical of the pre-revolutionary Chinese legal profession.

Question (Beijing Review Correspondent, 1983): Could you give a brief account of the historical development of the work of lawyers in China?

Answer (Tan Wenji, Ministry of Justice): Through 2,000 years of China's feudal society, there were no lawyers at all. The feudal land-

> lord rulers enforced a barbarous autocracy, extorted confessions by torture, arbitrarily declared the accused to be guilty, treated human life as if it were not worth a straw, forbade the accused to defend himself and provided no counsel for trials.
>
> It was not until modern times that the ruling classes in old China began to establish the work of lawyers, patterned after Western models. In 1912 the Northern Warlord government formulated a "lawyer statute" and in 1914 the Kuomintang government promulgated and enforced a "lawyers law."
>
> But, since old China was a semi-feudal and semi-colonial society in which only a few lawyers were upright and fair-minded and dared to speak for the people, the lawyers actually served the reactionary ruling classes.
>
> After the founding of the People's Republic of China, we abolished the old legal system of the Kuomintang government and established a new, socialist system. [June 6, 1983 at p. 19.]

Professor Suzanne Ogden has noted that the Chinese Communist Party inherited the traditional Chinese repugnance for lawyers. See S. Ogden, *China's Unresolved Issues: Politics, Development and Culture* (1992). This repugnance dovetailed with its desire to have the Party rather than the legal community make determinations of right and wrong. The early leaders of the PRC were thus culturally and ideologically predisposed to construct a minimalist legal system in pursuit of their own brand of socialist legality.

Not surprisingly, the private practice of law was banned and "bourgeois lawyers" were removed from the Chinese legal system in 1949. As the "new socialist system" for the Chinese legal profession emerged, it resembled that found in the Soviet Union. This model emphasized the preeminence of policy and politics over law. It ultimately led to the subordination of the Chinese legal system to the Communist Party. Early on, a significant number of collective "legal advisors offices" staffed by full and part-time "people's lawyers" were established. The work, pay and political conduct of such lawyers were directly supervised by the Ministry of Justice. The new formal legal system was just beginning to take root when the Anti–Rightist Campaign began in 1957. This campaign focused on intellectuals critical of the Party. Individuals with legal training were purged during the struggle and were removed from influential positions. They were severely criticized for advocating the adoption of Western legal institutions and for trying to eliminate the Party's control of law.

The role of the courts and procuracies was also undermined by the CCP during the Anti–Rightist campaign and the Ministry of Justice was abolished in 1959. The radical Maoist faction increased its influence within the CCP and, as a result, its control over the development of China's legal system. This faction's anti-legal bias was reflected in its preference for the mass line method of resolving conflicts. This method relies on the interchange of ideas between the CCP and the mass population as a way to deal with disputes rather than on a formal system of laws. In fact, many cadre, especially at the local level, saw the law as a hindrance in their fight against "enemies of the people." After 1957, the CCP and the police performed major roles in law enforcement and abuses of law by local officials increased dramatically.

Like the Anti-Rightist Campaign, the Cultural Revolution (1966–1976) had a devastating effect upon the legal profession. Many of the people's lawyers disappeared or labored in reeducation camps. By the early 1970s, the Chinese legal profession was virtually nonexistent. One measure of the effect of the Cultural Revolution upon lawyers can be seen in the field of legal education. Out of roughly 1,000 full-time law professors, only a little more than 100 were left in the late 1970s.

The rehabilitation of the legal profession began with the death of Mao in 1976 and the prosecution of the "Gang of Four" in 1980. This political trial publicly demonstrated the importance the Party ascribed to law and lawyers in the restoration of order in China. Popular demand for legal protection against arbitrary official behavior was evident. The Chinese leadership's emphasis on economic modernization after 1978 also called for a reevaluation of the legal system. This was especially true because of the reliance on economic contracts and foreigners as part of the development strategy. Such reliance required dealing with legal principles and practices that did not easily fit into the norms of China's socialist political order. Moreover, foreigners made it clear that the dearth of laws and the absence of a predictable legal system in the PRC made it an unattractive place to invest. Thus, in order to restore order after the breakdown of legal and traditional social controls during the Cultural Revolution and to advance China's economy, the decision was made to establish a more formal and complex legal system. This, in turn, required the training of competent legal personnel.

People's lawyers were soon being hailed as critical to the return of "socialist legality." Since the law schools were closed during the Cultural Revolution, the shortage of lawyers presented immediate problems. Trained personnel were needed not only to interpret the new laws, but also to assist in their initial formulation. In addition, legal professionals were needed to cope with the increasing number of foreigners doing business with China and to assist with disputes resulting from the decentralization of the economy and the development of the rural contract system. The government therefore increased the resources channeled into legal education and produced more lawyers. Nevertheless, in all of China with approximately 1.2 billion people, in 1992 there were about 50,000 lawyers, only one-third of the number of licensed attorneys found in the State of California. Professor Victor Li once posed the provocative question of whether there could be law without lawyers in China. See V. Li, *Law Without Lawyers—A Comparative View of Law in China and the United States* (1977). The question today is whether there are lawyers without law, or at least without the rule of law in the People's Republic of China.

EDUCATING THE POPULACE AND PROFESSION

By the end of the Cultural Revolution it had become clear to the general population that just as under imperial rule, it was largely power and relationships, not law, that determined a person's fate. Thus, once the leadership decided to focus on the development of the legal system, it was not surprising that the Chinese people not only lacked knowledge of the law but also a basic respect for its values. Legal education since the Cultural Revolution has proceeded on three main fronts: (1) education of the public at large; (2) training of judges, police, prosecutors, administrators, managers and others already involved in legal work; and (3) restoring and expanding university and institute law faculties and student enrollments.

Educating the populace about law has taken many forms, including radio broadcasts, travelling art troupes, videotapes and seminars. Continuing efforts are made through the press, television, the educational system and publicity of various kinds to raise the consciousness of the Chinese people of the law, legal rights and remedies, and the goal of conforming behavior to law. A "Propaganda Department" exists within the Ministry of Justice for these purposes and, in 1985, a five-year plan of popularization of common knowledge of law was adopted by the Chinese Communist Party Central Committee. The scale of this effort is monumental. By the end of 1986, for example, about 300 million citizens had been involved, with over 150 million law books published. A second five-year plan emphasizing China's 1982 Constitution has been undertaken. Like its predecessor, it is targeted at what the Party calls "legal illiterates."

On a more local level, a representative example is the "Legal Knowledge Publicity Day" that is held periodically in Beijing. This day is set aside for free legal advice and services from the Ministry of Justice and local government departments, legal advisory offices, and university law faculties. Lawyers and legal cadres answer hundreds of thousands of inquiries on this day. Another example is the general law course (focused upon criminal law and procedure) created for middle school students. There are tens of millions of students enrolled in these classes each year in China. The course was created at the request of the police to combat juvenile delinquency and standardized textbooks were approved by the Ministries of Justice and Education. Finally, by the early 1990s, several thousand legal advisory offices had been set up in cities throughout China.

Even prior to the 1957 Anti–Rightist Campaign, formal legal training in China was not a high priority. In the 1950s, Chinese law schools (four institutes and four university law departments) were expressly organized around the study of politics and law. Law was only seen as part of the study of politics and not as a separate discipline. For example, journals relating to legal issues were, in fact, journals on law *and* politics. The training of existing legal personnel since the Cultural Revolution has been China's most ambitious undertaking in legal education. Millions of judges, procurators, police and other security officers, and government administrators have received a legal education in "secondary schools of law" throughout the country. In addition, a selected number of "political and legal cadre" schools have been established specifically to provide in-service legal training. Although legal education of this kind is abbreviated when compared to what the universities are doing, it has served a vital function in restoring China's legal system. The "students" educated in this manner are the front line personnel in many Chinese legal institutions.

University and law institute legal education programs have been fully revived and, indeed, expanded. In 1987 over forty-five universities had law departments. There were also five Politics and Law Institutes under the direct supervision of the Ministry of Justice. Undergraduate law student enrollment has been increasing steadily. A much larger number of lawyers are being trained through correspondence law courses organized through the universities and the National Lawyers Correspondence Center run by the Ministry of Justice. The latter uses radio broadcasts as its primary method of teaching. Correspondence students travel periodically to universities for tutoring and examinations.

There is no shortage of law students in China. Persons are assigned to the academic study of law by government authorities. Because the status and pay of lawyers is generally low, university students usually do not prefer to major in law. However, in the late 1980s and early 1990s a more positive attitude toward the study of law has emerged. Part of the reason for the change may be the importance of lawyers in China due to increased foreign investment, and because contacts with foreigners offer possibilities of access to scarce goods and hard currencies. Once enrolled in law school, students now have their course examinations graded anonymously. This is a change from earlier ideological practices in the 1950s and 1960s which tended to identify and disfavor students from "bourgeois" family backgrounds.

The major problem in university legal education is a shortage of highly trained legal experts to teach in the newly reopened schools. Many of the legal scholars trained in prerevolutionary China and thus familiar with Western legal principles had either died or had their legal ability atrophy after years of nonuse. Some of these scholars, however, were politically rehabilitated in the early 1980s and tested to see if they were still knowledgeable about the law. Those who passed became teachers. Existing professors are frequently diverted from education by fee-producing legal practices organized through law firms associated with their universities. In 1986, the Ministry of Justice issued regulations intended to increase the amount of time spent on teaching and research by law professors. The Ministry banned their association in law firms. Professors may only form legal consulting departments to offer free services. Even so, a number of faculty-run law firms are said to continue to function. In order to improve the quality of legal education the Chinese have also relied on seminars taught by foreign scholars. A number of Americans, for example, have attempted to introduce U.S. law teaching methodologies, including socratic dialogue, problem solving and simulation. Such methods contrast with the tradition of lectures and rote learning used in Chinese legal education.

Legal education in China is a four-year "undergraduate education." Most of the curricula at university law departments and the Politics and Law Institutes reflect the contours of China's emerging legal system. Courses covering many of the major laws promulgated since the Cultural Revolution are required. Courses in philosophy, political economics, the history of the Chinese Communist Party and languages are also mandatory. Military training has, of late, been added to the curriculum in an attempt to instill greater discipline in students. Standardized and officially approved coursebooks for over fifty law school subjects have been created. There is little room for the intellectual priorities of Chinese law professors and students. Moot courts and three months of practical training are increasingly utilized. In sum, legal education at China's universities and law institutes is a substantial endeavor for students and faculty.

THE PEOPLE'S COURTS

Like most of China's legal institutions, the people's courts ceased functioning during the Cultural Revolution. Summary justice in the streets, before a band of Red Guards or at the point of a gun prevailed. Among those who were tried, convicted and sentenced as enemies of the people during that era were the judges and other personnel of the people's courts. While some perished or committed suicide, many others spent long years of "reeducation" at manual labor. It is little wonder that those judges who managed to return live with nightmares and now fear ideological mistakes in their decisions. Likewise, as the winds of change blow, newer colleagues on the bench operate in a climate of concern about rendering politically correct opinions. This is the human environment in which the people's courts function after Mao and Tiananmen Square.

The revival and restoration of the courts since the Cultural Revolution commenced in earnest with the 1979 Organic Law of the People's Courts. This Law creates the structure of the court system in China. There are four tiers of People's Courts: Basic Level Courts, Middle Level (Intermediate) Courts, Higher Level Courts and the Supreme People's Court. Specialty courts handle maritime, military, railroad, traffic and forestry matters. The traffic police courts, for example, have exclusive jurisdiction over auto accidents.

There are about 3,000 Basic Level People's Courts. These are city, county and district courts, each ordinarily divided into civil and criminal trial sections. The Basic Level Courts may refer particularly serious cases to a higher level court. Basic Level Courts are also responsible for the assistance of mediation committees in their areas. There has been a steady growth in the jurisdiction and specializations of the Basic Level Courts. Since the mid-1980s, many have "economic divisions" for economic crimes and commercial disputes as well as "enforcement divisions" which secure judgments.

In 1988, the development of "administrative divisions" to hear individual complaints against governmental actions was made a priority and many such divisions were established in the Basic Level People's Courts. Thousands of such cases, largely local in character, were soon filed. The right to initiate complaints challenging the legality of specific administrative actions is granted in numerous PRC laws and regulations. The Law on Prevention of Water Pollution, for example, allows citizens to challenge in court the imposition of administrative penalties by environmental agencies. Likewise, the Law on Sanitary Food permits similar challenges to decisions of local agencies suspending food production, imposing fines or revoking licenses.

In April of 1989, the National People's Congress adopted an Administrative Litigation Law (effective October 1, 1990) intended to broaden and reinforce the right of Chinese citizens to challenge specific governmental acts (but not the "legality" of the laws under which the officials acted). Corrective orders (supplemented by fines) may be imposed upon the offenders, and tort damages recovered. The right to sue the government (but not the Communist Party) now exists whenever there is an infringement of personal or property rights. Suit may also be brought whenever there is an unlawful detention, fine or adverse licensing decision, and when there are encroachments upon business autonomy. Recognition and facilitation of these rights is a remarkable milestone in the history of Chinese law and the people's courts. In the present repressive political environment, however, significant litigation against the government still seems unlikely.

There are about 300 Middle Level People's Courts in the PRC. Middle Level Courts operate in prefectures, autonomous regions and cities under central government control. Middle Level Courts have original and appellate civil and criminal jurisdiction. They also hear economic and administrative matters, including economic crimes and commercial disputes. Most cases involving foreign affairs or persons are brought in the Middle Level Courts.

There are twenty-nine Higher Level Courts which operate largely at the provincial level. The Higher Level Courts are divided into civil, criminal, administrative and economic sections. Higher Level Courts can act as trial courts in special cases, such as those referred to them by Middle Level Courts. The Higher Level Courts also serve as an appeals court from the Middle Level Courts, three to five judges sitting on the appeal panel.

The Supreme People's Court is the highest judicial body in the PRC. There are about ninety judges on the Supreme Court and each serves a maximum of two five-year terms. The Supreme Court has general supervisory control over all courts in the People's Republic. It also has original jurisdiction in specified instances and appellate review over Higher Level and specialty courts. The Supreme Court handles special prosecutions brought by the chief procurator, such as the trial of the "Gang of Four" after the Cultural Revolution.

THE ROLE OF THE SUPREME COURT

Supreme Court decisions are made by small panels of judges. Prior to 1985, these decisions were not disclosed to the public and were often unwritten. A Supreme Court communique of May, 1985 released four opinions intended to provide better guidance to local courts for correctly applying laws and decrees. More decisions have been released in issues of the "Bulletin" or "Gazette" of the Supreme People's Court. Clearly, however, the development of a systematic case reporting system for Supreme Court and other judicial opinions is in its infancy. Such a system would enhance the authority of the Supreme, Higher and Middle Level Courts, as well as promote uniformity of results in judicial proceedings throughout China. It would also give litigants and their lawyers a better grasp of the law and the likely results of appeals. While it is tempting for Westerners to argue the merits of case reporting systems, one must always remember the context within which the people's courts operate. For centuries, the courts in China have tended to individualize cases before them. There is no doctrine of binding judicial precedent in Chinese jurisprudence. Rather, the tradition runs the other way. In "seeking truth from the facts," as the people's courts are always admonished to do, there is considerable leeway to render decisions on the particular merits and circumstances of each case. In such an environment, case reporting systems may be less influential than an outsider might suppose.

The 1982 Constitution suggests that the people's courts were intended to be the least powerful branch of Chinese government. The Supreme People's Court is *not* authorized to interpret the Constitution and laws of the PRC. This is a function specifically reserved by Article 67 of the Constitution to the Standing Committee of the National People's Congress. Such interpretations function more like legislative amendments than judicial decisions, and may be undertaken at any time. However, under a 1981 Standing Committee Resolution on Strengthening the Interpretation of Law, the Supreme People's Court can give nonbinding "interpretations" on questions concerning the specific application of laws and decrees in judicial proceedings. These interpretations are now regularly issued not only in particular cases, but also in the form of replies to letters from lower courts posing specific questions of procedural or substantive law originating in matters before them. These replies are frequently published in the *Supreme Court Bulletin* and circulated throughout the judicial system.

Since the mid–1980s, the Supreme People's Court has begun to issue explanatory "Notices" and "Circulars" concerning PRC laws. The first three major Notices covered the Economic Contract Law, the Civil Procedure Law and the Foreign Economic Contract Law. An important Notice on the General Principles of Civil Law has also been released. All of these Notices, sometimes couched as "Explanations," expand upon the laws involved by covering matters not easily traced to their texts. The Supreme Court is creating new law even though the constitutional basis for issuing Notices is unclear. The Supreme Court may be merely exercising its supervisory administrative powers over the lower courts by guiding their decisions. In this sense, the lower courts are put on notice as to the Supreme Court's thinking about specific laws. On the other hand, these materials "interpret" existing PRC laws outside of the context of litigation. Such interpretative powers are clearly reserved to the Standing Committee of the NPC by the Constitution. Whatever the authority, the issuance of Circulars and Notices by the Supreme Court suggests a more active, more influential role for the court within China's emerging legal system. While, as mentioned, there is no formal doctrine of precedent in Chinese law, it is hard to imagine that lower courts will not treat these statements as binding upon them. In a politically influenced role, China's Supreme Court issued a circular two weeks after the massacre at Tiananmen Square instructing lower courts to expedite the trials of persons alleged to have engaged in counterrevolutionary activities or the creation of social turmoil.

JUDICIAL INDEPENDENCE

The 1979 Organic Law establishes the broadest mandates for the people's courts, mandates which an optimist might say seek to foster a rule of law in China. The people's courts have a duty to apply the law equally to all persons. Judicial decisions are to be rendered without discrimination on the basis of status, sex, nationality, religion, education or property. The courts are to administer justice independently, subject only to the law. They are to devote all their activities to educating the people in loyalty to their socialist motherland and conscientious observance of the Constitution and the law. These are some of the ideals, the aspirations, indeed the law to which the people's courts should adhere. Deviations in judicial practice have occurred and are likely to continue to occur, especially regarding judicial independence.

Professor Jerome Cohen highlighted the problem of judicial independence at an early stage in the evolution of China's court system. See Cohen, "The Chinese Communist Party and Judicial Independence: 1949–59," 82 *Harvard Law Review* 967 (1969). The provocative question at this time is whether deviations in PRC judicial practice are so frequent and fundamental as to undermine the very integrity of the court system. For example, one major deviation is the co-ordinated "speedy" approach of the police, procuracy *and* courts to the anticrime and anticorruption drives initiated by the Party in the 1980s. The same "speedy" treatment has been accorded to the 1989 Democracy Movement counterrevolutionaries. This approach strongly suggests that judicial independence in the PRC is more aspirational than operational.

The implementation of the mandates of the 1979 Organic Law of the People's Courts has been placed in the hands of the people's judges. Because of the nonadversarial nature of Chinese litigation, the quality of justice in the people's courts depends heavily on the calibre of its judges. Yet many Chinese judges have limited legal training and only a few have received a formal legal education. A number of judges are retired military, civil service or Party workers. The professionalization of China's bench is a critical long-term need upon which achieving the mandates of the 1979 Organic Law may ultimately turn. In the near-term, staffing and facilities problems have been evident despite the growth in legal training since the Cultural Revolution. Criminal statutes of limitations have even been extended because of the shortage of qualified judges.

A more general problem is the relatively low social and bureaucratic status and pay of people's judges. Although this is a problem which permeates the whole of the PRC legal profession, it is probably most acute in the judiciary upon whom Chinese justice heavily depends. Because China's judges rank near the bottom of the bureaucratic pay scale, their status and prestige is very low. This makes assignment to a judicial post unattractive and generally undermines the authority of the courts. It contributes to the low level of professionalism in the Chinese judiciary and increases the probability of Party interference with judicial decisions. In a society of scarce resources and pressing problems, it is sometimes difficult to see the wisdom of prioritizing China's judiciary. This wisdom is especially difficult to appreciate against a cultural history which eschews litigation out of fear of societal disharmony, corruption and physical abuse. But the times have changed, and the rule of law cannot be strengthened without independent, professional people's judges. China's judiciary, while it may remain the least powerful branch of government, should not also be its most ineffective branch.

The 1982 Constitution indicates that the people's courts are required to exercise their judicial authority independently and are not to be subject to interference by administrative organs, organizations or individuals. Judges on people's courts are, nevertheless, selected and may be removed without cause by responsible people's congresses or their standing committees. For example, because the Supreme People's Court is responsible under the Constitution to the National People's Congress and, in particular, to the Standing Committee of the NPC, its judges are selected by that Committee. In reality, selection and removal of people's judges is a Party prerogative to which the people's congresses accede. The Party is, of course, most concerned that people's judges should faithfully carry out its policies. To help insure this result, a high percentage of the judges are CCP members whose promotion and tenure within the Party are always at stake. Removal of judges from office for failure to fulfill unwritten, extra-legal Party obligations is rare. The Party's risks in this respect have been minimized by limiting judicial terms of office to a maximum of five years. The result is a Party-dependent judiciary with little of the assertiveness that might come from lifetime tenure.

Prior to the Cultural Revolution and shortly thereafter, the people's courts routinely submitted major decisions for review by local Party committees. An "examination and approval" system was used in death penalty cases, crimes involving foreigners, decisions relating to the Party's policies, cases with far-reaching implications, and instances when the police, procurators or judges were in conflict about proper procedures or results. The 1975 and 1978 Constitutions intentionally made no reference to an independent judiciary. In 1979, the Central Committee of the CCP issued an instruction officially abolishing the examination and approval system except for cases involving Party cadres above the prefecture level. This instruction was issued in conjunction with the promulgation in 1979 of the Criminal Law and the Law of Criminal Procedure. It was intended to promote judicial independence in criminal proceedings. Nevertheless, considerable evidence suggests that Party review is still the norm, and many judges feel more secure with it. Those nightmares and fears originating in the Cultural Revolution have not yet gone away.

The Party's "leadership" of the people's courts was strengthened in the months following the 1989 repression of the Democracy Movement. Just before martial law was lifted in January of 1990, the President of the Supreme People's Court announced: "In the course of last year's counterrevolutionary rebellion, some people hoisted the flag of 'judicial independence'.... Various levels of the people's courts must self-consciously accept Party leadership. It is a mistake to think that, because there is law, justice can be executed without the guidance of the [Party's] policies."

REGULATING LAWYERS AND LAW FIRMS

The 1980 Provisional Regulations On Lawyers, effective January 1, 1982, heralded the return of the legal profession in China. In general, these regulations were intended to define the role of lawyers in the legal system and to protect them from outside interference. The fact that two years elapsed between the initial formulation and implementation of these regulations suggests that they were the subject of prolonged debate. The regulations cover, for example, admission to the profession. Only PRC citizens with the right to vote may be certified as people's lawyers. University law graduates must apprentice for two years before admission to the bar. Persons with professional legal training, and those who have worked as judges or procurators, are also eligible. Indeed, anyone who has received a higher education, done at least three years of economic, scientific or technical work, and is proficient at lawyering tasks may seek to become a people's lawyer.

The shortage of lawyers in China has generally meant that all doubts about admission to the profession are resolved in favor of the applicant. Admission is by approval of judicial departments at the provincial level, which also have the power to expel "very incompetent" attorneys. There is no express provision for or against mobility of lawyers from province to province. Provincial bar examinations were generally cursory prior to 1986. In that year, the Ministry of Justice (MOJ) established a National Lawyers Qualification Examination. The passage rate on this exam was slightly above 50 percent. The exam has been openly criticized by older practitioners because it allows too many younger attorneys into an increasingly lucrative profession. Local judicial departments also resent the centralization of bar examinations and the implied mobility of lawyers.

Attorneys may lose their license to practice law if they are convicted of a crime, dismissed as a state official or, in cases when they are CCP members, expulsion has occurred. License revocation has been extremely rare, but this does not mean that lawyers who fall out of favor with the authorities fail to get the message. The 1980 Regulations require lawyers to "propagate the socialist system in all their work." This admonition is especially significant because, unlike judges and procurators, many people's lawyers are not CCP members. To insure the socialist commitment of lawyers, local Party committees regularly monitor their work. Informal censures from those committees are usually sufficient to cause most people's lawyers to conform their conduct to Party priorities and policies.

As a practical matter, few developments within the Chinese legal profession occur without the express authorization of its primary supporter and regulatory body, the Ministry of Justice. The MOJ has, in recent years, allowed a number of experiments to take place within the legal profession. Some of the most unusual experiments involve the operation of "law firms" in the PRC. The "work unit" of most urban people's lawyers is called a "legal advisory office" or, more recently, a "law firm." About 35,000 full-time and part-time lawyers are attached to approximately 3,000 such law offices. People's lawyers are salaried civil servants. Individual cases are assigned to them by their office, which collects the legal fees involved. Maximum domestic fee schedules are set by local bureaus of justice. These cover such services as advice, document drafting, civil or criminal litigation and settlement of estates. Since these schedules provide for a range of fees, bargaining between clients and Chinese law firms is not unknown. The Ministry of Justice has stipulated that fees charged foreign clients are to be negotiated "in accordance with foreign lawyers' fees." This "deep-pocket" approach has led to a wide discrepancy between inexpensive domestic and costly foreign fees. There is also considerable difference in what China's law firms charge foreign clients.

Many of the urban law firms in China have been experimenting with economic independence from the state. All of their expenses are covered by earnings. Small monthly retainers are used with business and government clients. Additional fees are charged for specific "outside counsel" legal services. The largest income source is economic contract work, often at a 1 or 2 percent fee measured against the value of the contract. By these means, Chinese law firms have acquired new offices, cars, higher salaries and bonuses. Other experiments involve law firms not affiliated with any government agency or legal advisory office and limited rights to engage in the "private" practice of law.

Lawyers are much less available in the Chinese countryside. This shortage of attorneys led to the creation in the 1980s of thousands of "legal services offices" in small towns and villages. Unlike China's law firms, these offices are generally not staffed by people's lawyers. Their personnel have limited legal training and handle simple individual and small business problems.

The people's lawyers are slowly evolving into a "free profession" capable of contracting individually with clients for services. Lawyers in some parts of China are thought to earn several times their state salaries by contracting with enterprises for their free time services. Substantial numbers of people's lawyers are also being employed as in-house counsel to government ministries and state enterprises. The Party appears prepared to allow the income and influence of lawyers to rise in this fashion. Over the long term, the privatization of China's legal profession could profoundly alter its power and status within society.

LAWYERS AS ADVOCATES

The Civil Procedure Law of 1982 (finalized in 1991) and the Criminal Procedure Law of 1979 make it clear that attorneys do *not* have a monopoly over representation of persons before the courts. Relatives, worker associates and other authorized persons may also perform this function. They often do so without fee. Large numbers of the criminally accused do not have lawyers as their advocates and retaining people's lawyers to engage in civil litigation is rare. Thus, it would appear that the Chinese are not fully persuaded of the utility of employing people's lawyers as litigators. This failure to utilize may partly be a question of expense, despite the nominal fees typically charged by people's lawyers. It may also be a product of lingering cultural reservations about lawyers or just simply the shortage of attorneys. More generally, however, there is a public perception that employment of an attorney is not likely to significantly alter the result in civil and, especially, criminal proceedings. One of the broad trends in post-

Mao China is the gradual erosion of this perception with a corresponding increase in the use of professional attorneys as advocates before the courts.

Even when employed, the people's lawyers labor under practical constraints. Under the 1980 Regulations on Lawyers, attorneys are given immunity from prosecution when they defend cases assigned to them by the state. However, frequently zealous advocacy on behalf of criminal defendants can create serious personal risks for people's lawyers. Here are three examples reported in the *Wall Street Journal* in 1987:

> A judge in Hebei province ordered his subordinates to handcuff a lawyer to a tree for 80 minutes. The lawyer's offense? He had persisted in asking the judge to handle a case that the latter had no wish to take on.
>
> In nearby Shaanxi province, a judge threw a robbery suspect's attorney out of court. The reason: The attorney had exposed glaring faults in the prosecution's evidence.
>
> A lawyer on Hainan island was arrested on the orders of the public prosecutor's office and detained for a month on charges of "conspiring with the accused" because of his staunch defense. [April 14, 1987 at p. 29.]

In these cases, the lawyers were seen as defending their clients too well, disregarding their duty to loyally serve the cause of socialism. Conditions were so bad for the people's lawyers in Guangdong Province that regulations were issued in 1987 expressly prohibiting their harassment by judges, procurators and police officers.

Client confidentiality with people's lawyers is a major concern and affects their role as advocates. Because the people's lawyers are state legal functionaries, monitored by Party committees, they face pressures to reveal incriminating evidence. Indeed, the Criminal Procedure Law provides that concealment by any person of evidence of a crime must be investigated. The 1980 Regulations on Lawyers refer to a professional duty to keep state and shameful personal secrets confidential. State secrets are still defined according to a 1951 statute. In essence, anything not published is a state secret, and therefore if a lawyer divulges the details of a case to anyone, he or she could be accused of a criminal act. Some have optimistically translated the Chinese character for "shameful personal secrets" more broadly to suggest a duty for people's lawyers to keep "individual confidences" of their client's secrets. However, as the preceding examples illustrate, this optimism may be misplaced in the context of a legal system where advocacy clearly has risks.

Apart from limited provisions in the 1980 Regulations, there is no Code of Professional Responsibility for people's lawyers. Such a Code could significantly enhance the profession's status, independence and effectiveness. It would also give clients a better basis for understanding what their people's lawyers can or cannot do for them, and just exactly how candid they can be.

Foreign attorneys can be found in Beijing, Shanghai, Guangzhou (Canton) and a scattering of other cities. To maintain their visas, some teach law to government cadres. Whether and to what extent foreign attorneys may practice law in the PRC has been under study by the government for many years. Competitive pressures add to the uncertain status of foreign attorneys. A number of Chinese law firms have been created to liaison with the government on behalf of foreigners. Many of these firms are directly linked to government agencies. Members of the China Global Law Firm, for example, work for the China Counsel for the Promotion of International Trade. The Ministry of Foreign Economic Relations and Trade (MOFERT) has established the Great Wall Law Firm. Some of these Chinese firms reportedly charge as much as some of the largest multinational law firms. They have not as yet displaced foreign lawyers in international business matters, though such a result may arrive in time. For now, they typically act as local counsel to the multinational law firms.

THE PEOPLE'S PROCURACY

The people's procuratorate or procuracy was the last of China's major legal institutions to be restored after the Cultural Revolution. During the "ten bad years," it was completely dismantled. It was officially revived by the 1978 Constitution. The procuracy occupies an especially sensitive position within the legal system. As heir to the supervisory role over government once fulfilled by the Imperial Censory, it is a potentially powerful institution having no direct analog in common law legal regimes. Public prosecutors in America, for example, play a much more restricted role than the people's procuratorate. Like their counterparts in the former Soviet Union and in the civil law nations of Europe, Chinese procurators perform a wide range of legal functions. As the 1982 Constitution provides, the people's procuratorates are "state organs of legal supervision." In this capacity, the procuracy is empowered to supervise the observance of socialist legality by all ministries, government agencies, enterprises, social organizations and civil servants. To its credit, the procuracy (with the acquiescence of the CCP) reexamined and redressed some cases of injustice committed during the Cultural Revolution, but it has done nothing to rectify the injustices associated with the repression of the 1989 Democracy Movement.

The Organic Law of the People's Procuratorates was promulgated in 1979. It governs procurators throughout China. Like the people's courts, the procuracy is divided into hierarchical levels. There are about 3,000 procuratorates staffed with well over 100,000 persons. The Supreme People's Procuratorate is at the top of the pyramid. It is responsible to the National People's Congress and the NPC standing committee. Likewise, each succeeding level in the procuracy is responsible to its corresponding people's congress and standing committee. At each level of government, election and removal rights over procurators are given to people's congresses and their standing committees. In addition, lower level procurators are responsible to higher level procuracy offices. This is known as the "dual control" (horizontal and vertical) system. It operates in addition to the Party controls discussed below.

The 1979 Procuratorate Law establishes the general duties of the people's procurators: suppressing treason and counterrevolutionaries; safeguarding orderly production, work, teaching, and scientific research; maintaining the "orderly life of the masses of the people"; protecting socialist and individual property; supporting the personal rights of citizens; and educating citizens to be law abiding.

PROCURATORIAL SUPERVISORY POWERS

Procurators make critical decisions in the Chinese criminal justice system. They have the power to supervise nearly everything the Chinese police and security agencies do, including investigations into detentions prior to arrest and allegations of the use of torture. If the procurators refuse to make a formal arrest, suspects detained by police or security agencies must be released. Procurators can order the police or security agencies to initiate criminal investigations or conduct further investigations. Since its reestablishment after the Cultural Revolution, as contrasted with the 1950s, the procuracy has approved the vast majority of applications for arrests and, implicitly, the confessions upon which they are often based. This can be explained in part by a kind of role reversal. Instead of the procuracy supervising the police, the opposite is achieved through widespread appointment of chiefs of police as heads of the Political and Legal (Party) Committees which "supervise" the police, procuracies and courts. Local government officials are also said to frequently interfere with procuratorial work. In such an environment, the independence of the procuracy is questionable if not a fiction.

An important task of the procuracy is to supervise the administration of reform and reeducation through labor assignments to the large number of labor camps scattered throughout China. Such assignments are said to have been significantly revived in 1989 to deal with democracy protesters. Labor camp assignments of up to four years are authorized. They can be given by court order or as a matter of police or security agency discretion (acting in consultation with local government officials) to "counterrevolutionaries," "hoodlums" and "antisocialist reactionaries." Labor assignments by the police occur without trial and cannot be appealed to the courts. However, complaints about them can be lodged with the procuracy in hopes of triggering supervisory review. If the procuracy undertakes such a review, it can order the assignment revoked. Not surprisingly, protests to the procuracy about labor and reeducation assignments do not appear to be frequent, despite the establishment of branch procuratorates in large reform and reeducation camps. When such assignments increased significantly after Tiananmen Square in 1989, the procuracy did not serve as a check on arbitrary police and security agency powers.

The decision to criminally indict a person is a responsibility of the procuracy. So too is the decision to go to trial. Despite the fact that its 1979 Organic Law requires the procuracy to "stress the weight of evidence, put little credence in confessions, [and] strictly forbid the extortion of confessions," confessions are frequent in China's criminal proceedings. Some are extracted through police torture despite an official campaign by the Supreme People's Procuratorate against "legal-disciplinary" cases. The predominant role of the procuracy and confessions in the Chinese criminal justice system is well illustrated by the fact that most controversy at trial focuses on sentencing.

The underlying assumption of the judges (and often defense counsel) is that the procuracy would not bring a case to trial without substantial evidence. Furthermore, that evidence may have already been reviewed by the court's internal "adjudication committee" under the practice known as "verdict first, trial second." This practice involves consideration of guilt in advance of trial. The adjudication committee (led by the court's president) meets without the presence of defense attorneys. In politicized cases, pretrial review is also undertaken by Political and Legal (Party) Committees as well as local government officials. By the time of trial, the verdict and indeed the sentence may have been communicated to the judge for execution. The trial becomes a formality for the record and its outcome poses no risk or threat to the political and legal establishment. It is not surprising, therefore, that nearly all criminal trials result in guilty verdicts.

Once a sentence has been rendered, the procuracy is still potentially involved in the criminal process. It has the power to supervise the legality of conditions and compulsory labor in China's prisons and detention centers. To do so, the procuracy stations officers in most such institutions. In this capacity, the procuracy has of late been willing to scrutinize some allegations of the use of torture in these facilities. Occasionally, this review has resulted in administrative sanctions and compensation to the victim.

Common law attorneys will find it remarkable that Chinese procurators can intervene in civil litigation in order to exercise supervisory powers. The procuracy, for example, can intervene in any private family, contractual or property litigation—the most common forms of civil litigation in China. Such intervention involves presenting the procuracy's views as to proper outcomes. This often results in securing an ideologically or politically correct solution, and is especially prevalent in litigation which has broad significance to the public or Party.

The 1979 Organic Law on the People's Procuratorate also grants local procurators the right to protest any "wrong" trial court judgment (even a private civil judgment). Such "protests" follow the ordinary appeal procedures. Any superior level procuratorate may protest a final judgment or ruling of a lower level court. The power of the procuracy to lodge protests against virtually all judicial decisions illustrates the scope of its supervisory powers over the Chinese legal system.

THE PROCURACY, THE GOVERNMENT AND THE PARTY

In theory, the procuracy has the power to supervise the legality of virtually *all* government acts, including legislative, regulatory and administrative decisions. Since the Chinese Communist Party supervises the government through its own system of parallel Party committees, an activist procuracy could threaten Party control. Conflicts between the Party and the procuracy arose in the 1950s, but were quickly eliminated by Party rebuke of procuratorial actions. In 1959, for example, the functions of local procuracies were taken over by the CCP's local level political and legal departments. Since then, and especially after their total destruction during the Cultural Revolution, Chinese procurators have learned to step lightly in exercising their supervisory powers over the legal system of the PRC. If the Party wishes to have the procuracy bring the government to heel, however, then there is much less potential for conflict. This is true of the Party's recent campaign against bureaucratic corruption which has led to the creation of a special anticorruption office and hot line in the Supreme People's Procuratorate and regional procuracies. Offense-reporting regulations have been issued which reward and protect China's whistle blowers. Early data indicates that approximately 30 percent of the corruption complaints received by the procuracy nationwide concern Party officials. A few of these complaints have actually led to public prosecutions of Party members.

As a matter of law and practice, the procuracy often finds itself in a delicate position. For example, it has the duty to protect the right of citizens to accuse state and Party officials of violations of law, while at the same time it must follow the leadership of the CCP in furthering socialist legality. Since nearly all procurators are Party members, adherence to Party leadership is expected and regularly obtained. Attempts have been made to insulate the procuracy from outside interference by the government and the Communist Party, an influence viewed by some as a problem. The 1982 Constitution, for example, specifies that procurators are to exercise their authority independently, according to provisions of the law, and are not to be subject to interference by administrative organs, organizations and individuals.

Similar provisions are found in the 1979 Procuratorate Law. In reality, however, procuratorial independence from Party influence is rare. Indeed, there has been substantial criticism and comment about high ranking Party members being practically exempt from prosecution. Breaches of Party discipline (including violations of law) by Party members are often dealt with by Party disciplinary committees through a private in-house system of justice. Party members, it seems, are only subject to public prosecution and the full force of Chinese law when the Party wishes this to occur.

NOTARIES

The Chinese notariat, like other branches of the legal profession, was a victim of the Cultural Revolution. Many notaries were killed, committed suicide or were "reeducated" during that period. The restoration of law and order after the Cultural Revolution brought China's notaries and notarial offices back into operation. Thousands of notarial offices are now scattered throughout the country. They notarize millions of documents annually. Today, Chinese notaries resemble the nation's barefoot doctors. They are the front line for many legal services, and they humbly guard the law.

Chinese notaries perform a wide range of significant functions. Like their European counterparts, they are an important branch of the legal profession. Most Chinese notaries have been trained or educated in the law since the Cultural Revolution. As state civil servants, they undertake important tasks within the PRC legal system. Indeed, notaries probably have more contact with the legal problems of ordinary citizens than the people's lawyers or procurators. They have even been known to make "house calls" to perform notarial acts.

Regulations issued provisionally in 1982 by the State Council regulate notarial work. Under these regulations, notaries may certify adoptions, birth records, contracts, death notices, educational degrees, familial relations, gifts, inheritances, marital status, personal status, property divisions, trusts, wills, work records, and the validity of a signature or seal. Notaries can also certify that copies, photocopies, portions or translations of a document are identical to the original. The 1982 regulations specifically provide that notaries may certify uncontested debts or rights to specific goods. This amounts to a summary writ of execution. The claimant may obtain compulsory process in the Basic Level Courts without lengthy litigation proceedings. Notarial fees for all of these services are fixed by the Ministry of Justice.

Notarization of a document in China signifies the accuracy of a signature. It may also certify the *legality* of the document or act to which the document pertains. In doing so, Chinese notaries investigate the legal sufficiency of the evidence put forward by the applicant seeking notarization. In some instances, notarial examinations involve careful scrutiny of legal questions. The notary may end up giving legal advice to the parties or actually drafting documents. In this way, notarization of documents in China may, as a practical matter, reduce the need for civil litigation. When a notary refuses to certify the legality of a document, the applicant may appeal this refusal. The Law of Civil Procedure requires the people's courts to recognize the validity of any judicial fact or document verified by a Chinese notary. However, if contradictory evidence is found, the certification may be annulled.

Notaries may represent persons in need of notarial services. They often, for example, represent foreigners because investment agreements and trademark registrations must be notarized. Notaries are also authorized to undertake other responsibilities in accordance with international custom. The regulations further provide that all notarial work done in a representative capacity should remain confidential. As with people's lawyers, there is great concern on the part of foreign clients about the degree of confidentiality they enjoy with Chinese notaries. They have no desire to see their notaries serve as watchdogs for anyone. Chinese notaries, meanwhile, are caught in the middle. They are civil servants with duties to the state and their loyalty is monitored by Party committees. In a crunch, these duties and loyalties would most likely prevail over the confidences of the persons they represent.

NOTARIZATION OF ECONOMIC CONTRACTS

The notarization of domestic economic contracts, though not often mandatory, has become commonplace. It is the most important of all notarial tasks. Notarization helps insure orderly relations among state, collective and private enterprises in China's hybrid economy. The popularity of notarized economic contracts is partly explained by the evidentiary certainty that accompanies any notarized document. More importantly, once the contract is notarized, the legal rights and obligations of both parties are validated and recorded.

Notaries may require certain terms in economic contracts in order to insure completeness, accuracy and conformity to the law and prevailing government plans. They often engage in lengthy investigations of economic contracts. Tung–Pi Chen has indicated that notaries must:

> Investigate whether the applicants possess the required legal personality and, in the case of a business enterprise, whether it is legally registered with and licensed by the industrial and commercial administrative bureaus of the local government;
>
> Ensure that the subject-matter of the contract is within the scope of the authorized business activ-

ities of the applicants, and that the signing officers of the parties concerned are acting within the scope of their authority;

Verify that the contract complies with the Economic Contract Law and regulations, and in particular that it contains clearly and unambiguously all essential terms and conditions including: a) the description of the subject-matter of the transaction, b) the quantity and quality, c) the price or remuneration, d) the time, place and method of performance, e) the liability for breach of contract, and that the terms and conditions are all consistent with Party policy;

Ascertain the practicality of the contract, i.e., that it can realistically be carried out by the parties concerned, for example, in the purchase and sale of goods, suppliers must have the capacity to produce while buyers must have the ability to pay;

Satisfy themselves that the parties freely entered into the contract as legal equals irrespective of their administrative hierarchies, and that they abide by the fundamental principle of 'equality and mutual benefit' in the sense that each derives reciprocal rights and obligations from the contract; and

Undertake frequent field supervision to ensure the unfailing performance of an executory contract. Tung–Pi Chen, "The Chinese Notariat: An Overlooked Cornerstone of the Legal System of the People's Republic of China," 35 *Interna-*

tional & Comparative Law Quarterly 63, 77 (January 1986).

Notaries also monitor economic contracts to help prevent illegal or false terms and conditions, such as profiteering or bidrigging. When a notary discovers criminal activity, a report is made to the local procuracy or police. Notaries are thus important guardians in the Chinese legal system, especially in the economic sector.

In sum, the Chinese legal profession has come a long way in a hurry. Its progress from the reeducation camps of the Cultural Revolution to the China Global Law Firm, procuratorial supervision (at least in theory) of the entire Chinese legal system, and notarization of fundamental legal documents has been extraordinary. Nevertheless, much work remains before the people's lawyers, procurators and notaries will be able to function as independent professionals in service of the Chinese legal system.

CHAPTER IV

CRIMINAL JUSTICE

The prevailing Western image of the criminal justice process during the last century of the Qing Dynasty is as an instrument of state control, with little concern for the realization of individual justice. Numerous commentators have characterized the process in this manner, either directly or by treating the entire late imperial state as an authoritarian monolith essentially uninterested in law, other than as a command mechanism. Although recent evidence suggests that criminal justice during this period may be richer and more complex, this evidence has not yet led to a significant revision of the way in which the formal criminal justice process is typically portrayed.

Professor William Alford has argued that research in Chinese legal history remains at too preliminary a stage to warrant conclusive judgments about the theory or operation of the formal criminal justice process during the Qing Dynasty period. This inability may be attributable to the lingering effects of the seeming disdain of Confucian-oriented scholar-officials for law, to the absence of systematic official case reporting, or to the difficulty of securing, reading, and evaluating original source materials.

In many respects the technical rules and institutional framework for the administration of criminal justice in the PRC are similar to the inquisitorial system prevalent in continental Europe. That system was introduced into China in the first half of the twentieth century before the communists came to power in 1949. Notwithstanding surface similarities, China's criminal justice system has its own distinctive features that are tailored to its imperial roots, ancient culture and political ideology.

The criminal justice system that exists in the PRC today is in large part a reaction to the Cultural Revolution (1966–1976) and the radical fluctuations associated with earlier periods. The revolutionary fervor of the Cultural Revolution led to the wholesale disregard of law and to the dismantling of legal institutions. With the death of Mao in 1976, his successors determined that reform of the criminal justice system was essential. In 1978, the Communique of the Central Committee of the Communist Party of China set the general goals of the PRC's legal reform: "In order to safeguard people's democracy, it is imperative to strengthen the socialist legal system so that democracy is systematized and written into law in such a way as to ensure the stability, continuity and full authority of this democratic system and these laws; there must be laws for people to follow, these laws must be observed, their enforcement must be strict and law breakers must be dealt with." One of the major themes reflected in this communique is the restoration of order by means of law.

LAW ON THE BOOKS VERSUS LAW IN PRACTICE

A critical examination of any legal system will reveal differences between the criminal law on the books and the criminal law in practice. In Western systems, these differences usually are found at the operational or enforcement level and not at the more general policy level. In China, the differences can be detected at both the operational level and at the general policy level. But this phenomenon is not new. For example, perhaps the most conspicuous single Confucian influence on the Qing Code of imperial China was the principle of legalized inequality where individuals, depending on their status and their relation to the victim, were held to different standards and punishments. This legacy can be seen today. What emerges is a system of criminal justice that operates at two levels, one which is normative and the other prerogative. This two-level quality, perhaps more than any other, distinguishes the criminal justice system in the PRC from other Western systems.

With respect to "ordinary" criminal defendants, the criminal justice system tends to operate as stated in the criminal laws. Variations between law on the books and law in practice can be discovered at the operational level, however. With respect to non-ordinary criminal defendants, which typically involve "political" matters, the system operates in a prerogative fashion. The protection afforded the non-ordinary criminal defendant may be either reduced or enhanced depending on the particular circumstances and the status of the defendant. When the criminal justice system operates in a prerogative manner without demonstrating a compelling reason, the system fails to provide the stated constitutional protection of equal protection before the law for all Chinese citizens.

The events surrounding the suppression of the 1989 Democracy Movement directly assaulted the idea that criminal law and procedure exist in China. The normal provisions of the PRC's Criminal Law and Criminal Procedure Law were not followed notwithstanding the fact that most of those involved were exercising their rights to demonstrate and to protest as guaranteed by the 1982 Constitution. In the aftermath, many individuals were denied their legal rights as Chinese citizens.

The Supreme People's Court endorsed the counterrevolutionary classification of the demonstrations. This action effectively foreclosed the possibility of contesting this characterization in lower court criminal proceedings. The Supreme Court also instructed all courts to "swiftly try the cases involving counterrevolutionary ringleaders and serious criminals who beat, smashed, looted, burned and killed, and severely punish the culprits according to law."

The legal requirement to proceed according to Chinese law was not followed. The 1982 Constitution prohibits unlawful deprivation or detention of a citizen, and the Criminal Procedure Law details the process to be used in handling suspects, including the use of arrest warrants, notification of arrest and detention, and time limits for detention during an investigation. The Criminal Law specifies the types of available punishments, including minimums and maximums.

The authorities detained large numbers of citizens incommunicado in violation of both the Constitution and Criminal Procedure Law. Confessions were exacted through torture and other forms of police mistreatment. Prosecutions were rushed through the courts, with little or no time for consultation with or the assistance of counsel or for the adequate review of the record established at trial by higher authorities. Sentences were imposed that were disproportionate to the terms of the Criminal Law. For example, the three men who were charged with throwing ink and paint-filled eggshells at Mao's portrait in Tiananmen Square were sentenced to prison terms ranging from sixteen years to life. The death penalty was implemented quickly under expedited proceedings. Some defendants accused of crimes allegedly committed on June 5–6, 1989 were tried, sentenced and publicly executed within two weeks. Chinese citizens being humiliated and abused were paraded before "courts" and seen on television worldwide. The fact that little or no attention was paid to the procedural requirements of Chinese law vividly illustrates the criminal justice system operating at the diminished prerogative level.

But the criminal justice system can also operate selectively, where individuals are treated as above the law. The area of economic crimes illustrates this aspect. Any criminal act that violates an economic law or regulation, or undermines or endangers the socialist legal order can be considered an economic crime. Smuggling, bribery, speculation or profiteering—such as selling state goods obtained at below market prices on the open market or trading on the black market—swindling, diverting foreign exchange, trademark counterfeiting, and tax evasion are illustrations of the activities included within the category of economic crime.

Since the early 1980s economic crime in the PRC proliferated. The decentralization of economic decisionmaking, greater access to foreign goods and foreign exchange, official approval of the concept of profit, the changing definition of economic crime as a consequence of changing political attitudes or ill-defined economic goals, and many other factors related to the reform of the Chinese economy created a greater opportunity for individuals to commit economic crimes. While there are many reasons for the actual increase in economic crime, the growth of corruption and proliferation of economic crime, in large measure, is testimony to the virtual immunity of senior Party and other government officials from the reach of the criminal law. The Party Constitution effectively grants the Central Discipline Inspection Commission and its provincial and local branches priority over the judiciary in examining and dealing with Party members involved in criminal activity, including economic crime.

Certain high ranking Party members who violate any law may avoid legal punishment entirely and be dealt with according to internal Party procedures which may result in disciplinary but not criminal sanctions. This practice of substituting Party disciplinary sanctions for legal sanctions is widespread and examples commonly appear in Chinese newspapers and magazines. Various reports from the early 1980s indicate that only approximately one-third of the economic crimes being investigated and prosecuted in various cities were committed by members of the CCP, who often held important government positions. Given the widespread problem with economic crime, this percentage seems disproportionately small. Reports also indicate that when challenged or arrested for economic crimes, CCP members are often treated more leniently than those who are not members of the CCP. As part of a Party rectification campaign from 1983–87, the leadership targeted several groups within the CCP for reeducation and possible loss of Party membership. Among those groups were corrupt Party officials who had used their positions for personal gain, including protection from prosecution. In spite of this campaign, abuses of political power continue. The insulation of Party officials from the normal reach of the criminal law by substituting internal Party procedures and treating them differently illustrates the enhanced prerogative of the criminal justice system.

CRIMINAL PROCEDURE

During the Qing Dynasty, a criminal trial consisted of interrogation of the accused by the magistrate, who had substantial powers. The administration of justice was exclusively within the preserve of the state, and no independent actors, such as defense counsel, were allowed to intrude in the process. The legacy of this general approach is evidenced in the PRC's approach to criminal procedure today. The approach to criminal procedure, as well as the substantive criminal law, also has certain socialist characteristics that are traceable to criminal law and procedure in the Soviet Union. Although criminal justice in the PRC is generally modeled on Soviet law, it differs in important respects. Thus, for example, criminal investigations are normally conducted by the police in the PRC, not by the procuracy. See Berman, Cohen, Russell, "A Comparison of the Chinese and Soviet Codes of Criminal Law and Procedure," 73 *Journal of Criminal Law & Criminology* 238 (1982).

Prior to the adoption of the Criminal Procedure Law (CPL), which became effective in 1980, the PRC did not have a comprehensive code of criminal procedure. An "informal" approach to criminal procedure was used during the Cultural Revolution. This was a reflection of Mao's preference for a societal model of law and the rejection of a formal or juridical model of legal process. The adoption of the CPL was one of the many positive steps taken to reestablish and strengthen the legal system following the Cultural Revolution.

The CPL is the most important law dealing with criminal procedure in the PRC. It is not, however, the only source of law on criminal procedure. A variety of statutes adopted by the national and local legislatures, such as the Organic Law of the People's Court 1979, the Organic Law of the People's Procuracies 1979, the Regulations Governing the Arrest and Detention of Persons Accused of Crimes 1979, and Decisions Governing the Speedy Trial of Crimes that Seriously Threaten Public Security 1983, also contain provisions affecting criminal procedure. The expedited procedure for threatening public security was widely used in connection with those accused of crimes at Tiananmen Square.

The stated objective of the CPL is to guarantee the correct enforcement of the criminal law. The CPL is both a law of punishment and of protection. This dual feature distinguishes it from earlier laws dealing with criminal procedure that stressed the principle of punishment. The CPL is divided into four general parts. Part 1 contains general principles; Part 2 deals with the filing of a case, investigation and filing a public prosecution; Part 3 consists of articles dealing with trial; and Part 4 pertains to "execution of judgments."

Several features about criminal procedure in the PRC today are notable. First, the traditional social aversion to the formal legal system still persists. The CPL permits minor offenses to be privately prosecuted and the civil aspects of the case to be mediated under the auspices of the criminal court. When this occurs, the victim of the offense acts as the prosecutor in bringing the accused to court. Appeals from this process may also be mediated. As a result, an informal system operates side by side with the formal system.

Second, the CPL is remarkably brief and general. It only contains 164 articles. For purposes of comparison, the criminal procedure provisions of California Penal Code contain close to 950 sections. These features of brevity and generality, which are characteristic of much of Chinese law, grant substantial discretion to the authorities charged with administering the criminal procedure laws.

Third, China has adopted the general features of the inquisitorial system, which is normally associated with the civil law tradition. The inquisitorial system derives its name from the active role assumed by the judge who acts as an "inquisitor" in the search for the truth rather than being, as is the case in the common law system, an impartial referee between the state and the accused. Judges in China not only direct the examination of the witnesses and the accused by others, but they also personally question them. In the PRC, the public investigator has the duty to gather evidence for both the prosecution and the defense. Similarly, the public prosecutor is obligated by law to present evidence both for and against the defendant. But unlike the criminal process in most civil law countries which follow the inquisitorial system, China uses the criminal process as a educative tool. As was the case during the imperial period, strong emphasis is placed on the rehabilitation of the offender throughout the entire process.

Fourth, lawyers—including defense lawyers—are viewed as responsible to the court and socialist legality, not to the client. They are envisioned as performing a public function. Defense counsel has the obligation under the CPL to assist the court in the search for objective truth: "to present materials and opinions proving that the defendant is not guilty, that his crime is minor, or that he should receive a mitigated punishment or be exempted from criminal responsibility." If an accused has confessed guilt, the defense counsel is ethically obligated to plead the client guilty to the offense. The Criminal Law (CL) provides "(a)ny judicial worker who ... deliberately shields a guilty person and saves him from prosecution stands truth on its head and perverts the law will be sentenced to detention or imprisonment...." Both the role and the involvement of the defense attorney, especially prior to trial, is significantly more limited under Chinese law than it is under United States law.

Fifth, the CPL guarantees the criminal defendant the right to appeal adverse decisions without the risk of increased punishment. The procurator also has the right of appeal. An appeal results in a *de novo* determination, and the process is inquisitorial. Absent review through the process of adjudicatory supervision, the judgment of the court of second instance is final. However, as discussed below, the principle of finality and the protection against increased punishment is not absolute.

Sixth, under the Criminal Law and Criminal Procedure Law, as amended by a 1983 resolution of the NPC Standing Committee, a person charged with one of the violent or serious crimes can be executed within eight days or so, including arrest, investigation, prosecution, sentencing, appeal, and execution. See Shao–chuan Leng and Hungdah Chiu, *Criminal Justice in Post–Mao China* (1985). As outlined below, the speed with which each phase of the criminal process must be conducted is contained in the CPL. Nevertheless, the right to speedy trial is not an end in itself. Excessive speed in adjudicating a defendant's guilt and severely limiting the time within which an appeal or protest can be made can compromise the very essence of a criminal defendant's right to a trial.

Seventh, the absence of a significant number of lawyers to administer the criminal justice system and the absence of published judicial opinions that reveal the CPL in actual operation makes it difficult to assess the extent to which the stated provisions of the CPL generally are being implemented. Thus, despite the existence of many stated procedural safeguards, it is not possible to conclusively state how closely the Chinese judicial authorities follow them.

FILING, INVESTIGATING AND PROSECUTING CRIMINAL COMPLAINTS

The pretrial proceedings of the criminal process are composed of two parts: detention and arrest, and investigation. As with most criminal justice systems, filing a complaint for investigation and possible prosecution is the first procedural step in the typical criminal case. As a practical matter, reports from the public or victims are the main source of information concerning suspected criminal activity. Two different methods of responding to a suspected criminal act exist depending on whether the complaint is made before or after the detention or arrest of the suspect.

The first procedure provides that upon discovery of a possible criminal violation, the complainant has the "right and duty" to report the matter to the police, procuracies, or courts. These receiving agencies then have the duty of accepting and registering the complaint for possible investigation. If the complaint falls outside the receiving agency's jurisdiction, the complaint must be transferred to the organization having jurisdiction. A complaint may be oral or written. If the complaint is oral, it must be reduced to writing and attested to by the complainant. Legal sanctions exist for making false complaints or accusations. After receiving a complaint, the government agency reviews the facts of the accusation and determines whether to initiate an investigation, which may, in turn, lead to formal charges being prepared. If rejected for further criminal investigation, the receiving agency is supposed to inform the complainant of the reason. A dissatisfied complainant then has the right to apply for reconsideration of the decision rejecting the complaint.

The second procedure for bringing offenders in front of the appropriate authorities for criminal investigation and possible prosecution occurs when a suspect is arrested and taken into custody before an actual complaint is filed. The CPL permits the immediate apprehension and taking into custody of a criminal suspect by a public security officer (police officer) or citizen under certain circumstances, such as being caught in the process of committing a crime. When a citizen is allowed to seize and detain an offender, the citizen is required to turn the suspect over to the police, local procurator (prosecutor), or people's court for appropriate disposition.

The CPL encourages the reporting of criminal activity by providing a simple method of filing oral and written complaints. The complainant's anonymity can be protected during the investigation phase, which encourages the reporting of suspected criminal activity. Chinese law allows the joinder of "supplementary civil actions" with criminal prosecutions in order to permit a victim suffering material loss to recover compensation. As a result, victims are encouraged to report a crime to the authorities since the matters can be joined.

Generally, the initial screening of most criminal complaints is done by the police, not by procurators. The CPL gives the police discretion to decide whether to initiate a preliminary investigation into certain complaints they receive. For example, if the facts of the crime are obviously minor and do not necessitate the investigation of criminal responsibility, then the police are not obligated to investigate the matter. The police also have the discretion as to whether to recommend to the procuracy the arrest of a criminal suspect. The police or "public security bureaus" conduct most of the preliminary investigations of criminal complaints.

The procuracy has the authority to investigate certain types of crimes, such as bribery, embezzlement, and other economic crimes. In addition, the procuracy has the overall authority to decide whether "arrests" should be made and whether prosecutions initiated. The CPL provides that, in reviewing a case, the procurator must ascertain, among other things, whether the facts surrounding an alleged crime are supported by reliable and complete evidence, whether criminal conduct has been omitted from the charges, whether other persons connected with the alleged crime should be investigated, and whether the investigation by the police was lawful. When the procurator thinks that the facts of the complaint, as supported by the investigation, are "reliable and complete," he or she then initiates a prosecution in the appropriate people's court.

The CPL also gives the procurator the latitude to exempt a case from prosecution "in cases where, according to the provisions of the Criminal Law, it is not necessary to impose a sentence of criminal punishment or an exemption from criminal punishment may be granted...." Cases that are exempted from trial are internally reviewable by superiors in the procuracy. The public security bureau which initially investigated the case and transmitted it for prosecution has a right to be informed of the decision to exempt the case from prosecution and to request that the decision be reconsidered. Similarly, the crime victim has the right to be advised of a decision not to prosecute and to request that the local prosecutor review its own decision.

Finally, the procurator has the authority either to conduct a supplementary investigation into the facts and circumstances surrounding the case or to return the case to the public security bureau for further investigation. Thus, the Chinese procurator has considerable discretion to screen out cases that do not warrant criminal prosecution.

The people's courts also screen criminal cases before they reach the trial stage. The court, which receives a case after the decision to prosecute is made by the procurator, is required to conduct a threshold *ex parte* review to determine whether the case is ready for adjudication. This review of the case can be perfunctory or it can consist of "inspection, examination, search, seizure and expert evaluation." The case may be referred for adjudication only after the court has determined that "the facts of the crime are clear and the evidence is complete." The judge has the power to remand the case to the procuracy for supplementary investigation or to direct the procuracy to withdraw the prosecution.

As outlined above, the facts of each case involving suspected criminal activity are thoroughly reviewed. Before a case is tried, it is reviewed by the police, prosecutors, and people's court. Although each authority has the right to screen out the case from the criminal process, the exercise of this right is reviewable and thus not unlimited.

Many criminal suspects are detained in custody during the pretrial investigation and pending the decision to prosecute. The procedural safeguards against prolonged and arbitrary detention before trial are contained in the CPL, but no empirical evidence exists to determine how closely these safeguards are followed. The law distinguishes between the "detention" and the "arrest" of a criminal suspect. Detention involves the confinement of the suspect, without an arrest warrant, for the purpose of investigating whether sufficient evidence exists to justify arrest on formal charges. In contrast, an arrest is made on the basis of a warrant. After the arrest is ordered either by the procuracy or the people's court, the suspect is then apprehended and confined, or confinement continued, pending the investigation of whether the evidence supports prosecution.

The police may detain a suspect for up to three days. This period may be extended from one to four days under special circumstances. Thereafter, the detained suspect can be held for a longer period during the pretrial investigation if the prosecutor approves the arrest of the suspect within three days. Criminal suspects who are not arrested and formally charged within ten days of being detained in custody must be released. If arrested, the suspect may be held for an additional two months. When the investigation cannot be concluded within that time period, the pretrial detention may be extended for an additional month, with the approval of the procuracy at the next-higher level of administration. Additional detention extensions may be given only in "especially major or complex cases" and, then only by the Standing Committee of the NPC and at the request of the Supreme People's Procuracy.

In the United States, most state constitutions or statutes give a criminal suspect the limited right to be released from pretrial detention on payment of bail. Under Chinese law, a criminal suspect "summoned for detention" may be released during pretrial investigation by securing a guarantor of his or her continued availability or by living at home. If restricted to home the suspect is not free to leave the designated area, but is under "house arrest." The CPL does not specify when these alternatives to pretrial confinement may or should be granted. The right to authorize these alternatives is given to the people's courts, procuratorates, and public security organs. In pratice, the agency that caused the arrest or detention has effective authority.

The 1982 Constitution provides that arrests must be approved or ordered by the procuracy or the people's court, and the CPL contains a similar provision. Before the police can arrest a person, they typically first fill out and submit to the office of the procurator an arrest application, together with supporting materials and accompanying evidence. The procuracy may then either approve or disapprove arrest, or may order a further investigation. The police must immediately release a detained suspect, if the procuracy decides against the suspect's arrest. The police are required to produce an arrest warrant in arresting a suspect. The family of the arrested suspect or his or her residency unit must be notified of the arrest within twenty-four hours, the reasons for it, and the place of confinement. Exceptions to the notification requirements exist when notification would hinder the investigation or when it is impossible. Interrogation must be conducted within twenty-four hours of arrest, unless it has already taken place.

Search and seizure procedures are outlined in Articles 71 through 87 of the CPL. As a general matter, they are far simpler than U.S. search and seizure law. Under Chinese law, the police and the procuracy exercise powers most often assigned solely to the judiciary in Western countries. Investigators are authorized to conduct searches of the person, articles, residences, and other relevant places when carrying out an arrest or detention. A search warrant must be shown to the person being searched, except when the arrest or detention occurs in an emergency situation. But, no constitutional or statutory provisions exist in Chinese law requiring prior approval by the procuracy or the people's court of a search by police. Thus, the search warrant requirement does not adequately protect against arbitrary police conduct, such as "sniffing expeditions," since the police can issue a warrant to their own investigators whenever they choose.

An accused may not know the specific charges against him or her during the pretrial investigation or during interrogation. Nevertheless, a criminal defendant has the right to be informed in advance of the trial of the nature and the factual basis of the accusation. Under Article 110 of the CPL, the defendant may not be informed of the bill of prosecution until after the decision to prosecute has been made, and, in any event, no later than seven days before trial. Only after the accused is informed of the bill of prosecution does counsel for the defendant acquire the right to inspect the prosecution's evidence.

Both the 1982 Constitution and CPL give an accused the right of defense, but this right does not translate into the right to court-appointed counsel or the right to a lawyer. The CPL states: "In addition to exercising the right to defend themselves, defendants may also authorize the following people to defend them: 1) Lawyers; 2) Citizens who are recommended by a people's organization or by the defendant's unit or who are authorized by the people's court; and 3) Close relatives or guardians of the defendant." This right of defense is effectively undermined by the failure to give the accused and his or her counsel timely notification of the bill of prosecution. As a practical matter, an accused who has been in pretrial detention may not be able to contact a defense lawyer until shortly before trial. The restrictions on the timely access to a lawyer are difficult to justify. Presumably, they rest on the dubious assumption that the defense counsel may interfere with the investigation or that counsel is unnecessary prior to the decision being made to prosecute the accused because of the inquisitorial nature of the system. One of the more fundamental reforms that would improve the CPL would be advancing the point at which a suspect is permitted to retain the presence of counsel. If suspects were given the right to counsel upon commencement of the preliminary investigation, their constitutional right to defense would be significantly enhanced.

The general shortage of trained lawyers to assist individuals accused of crimes is also a significant limit on the right to defense. As a practical matter, most accused persons defend themselves or rely on persons not trained in the law. Notwithstanding this situation, there has been an increasing tendency, at least in the larger cities, for persons accused of more serious crimes to rely on legal counsel.

TRIAL AND SENTENCING

No person can be convicted of a crime without evidence produced at trial in a court of competent jurisdiction. Each of the four court levels (Basic, Middle (Intermediate), Higher and the Supreme People's Court) has a criminal branch or division. The Basic People's Court is the court of first instance for the ordinary criminal case. The court may be composed of "from one to three judges and from two to four people's assessors". Normally, the court consists of a professional judge and two people's assessors (laypersons). When the matter before the court is considered "petty," one professional judge may hear the case. The people's assessors have equal rights with the professional judge, although, as a practical matter, the people's assessors are usually influenced by the professional judge. People's assessors are used in most trials before the people's courts. They symbolize justice at the hands of the people, but have neither the power nor influence associated with common law juries. Any citizen over twenty-three years of age who is eligible to vote may become an assessor. People's assessors are elected for three-year terms and they sit on a part-time basis. Parties to a case before the people's courts may seek to have a professional judge or an assessor recused for bias. The chief judge of the court decides such petitions. This example, given by a man who served as a people's assessor for several years and reported by Amnesty International, captures the essence of many Chinese trials:

> In March of 1986 I was informed by the court that I was to perform my first period of service as a people's assessor at a trial. Before the trial commenced the judge informed us (there was also a woman comrade there) that, since things were a bit rushed, there would be no time for us to familiarize ourselves with the details of the case in hand. [He said:] "you must just listen to what you are told to do." During the discussions of the collegial panel, the judge also said that the court president (*yuanzhang*) had already issued a directive regarding both the verdict and the level of sentencing that was to be applied. Thereupon, he took out a pre-written verdict sheet (*zao yi xiehao de panjueshu*), read it out once, and asked us whether we had any comments to make. I ask you, what comments could we be expected to have?! So, although we felt somewhat uncomfortable about it, the case was simply "collegially" decided upon in this way. [August, 1989]

In China, the court decides both guilt and punishment as there are no juries.

The CPL requires all trial judges, both professional and lay, to review the pretrial investigative file, which includes among other matters prior convictions. This requirement has the potential for influencing judicial decision making on the issue of guilt when the defendant is tried. Although the judges are required to decide the defendant's guilt or innocence based on the evidence produced at trial, some mechanism should be devised to prevent the collegiate panel from prejudging the facts of the case based on the pretrial investigative file.

Generally, illegally obtained evidence is excludable from trial under Chinese law. However, evidence obtained or derived from illegally obtained evidence, which most United States attorneys know as the "fruit of the poisonous tree," is not excludable. Thus, Chinese law does not provide the defendant protection against potentially damaging information obtained from otherwise inadmissible evidence. The protection afforded by the CPL could be enhanced by broadening the exclusionary rules in this context.

The CPL provides that criminal trials are generally to be held in public. The right to a "public trial" does not extend to pretrial proceedings. Exceptions exist however. For example, cases involving state secrets and the intimate affairs of individuals or juveniles are not subject to this requirement. Whenever a case is not heard in public the reasons for its being closed must be announced in court. While it is a defensible policy to close trials when matters of national security are involved and in other instances, there does not appear to be any mechanism whereby members of the public can challenge the determination to close a trial. As a result, cases with political implications may be easily closed to the public by the authorities. The absence of statistics on the number of public and nonpublic trials makes it difficult to ascertain whether the general requirement is closely followed. Since there is no practical reason for the courts to resort to closed trials in the typical criminal case and very few citizens are interested in attending trials unless their relatives or close friends are involved, the public trial requirement is probably followed in most criminal cases.

The 1982 Constitution creates constitutional rights for minorities appearing before people's courts. Citizens of all of the nationalities of China have a right to use their own spoken and written languages in court. The people's courts must provide for interpreters as needed. Where minorities live in compact communities or where a number of minorities live together, the hearings before people's courts must be conducted in the local language. Indictments, judgments and notices must also be in that language. It is difficult to evaluate whether these procedural rights are being implemented by the people's courts. The repeated repression of Tibetan demonstrations for greater autonomy and independence suggests that protection of minority rights is not a legal theme having much operational currency in the PRC.

The trial phase of the criminal proceeding begins with the administrative review of the case by the people's court. Once the case is accepted for trial, the three-judge trial panel is convened. The trial begins with the court confirming the identity of the defendant and with the fact that the parties are ready to proceed. The prosecutor then reads the bill of prosecution outlining the charges. Following this formal notification of the charges, the examination of the defendant begins. The trial panel starts the questioning, followed by the procurator, and finally by defendant's counsel. Witnesses do not testify under oath, but they are admonished that giving false evidence or concealing evidence are criminally punishable offenses.

Once the judicial investigation of the facts is complete, the prosecutor may comment on those facts from the state's viewpoint. The victim is then given the chance to address the court. Thereafter, the defendant may present any witnesses. A "debate" between the prosecution and the defendant's attorney follows. The "debate" focuses on both the question of the defendant's guilt and appropriate sentencing. It frequently is the most exciting part of the proceeding. After the "debate," the defendant has the right to make a final statement before the court retires to make its determinations. A majority of the court is needed to convict the defendant. The court may announce its judgment at the conclusion of the trial or it may delay making the announcement for "no later than one and a half months after receiving the case."

The CPL provides, in part: "In the decision of all cases, the emphasis should be placed on evidence and investigative research, and credence should not be readily given to oral statements. In cases where there is only the testimony of the defendant and there is no other evidence, the defendant cannot be found guilty and sentenced to criminal punishment...." The CPL does not expressly refer to any "presumption of innocence." If a defendant decides not to testify, this choice is not subject to any contempt penalty. As a practical matter, it would probably be viewed by the adjudicators as a silent confession of guilt since the case has been carefully reviewed by the police, procurator, and investigating magistrate prior to being referred to trial. Silence is also likely to be taken into account at sentencing since it is indicative of the person's unrepentant attitude toward the crime.

The debate as to whether China adheres to the "presumption of innocence" has continued since the enactment of the CPL. On the one hand, if one includes within the concept of the presumption of innocence many of the understandings associated with the adversary system—for example, that the accused has no burdens at all, no duty to cooperate with the state, and that he or she may affirmatively utilize procedures designed for an accused's protection to obscure or obfuscate the truth or impede the prosecution—there is little support for the proposition that Chinese law has adopted the presumption of innocence, at least as the term is used in Western law. On the other hand, if one stresses the fact that judgments of guilt must be founded on the evidence, not on subjective assumptions of guilt, then an argument can be made that something like the presumption of innocence exists.

A guilty plea by the defendant does not have the same procedural significance that it has in United States law. The guilty plea is the most common basis for criminal convictions in the United States. It almost always is produced in response to negotiations between the prosecution and the defense attorney over such matters as the charges or possible sentence. In contrast, when the defendant enters a guilty plea under Chinese law, the prosecution still has the obligation to prove the guilt of the defendant. Evidence other than the confession of the accused should support the conviction. Consequently, the Chinese court must look beyond the guilty plea to other supporting evidence before determining the defendant's guilt.

In order for a confession to be reliable it has to be free and voluntary. Consistent with this principle, the CPL provides: "The use of torture to coerce statements and the gathering of evidence by threat, enticement, deceit or other unlawful methods are strictly prohibited." This would seem to prohibit the use of coerced confessions. But the above quoted language leaves open the question of whether the use of psychological coercion or other subtle forms of encouragement to obtain confessions is also prohibited. Moreover, the practical protection afforded by this provision of the CPL is directly affected by the legal requirement that "the defendant shall answer the questions put by the investigation personnel according to the facts." It is not clear to what extent a defendant may maintain his or her silence during the pretrial investigation in light of this requirement to answer questions. Confessions are produced during the pretrial investigative process in China, not in response to negotiations between the prosecution and the defense as is typically the case in the United States.

The CPL requires the court, as well as the procuracy and police, to base their decisions on facts. No specific reference exists in the CPL that prohibits repeated prosecutions of the same defendant for the same offense, which in the United States is precluded by the doctrine of double jeopardy. In theory, an individual who has been tried for a crime and "wrongly" acquitted could be retried for the same crime.

APPEALS

Under Chinese law the criminal defendant has the right of appellate review. Two methods of reviewing a trial decision exist. One method involves the review of the case by the next-higher-level court through the process of appeal or protest. In this type of review, the appellate court is not bound by the scope of the matters appealed or protested. It has the power to conduct a complete review of both the facts and the law that was applied. However, no additional appeal beyond this next-higher-level is permitted. The appellate review is normally conducted by a panel of three to five law-trained judges.

Appeals may be made by either the defendant or the procurator. They must be made within ten days of a judgment or within five days of a judicial order. Typical grounds for an appeal include erroneous determination of facts or erroneous application of the law to the facts, violation of lawful procedures, and too lenient or too severe a sentence given the facts. The appellate court can reject the appeal and uphold the original judgment or order, or revise the original judgment when the court of first instance made an error in applying the law to facts. It may also remand the case for a new trial.

To avoid the impression that appellants are penalized by exercising the right of appeal, the CPL provides that the appellate court retrying a case may not increase a defendant's punishment when the defendant appeals. This limitation does not apply when the procuracy protests the decision. For example, a procurator who thinks that the sentence of the lower court was too lenient may appeal and successfully have the original judgment reopened. In this case, a more severe sentence could be imposed on remand.

The second method of review is by "adjudication supervision." This system of review seeks to ensure that erroneous or unjust judgments are corrected and that criminal offenders are duly punished. Under this type of review, parties to a criminal action, victims and their family members, and even interested third parties—irrespective of whether they participated in the case—may go to the people's courts or people's procuracies and present petitions regarding final judgments or orders. In addition, the people's court must reopen a case for adjudicatory supervision whenever they find an error.

The decision to review a case by adjudication supervision is discretionary. No legal right exists to have the case reviewed in this manner. Review by adjudication supervision is not restricted by any statutory time limits. Because a case could be reopened through adjudication supervision at any time after a "final" judgment of the lower court, this opportunity to reopen the matter effectively weakens the protection afforded by the principle of finality of judgments. A defendant theoretically could be subject to another trial on the same bill of prosecution.

A supervisory review hearing is conducted by the "presidents of the people's courts at various levels" or by the Supreme People's Court. Three different kinds of action may be taken when a case is reopened under adjudication supervision: (1) the court committing the error may refer it to its adjudication committee for handling; (2) the Supreme People's Court and higher level courts may review the case and correct the errors by reversing or modifying the judgment or ordering the people's courts at lower levels to conduct a retrial; and (3) the Supreme People's Procuracy or some higher-level procuratorate other than the one which originally prosecuted the case may protest the judgment in accordance with the established procedures for adjudication at the court level of first instance.

Some insight into criminal appellate practice can be derived from China's *Supreme Court Gazette,* which published 24 selected criminal cases reviewed by the Judicial Committee of the Supreme People's Court during the period 1985–87. In the majority of cases, 17 out of 24, the court of second instance reviewed the case pursuant to an appeal. Out of those 17 cases, one or more of the defendants appealed the lower court decision in 15 situations; the defendant filed an appeal and the procurator a protest in one case; and, the procurator appealed one case. Out of the same 17 cases, 14 cases were affirmed, none were reversed, and in 3 situations the sentence modified—in one instance, pursuant to a procurator's protest, the appellate court eliminated a two-year reprieve on a death sentence, and thus increased the sentence. Assuming this to be a representative sampling, these statistics on the one hand suggest that appellants do not fear that they will be penalized for accessing the appeals process. On the other hand, the statistics also reveal a low success rate for appellants.

In addition to these two methods of reviewing criminal judgments, a special review procedure exists for death penalty sentences. A death sentence must be approved by the Supreme People's Court or by the higher court at the provincial level. Since 1981, the Higher People's Court is authorized to approve the death penalty in cases of murder, robbery, rape, bombing, arson and sabotage.

CRIMINAL LAW

The PRC did not have an integrated criminal code prior to the adoption of the 1979 Criminal Law (CL). Scattered statutes covering specific crimes, such as counterrevolution and corruption, and unpublished regulations on penalties for murder, rape, and other antisocial acts, have existed since the founding of the PRC. Prior to the adoption of the CL, those charged with administering the criminal justice system, as well as those subject to it, were not always able to determine whether certain conduct was criminal. The absence of an integrated criminal code produced uncertainty. The authorities might treat the same conduct differently. The matter might be submitted to mediation by the offender's residency committee or work group, or it might be subjected to the application of administrative sanctions by the police, or it might be the basis of a criminal prosecution.

The adoption of the CL was one of the major changes following the end of the Cultural Revolution. The positive impressions associated with its adoption were weakened, however, with the Decision of the Standing Committee of the NPC Regarding the Severe Punishment of Criminals Who Seriously Endanger Public Security. This 1983 Decision effectively amended the CL so as to permit a campaign against serious crimes to be conducted with greater severity and with less constraint. Notwithstanding this Decision, the CL was a positive step toward reforming the criminal justice system.

One distinctive feature of the criminal law in the PRC is the concept of crimes by analogy. The principle of culpability by analogy is not a recent phenomenon. It can be found in the legal codes of the Tang (618–906), the Ming (1368–1644), and the Qing (1644–1911) dynasties. Under the general reach of this principle, a person who commits a socially dangerous act not expressly prohibited by the law can be punished under a provision that prohibits analogous acts. The Act for the Punishment of Counterrevolutionaries (1951) first articulated the PRC's intent to adopt the controversial principle of culpability by analogy. This Act provides that persons who undertook acts with counter-revolutionary intent that were not specified in the law were to be prosecuted and punished as though those acts were crimes. The CL reaffirmed the commitment to the principle of crimes by analogy: "A crime that is not expressly stipulated in the Special Provisions of this Law may be determined and punished according to the most closely analogous article of the Special Provisions of this Law, but the matter shall be submitted to the Supreme People's Court for approval." Crimes by analogy contravene two basic principles found in maxims of Western criminal law: no crime without law (*nullem crimen sine lege*) and no punishment without law (*nulla poena sine lege*).

Another distinctive feature of criminal law in the PRC is the use of administrative police sanctions. The Labor Reform Statute (1957), which is still in effect, allows the police to impose administrative (nonjudicial) sanctions against those "without legitimate employment, hoodlums or irresponsible characters ..., those opposing security control and those who have been unsuccessfully reeducated," as well as "counterrevolutionary elements ..., anti-socialist reactionary elements ..., those who impede social order [and] those who constantly make trouble or impede official matters." These administrative sanctions can be brought to bear against a wide variety of antisocial behavior. The police can incarcerate individuals for up to four years by following administrative procedures. Those who are subjected to such nonjudicial sanctions have no judicial recourse.

The 1979 Criminal Law became effective January 1, 1980. It is supplemented by a number of rules dealing with public order and state security. For example, state security matters are dealt with in the Organic Rules of Public Security Committees and Rules for Organization of People's Mediation Committees, and Organic Rules of Neighborhood Offices and the Organic Rules of Urban Residents Committees. In addition to these Rules, the NPC adopted the Security Administration Punishment Act in 1986.

The CL, which consists of 192 articles, follows the civil law format—a General Part that establishes the general principles of crime and punishment, and a Special Part that specifies particular crimes. In many respects, the CL resembles the 1960 Russian Soviet Federated Socialist Republic (RSFSR) Code. Notwithstanding the resemblance to the Soviet Code, it has distinguishable features. For example, the CL emphasizes the punishment of wrongdoers rather than wrongful acts. It uses moralistic terms, such as "heinous" and "monstrous," in describing some offenses. It also covers crimes that are germane to Chinese circumstances. In a broad sense, the CL reflects a highly moralistic and reformative tone.

A third distinctive feature of the CL, at least by Western standards, lies in the generality and brevity of the definitions of crimes. There are a number of examples. The entire law of intentional homicide is contained in a single sentence: "Whoever intentionally kills another is to be sentenced to death, life imprisonment or not less than ten years of fixed-term imprisonment...." Crimes against the person are contained in eleven articles, whereas for purposes of comparison the California Penal Code contains approximately eighty provisions. Crimes against property are delineated in seven articles. The California Penal Code has about 140.

There are at least two significant consequences associated with such generality and brevity. First, more ambiguities in defining criminal conduct exist. For example, the CL provides penalties for "whoever makes a regular occupation of smuggling or speculation or smuggles or speculates in huge amounts...." In this instance, ambiguities exist in determining the meanings of "regular" and "huge." In more general terms, there are predictable difficulties in determining which acts are appropriate for mediation or for administrative sanction ("rehabilitation through labor") or for criminal prosecution. Second, the authorities charged with implementing the criminal law have greater discretion, which in turn increases the opportunities for abuse of power.

Protection of the socialist order and the personal rights of the citizens of the PRC are the principle objectives of the CL. The CL identifies the following goals: "to use criminal punishments to struggle against all counterrevolutionary and other criminal acts in order to defend the system of the dictatorship of the proletariat, to protect socialist property owned by the whole people and property collectively owned by the laboring masses, to protect citizens' lawful privately-owned property, to protect citizens' rights of the person, democratic rights and other rights, to maintain social order, order in production, order in work, order in education and scientific research and order in the lives of the masses of people, and to safeguard the smooth progress of the cause of socialist revolution and socialist construction." Some of these objectives are similar to the objectives of most criminal justice systems. Nevertheless, there are distinguishable features, such as the class struggle emphasis and the use of positive commands to prescribe desired societal results.

The concept of crime includes any act endangering society's protected interests and punishable by law. For an act to be criminal three criteria must be satisfied. First, the act must endanger society. The emphasis is on socially dangerous acts. Second, the actor must have the requisite mental state. To constitute a criminal offense, the socially dangerous act must be committed intentionally or negligently. A person who is mentally ill and who is unable to recognize or control his or her conduct cannot be criminally responsible. However, an intoxicated person who commits a crime is treated as criminally responsible. A number of affirmative defenses exist under the CL, such as self-defense and necessity. These defenses exculpate an actor from criminal liability only when the measures taken are proportionate to the social danger against which the defense is used. Third, the act must be punishable by law. An act that violates the civil law or administrative regulations is not a crime. Only an act that endangers society seriously enough to be in violation of the Criminal Law is an offense.

Under United States law, entrapment occurs when the intent to commit the crime originated not with the defendant, but rather with the creative activities of law enforcement officers. It is presumed that the legislative intent does not cover the conduct, so the conduct is not treated as being criminal. The affirmative defense of entrapment is not recognized in China. Thus, for example, if a member of the security bureau approaches an American tourist in Beijing, who has no predisposition to exchange currency in the black market but is induced to make the illegal exchange, the tourist cannot then plead entrapment as an affirmative defense.

The CL lists eight general categories of crimes and their penalties: (1) counterrevolutionary crimes; (2) crimes endangering public security; (3) crimes undermining the socialist economic order; (4) crimes infringing upon the personal rights or democratic rights of citizens; (5) property crimes; (6) crimes disrupting the order of social administration; (7) crimes disrupting marriage or family; and (8) crimes of dereliction of duty or malfeasance. A variety of different types of crimes are included within each general category. Thus, for example, the crimes of counterfeiting national currency and valuable securities are included within the category of crimes undermining the socialist economic order. Some crimes are particular to the socialist ideology, while others are typical to Western criminal codes.

Crimes of counterrevolution, which are reminiscent of the sweeping provisions of the 1926 Russian Criminal Code, appear first in the CL and deserve special comment. Counterrevolutionary crimes are defined as "all acts" involving any means "committed with the goal of overthrowing the political power of the dictatorship of the proletariat and the socialist system." Culpability is described in terms of acts that "endanger the sovereignty and territorial integrity of the state, endanger the system of the dictatorship of the proletariat, undermine the socialist revolution and ... undermine social order ... [or] endanger society." The operative terms, such as "endanger" or "undermine," are not defined in the CL and are not self-defining. This failure effectively gives the authorities the latitude to suppress legitimate conduct and opinion in an omnibus manner by manipulating it into the crime of counterrevolution. Although some counterrevolutionary crimes and punishments are more specifically defined elsewhere in the CL, the elastic nature of key terms generally insures the authorities will have the legal grounds for suppressing any political dissidence that they find objectionable. For example, the demonstrations in the spring of 1989 were defined as "counterrevolutionary" by the Chinese government even though the protesters did not have the goal of either overthrowing the socialist system or Communist Party.

Crimes against the socialist economic order include a wide variety of acts, including speculation, violation of the customs laws, and tax evasion. Although economic crime, which falls within the category of undermining the socialist economic order, was officially prohibited when the CL became effective in 1980, national attention was not focused on this type of activity until 1982 when the NPC adopted a resolution increasing the penalties for the perpetrators of economic crimes. By the end of April 1983, more than 192,000 cases involving economic crime were being investigated, and over 71,000 Party members were implicated. The government established a crime reporting system in the second half of 1988. Within this period more than 24,000 high officials and Party members were reported for committing irregularities. Between July and November 1988, more than 101,000 white-collar crimes were reported to the Procuratorates. As reported in a 1989 *Beijing Review* article, graft and bribery constituted over 50 percent of China's economic crimes. Despite two focused campaigns against economic crime during the 1980s, economic crime and corruption continues to be a significant and pervasive domestic problem.

China has an increasingly extensive bureaucracy for combatting economic crime. A number of ministerial-level agencies are active in detection and enforcement aspects of this type of crime. The Customs Administration is responsible for uncovering smuggling cases as it monitors imports and exports. Tax bureaus under the Ministry of Finance conduct investigations and refer cases to public security and procuratorial authorities for action in connection with suspected tax offenses. The State Administration for Industry and Commerce (SAIC), which grants business licenses, assists in uncovering individuals and enterprises unlawfully engaged in business activities or earning illegal profits.

The China Audit Administration (CAA) was established in 1983 to monitor State tax and other economic affairs. It is responsible for auditing the finances of China's enterprises in their use of State funds. In conjunction with other agencies, it has uncovered serious cases involving tax evasion, violations of State pricing laws, and illicit bonus payments to employees.

In 1987, the Ministry of Supervision was established as a watchdog agency. It is charged with reviewing and supervising the performance of government departments, government workers, and government-employed factory managers. In its capacity as a watchdog agency, it supervises contracts signed with foreigners and it also deals with bribery, corruption, and malfeasance of government employees, including divulging State secrets by selling or otherwise revealing internal economic information to foreigners. Through October 1987 it had reviewed some 10,000 contracts.

Crimes infringing upon the rights of the person include a number of crimes U.S. courts would treat as major felonies, such as intentional killing, rape, kidnapping and so on. The CL also includes within this category a number of crimes not commonly found in the U.S. For example, the "use of big character posters" or "small character posters" to publicly insult another person is a crime.

The category of property crimes covers stolen private and public property. Criminal conduct such as theft, swindling, forcible seizure, blackmail and extortion and embezzlement by state personnel who take advantage of their office are prominent among such crimes that draw heavy punishments.

Crimes of disrupting marriage and the family are similar to those found in most American jurisdictions. These include, for example, bigamy, spousal and child abuse, and refusal to support aged, young, or disabled family members. There are some interesting family law crimes that reflect cultural differences, however. Examples of these include cohabiting with "the spouse of a member of the armed forces in active service" or interfering with "the freedom of marriage of others," which is a prohibition directed at China's feudal past.

PUNISHMENTS

In China, punishment for wrongful and illegal behavior is divided into two categories: "administrative," which may be formal or informal, and "criminal." "Informal" administrative sanctions, such as warnings and criticism ("censure") are social control measures. Administrative sanctions can be more than just mild forms of reprimand. For example, the formal administrative procedures contained in the Labor Reform Statute and Administrative Punishment Act of 1957 allow state security authorities to incarcerate persons in either local detention centers, which are similar to county jails in the United States, or "education through labor" camps. In 1990, the Committee on Foreign Relations of the U.S. Senate received testimony conservatively estimating that about 700,000 persons a year are sent to such centers or camps for terms of less than four years. This type of administrative procedure supplements, and often is a substitute for, criminal prosecutions. Individuals subject to Administrative Punishment Statutes have no recourse to judicial review because their "reeducation" is administrative, not criminal.

Criminal sanctions are divided into principal punishments and supplementary punishments. The five principal punishments include: (1) "control" as a type of supervised probation that can last from three months to two years; (2) "criminal detention," which should not be confused with pretrial detention discussed in the criminal procedure part of this chapter, involves short-term deprivation of freedom in a detention house and can last from fifteen days to six months; (3) "fixed-term imprisonment" involves imprisonment from six months to fifteen years; (4) life imprisonment; and (5) the death penalty, which is discussed more fully below. The first two types of punishment, control and criminal detention, are imposed for minor offenses. The term "imprisonment," which is imposed for offenses considered serious, is synonymous with "reform through labor" and can be carried out in a prison or a labor camp. In 1990, testimony given the U.S. Senate estimated that one million persons were incarcerated in prisons or labor camps. The function of "reform through labor" camps is not explained in the Code.

The CL provides for three "supplementary" punishments: (1) fines; (2) deprivation of political rights, such as the right to vote or hold office or leading position in "any enterprise, public institution, or people's organization"; and (3) confiscation of property. Additional penalties specified in other provisions of the CL are deportation, which applies only to foreigners, and restitution made to a victim suffering an economic loss from the crime.

Ordinary offenders can be treated with leniency, which most often occurs when the offender is repentant. The CL permits a convicted offender to be sentenced to a milder punishment than the minimum generally set by law when the court thinks such a sentence would inflict too severe a punishment given the circumstances of the case. Under certain circumstances, sentences can be "temporarily executed outside prison" or suspended. A sentence can be suspended when the offender, who has been sentenced to criminal detention or to a fixed-term imprisonment of not more than three years, demonstrates sincere repentance and presents no further danger to society. When a sentence is suspended, the offender is placed on probation. Parole for persons sentenced to fixed-term imprisonment is also permitted when not less than half has been served, or for persons sentenced to life imprisonment when at least ten years have been served and when the offender demonstrates true repentance and release will not endanger society. A parolee remains under the supervision of the police, and revocation of parole is possible if the parolee commits additional offenses.

The use of capital punishment continues virtually unchallenged in China. In 1986, Deng Xiaoping argued that execution is one of the indispensable means of education. Capital punishment is used more frequently by the authorities in China and is available for a wider range of crimes than is the case in the United States. In late 1990, Amnesty International reported that close to 900 people were known to have been executed from January 1990 through early December 1990. They also observed that the actual number of individuals executed during this period was believed to be much higher because the government does not publicly report the number of executions. During the anti-crime campaign of 1983, the number of executions was estimated to be in the range of 5,000 to 10,000.

The CL authorizes the use of capital punishment for a wide variety of crimes: crimes of counterrevolution, intentional homicide, aggravated intentional injury, robbery resulting in great bodily injury or death, "habitual" theft of "huge amounts," aggravated smuggling or speculation, aggravated theft and export of cultural relics, aggravated sale of narcotics, arson, aggravated rape, illegal manufacture and sale of arms, corruption while in public office, and luring or forcing women into prostitution. It is imposed only for "serious" offenses, but serious offenses are both broadly defined and include nonviolent crimes. Thus, for example, the death penalty was imposed recently against a number of persons who were dealing in pornographic materials and against a customs agent who had accepted a $173,000 bribe. In late 1990, 64 individual were executed in one day in Guangdong province: 24 robbers, 20 thieves, 14 murders, four weapons dealers, and two "hooligans."

Death sentences are sometimes handed down at mass rallies to "educate" the public. In mid–1990, a story in *The Washington Post* reported that Chinese radio said that in the northeastern town of Jinzhou, a rally attended by nearly 20,000 people was held to sentence criminals guilty of serious offenses. According to the radio report, 12 criminals at the stadium were given the death sentence. It is usual for those sentenced to be taken immediately from such rallies to an execution site. Executions are usually by a single shot in the back of the head.

The Criminal Law purports to place limits on the use of the death penalty. Persons under eighteen years of age and women who are pregnant during trial are exempt from capital punishment. Under certain circumstances, a "two-year suspension of execution may be announced at the same time the sentence of death is imposed, and reform through labor carried out and the results observed." At the end of the two-year period, the death sentence may be reduced to life imprisonment. This was the sentence handed down on January 25, 1981 to Jiang Qing (Mao's wife) and Zhang Chunqiao, two members of the "Gang of Four."

Judicial review of death penalty cases is also provided by the Criminal Law: "Except for judgments made by the Supreme People's Court according to law, all sentences of death shall be submitted to the Supreme People's Court for approval." In 1984, it was reported that the Supreme People's Court had transferred the right to examine and approve some death sentences to the Higher People's Courts. The speed with which some individuals were executed after Tiananmen Square raises serious questions as to the adequacy of judicial review of death sentences in China.

CHAPTER V

CIVIL JUSTICE

The forms and techniques of civil or private dispute resolution adopted by any state tend to reflect the values and authority relationships within it. Thus while there are some surface similarities, contemporary civil dispute resolution in China differs substantially from traditional techniques. Since 1949, the communists have sought to replace older Chinese values with their own. For example, there is a focus on struggle to overcome obstacles and meet specific goals rather than on harmony and compromise. The communists have also reorganized Chinese society by weakening traditional forums associated with dispute resolution such as the family, clan and village. In their place are mediators and mediation committees whose focus is frequently as much on settlement of the dispute according to correct political standards, such as promoting national over local values and interests, as on a resolution that reflects a compromise aimed at individual preferences and maintaining societal harmony.

In general, the communists have used civil dispute resolution as part of their ongoing effort to change Chinese society and mobilize support for Party policies. It is, of course, impossible for the

Chinese Communist Party to control effectively all individual behavior in China. It is when behavior no longer conforms to societal and CCP norms and laws that the judicial process becomes most significant. The focus of the prior chapter was on criminal justice and the resolution of disputes primarily between the Party and state on the one hand, and individuals, entities and groups on the other. This chapter surveys civil justice and dispute settlement procedures and issues in the People's Republic of China. Its primary focus is upon the process of mediation, arbitration and civil litigation. These processes are critical to the realization of the substance of the PRC civil and economic law detailed in the succeeding chapters on People and Property, Business and Labor, Contract and Tort and Foreign Trade, Investment and Technology.

THE PREFERENCE FOR MEDIATION

In the litigious United States, there is growing acceptance of "alternative dispute resolution" (ADR) techniques. More and more family, civil and commercial disputes are being settled outside the courts with the help of mediators, conciliators and arbitrators. In China, these techniques represent the mainstream, and recourse to litigation is the alternative. Mediation and conciliation are the predominant forms of civil and (to a lesser extent) commercial dispute settlement in the People's Republic of China. This is true for international as well as domestic matters. In both arenas, the Chinese have evidenced a strong preference to avoid adjudicatory methods of dispute settlement. The prevalence of mediation has been a source of pride among many Chinese lawyers. Within the People's Republic it is frequently regarded as one of the "Chinese characteristics" of the legal system.

Mediation and conciliation are often perceived to be the same thing. Both involve third persons assisting the parties in reaching settlement. Traditionally, conciliators merely act as "go-betweens." Conciliators do not make settlement recommendations to the parties, whereas mediators do. A mediator's recommendations, however, are not final or binding. In addition, the Chinese distinguish "people's mediation" from "judicial mediation." The most important difference is that judicially mediated agreements are enforceable by the courts. The results of mediation by village or residents committees, and work or agricultural units, are enforced principally by accompanying social and political pressures.

The significance of mediation as a method of dispute settlement is illustrated by statistics from the Chinese Academy of Social Sciences. The Academy estimated in 1981 that mediation committees dealt with thirteen times more civil and minor criminal cases than the Basic Level People's Courts. Approximately 860,000 mediation committees disposed of nearly 8.2 million civil disputes. The Academy calculated that nearly 90 percent of the civil disputes of 1981 were resolved by mediation. About four million older women (*lao taitai*) acted as mediators in this work. By 1989, the number of mediation committees had increased to over 1 million with a staff of 6.5 million mediators. In Beijing, this amounts to about one *lao taitai* for every 20 families. Very little transpires (from the presence of overnight guests to child abuse) that these older women do not observe.

The Chinese preference for mediation is deeply rooted in the Confucian philosophy stressing that social conflict disrupts the natural order of life. In prerevolutionary China, mediation brought respected family, clan, village or guild leaders into dispute resolution. The Confucian goal of harmony was most often achieved through bargained compromises, each side yielding a little to the other. These philosophical and cultural tenets, combined with the brutality (torture was reasonably frequent) and corruption of the imperial courts, produced a remarkable preference for mediation of disputes. To enter a court of law, says an ancient Chinese adage, is to "enter a tiger's mouth."

In postrevolutionary China, Mao desired to "mobilize" the populace behind communist goals and policies. He quickly saw in China's traditional preference for mediation a way to implement this desire and to consolidate the Party's power. While mediation was supposed to be "voluntary," in practice disputes became politicized and the pressure to participate and to conform to Party-directed conduct was enormous. Party cadres and local activists were recruited to serve as mediators. On the one hand, they functioned as guardians of the law and thus helped to reduce the case load of the people's courts. On the other hand, they served as Party snoopers, a role that has recently been reemphasized in searching out the 1989 Democracy Movement leaders and in requiring advance approval of most group meetings. The *lao taitai* also keep "offenders" under close scrutiny.

In the mediation process under Mao, the goal was to educate, convert and ultimately control China's people. Good and bad class origins of the disputants heavily influenced the outcome, which was often expressed in terms of politically correct solutions. Powerful political, economic and social pressures were thus brought to bear under Mao's practice of mediation. Examples have been reported of as many as 150 meetings between mediators and the parties during a six-month period. It still is common for mediators to threaten or actually contact an employer or the police to achieve conformity.

Professor Stanley Lubman has described the following 1959 dispute which illustrates both traditional and Maoist mediation practices:

In a large city in South China in 1959, an employee of an enterprise rented a room from the agent of an overseas Chinese for ten yuan monthly. It was understood that the tenant would also have the use of another room in the same apartment, except when the landlord's agent wished to use it. Soon afterwards, additional members of the tenant's family came to live with him, and he put them up in the second, "empty" room. The agent demanded that the rent be increased to twenty yuan monthly, because the tenant and his family were now occupying twice the space rented. The tenant refused, arguing that the agent could still sleep in the second room whenever he wanted. The agent demanded that the family vacate the premises and refused to accept ten yuan monthly.

When the tenant and his family refused to move, the agent went to the local street business office, which sent a woman to mediate the dispute. The mediator, who was addressed by the two parties as "Sister" Chang, heard the parties explain their positions as stated above, and then said that it appeared to her that the tenant was really living in two rooms, not merely the one for which he was paying rent. She suggested that she did not think it was right for the tenant to pay no rent for the second room; nor did she think it was right for the agent to make them all move because of the disagreement. She suggested that it would be best if both sides "yielded a little" (*jang i-tien*) and arrived at a compromise. The agent adamantly refused to agree (in a Hong Kong interview, the former tenant stated that he thought the agent suspected Sister Chang was favoring the tenant, a resident of the same street, against an absentee landlord) and initiated proceedings in the district people's court, which summoned both parties.

When the tenant went to the court on the appointed day, he showed his letter to a policeman, who directed him to an office. In the office was a cadre who identified himself as the person in charge of mediation (*t'iao-chieh chu-jen*) and a clerk. The agent arrived, and the mediator heard both sides, interrupting to ask questions. Then he proposed a solution.

The cadre stated that since the tenant was a cadre and the landlord an Overseas Chinese, the two men had obligations to help and understand each other in the interests of the revolution. He proposed that the tenant pay an additional four yuan monthly for the use of the second room, and that the parties continue to observe their agreement that the tenant and his family would move out of the room whenever the agent wished to use it. The parties agreed to this proposal, and their dispute was thus resolved. Lubman, "Mao and Mediation: Politics and Dispute Resolution in Communist China," 55 *California Law Review* 1284, 1344–45 (1967).

In this example, Sister Chang utilized a traditional Chinese mediation approach, "yielding a little." Nothing in her approach is openly political or ideological. It fails. The court's mediator identifies the parties by their political status and clearly suggests that the revolution requires a solution to their dispute. The implied threat is that both parties might be seen as "counterrevolutionaries" if they do not agree to the terms proposed by the court's mediator. The politicization of the dispute ideologically "educates" the parties and coerces a settlement surprisingly consistent with Sister Chang's proposal that each side yield a little.

The use of people's mediation continues to be favored by the Chinese Communist Party because it exemplifies communal thinking. Though less evident today, the Party traditionally has seen the courts as prerevolutionary institutions for class manipulation. The Marriage Law of 1980 and other laws make mediation compulsory prior to judicial proceedings. Mediation is also perceived as the "first line of defense" against "disputes between friends" turning into "disputes between enemies." A mediated result following Party policies is a "victory" over "wrong-thinking," "wrong-behavior" and other early signs of criminality. Thus, both Confucian philosophy and Communist ideology help explain why mediation is the predominant method of dispute settlement and social control in the PRC.

Practical and traditional considerations also encourage ordinary Chinese citizens to use mediation not litigation. The tradition in China is that the courts are associated with the enforcement of state power. Their primary function has been to recognize *duties* not rights. The courts have not been very open to the settlement of private disputes. China has generally pushed such disputes back into society and out of the judicial system. Practical considerations also tend to make mediation the most effective method of settling disputes in the PRC. For example, lawyers are scarce and judges generally are undertrained. Judges are required by law to "stress mediation" and, if litigation ensues, the Party can influence judicial decisions. At present, therefore, private litigation is replete with traditions and hazards which make mediation attractive.

MEDIATORS AND THEIR RULES

Many disputes typically litigated in the Americas or Europe are resolved in China by mediation. Some mediation and conciliation occurs outside formal state mediation procedures. As in the prerevolutionary past, family elders, neighborhood leaders and friends normally function as mediators. Such informal efforts at avoiding disharmony have been a hallmark of Chinese culture for millennia. Informal mediation also has the distinct benefit in modern times of not involving the State or Party in the dispute. A modicum of privacy is preserved.

Formal mediation in the countryside initially occurred within production teams on agricultural communes. Because of the agricultural reforms undertaken after the Cultural Revolution, mediation now involves "rural contract-operation households," not production teams. A Village Committee Law, implemented in 1987 on a trial basis by the Standing Committee of the National People's Congress, establishes village committees throughout most of rural China. These committees conduct the mediation of local disputes.

In urban areas, formal mediation is undertaken by committees created in neighborhoods, residential areas and work units. For example, each factory, store, government office and school is likely to have a mediation committee. These committees resolve the civil and minor criminal disputes of urban Chinese. Disputes concerning pay, dismissals, productivity and occupational safety are resolved in these forums. Domestic disputes concerning petty theft, housing, neighbors, safety, inheritance, family life and verbal abuse are also mediated by such committees.

Both the informal and formal mediation processes operate on the premise that disputes are frequently conflicts in a family or between neighbors and that these situations can be resolved fastest and most equitably by individuals who live within the community and act as mediators. Thus, there is a focus on grassroots mass organizations. For example,

> if a person steals a bicycle, the family is notified, and the family elders impose minor disciplinary action. If the person refuses to admit his or her wrongdoing or refuses to accept the sanction from the family, the neighborhood committee

becomes involved. The leaders of the neighborhood committee then guide a group of neighbors in attempts to reeducate the offender. If the person is a first-time offender and confesses to the wrongdoing, the action is usually forgiven, and the individual is given a chance to amend his or her behavior under the supervision of the group. If the person repeats the deviant act, the public security unit is called in. The public security, or police, do not jail the individual but instead attempt reeducation. Only the incorrigibles are incarcerated in labor reform camps. J.C.F. Wang, *Contemporary Chinese Politics: An Introduction,* 127 (1992).

Nationally promulgated rules govern formal mediation in China. The Provisional General Rules for Organization of People's Mediation Committees ("General Mediation Rules") apply throughout the nation. Other major regulations in this area concern Urban Residents' Committees and Village Committees. Some of these rules date from as early as 1954. Many were reinstated and officially republished after the Cultural Revolution. The Urban Residents' Committee Regulations were enacted into an Organic Law in December of 1989. This action was widely perceived as part of the backlash to the 1989 Democracy Movement, and was a further attempt at legitimizing the Party's use of these Committees to root out counterrevolutionary tendencies.

The General Mediation Rules are summarized below. How many of China's millions of mediators have ever read or have any knowledge of these rules is uncertain. Clearly there are differences between the General Mediation Rules and the practice of mediation. This is especially evident in the contrast between the voluntary, noncompulsory approach taken in the General Mediation Rules and the use of coercive, politicized mediation practices. Nevertheless, given the monumental significance of mediation to dispute settlement in China, the General Mediation Rules constitute a desirable effort at harmonizing mediation practices. They attempt to create a law of mediation.

The people's mediation committees are authorized to handle civil and minor criminal disputes while "propagating policies and laws." They are supervised by the Basic Level People's Courts and local governments. Mediation committees normally have three to eleven members whose "political backgrounds are pure." Committee members are elected by local governments (i.e., selected by local Party committees) for one-year terms. They may be recalled at any time if delinquent or incompetent. Mediation is supposed to commence only after obtaining the consent of the parties. It is not supposed to be compulsory. Officially, at least, mediation is not a prerequisite to recourse to the courts, absent a specific law to that effect. However, the Law of Civil Procedure requires all courts to "stress mediation."

People's mediation committees are prohibited from taking bribes, showing favoritism, punishing or detaining the parties, or using "oppression or retaliation." Mediation committees should hear the parties' concerns, investigate facts, be polite and patient, and employ "the method of persuasion." They are to persuade all involved to follow current Party policies, which are not necessarily embodied in Chinese law. Successful mediations are recorded and often subject to written agreement. The Law of Civil Procedure instructs the courts to override mediated results that violate Chinese law or policy. The General Mediation Rules also commit the courts to supervision and assistance of people's mediation committees. Mediation committees may refer serious matters to the courts or local prosecutors. The General Rules indicate failure of people's mediation does not prevent litigation.

The East China Institute of Politics and Law has prepared some mediation case studies from the 1980s suggesting that more legal analysis and less political determination is being employed than in the past. These cases also suggest that the General Mediation Rules may be having a salutory effect on people's mediation procedures, rendering them less ideologically coercive though still intimidating when borderline criminal behavior is involved. "Case Three" provides a good example of these trends:

> Teng Yigong (Yigong) and Teng Wanjuan (Wanjuan) are cousins who live together in a house of three rooms. They lived peacefully together be-

fore 1965, when they tried to divide the property of the family, and disputes arose about the ownership of the house. From then onwards, they started to quarrel and relatives gradually became enemies. Wanjuan directed his kitchen chimney towards Yigong's room, and Yigong put the trash on Wanjuan's corridor. They quarreled almost every day, even at night, so that the neighbors were harassed. Sometimes, even the old people and the children of the two families would come out to fight. This dispute was not resolved for many years. Once Wanjuan thought that Yigong was making trouble intentionally, he called the crematory saying that one person in Yigong's family died and asked the crematory to send a car to Yigong's home. When Yigong heard about it, he also called the fire brigade to report a fire in Wanjuan's home. Both the crematory and the fire brigade sent out vehicles to the cousins' homes to find that reports were false. The cousins were criticized by their working units and they were fined. But the disputes between the two families were not solved. During those years, the mediation committee had done some work which was not very effective. Some mediators said they would give up and let the court handle it.

The mediation committee held a meeting, summing up the work done relating to this dispute. They thought that there were two problems in doing this work: the mediators were afraid of being in a tangle, so they were mediating off and on; the mediators were just trying to smooth things over without discerning between right and wrong.

On summing up the previous work, the mediators went to the two families again. They talked to the family members about the situation, the related laws and regulations. Through several patient talks, the family members began to recognize their mistakes. They said: "The present primary task is stability, unity and the construction of four modernizations. We have been quarreling for many years over this house. What we have done is harmful to this task." Through the study of laws and regulations, they admitted that their conduct, especially the two false reports, was prohibited by law. The mediators also told them some real cases in which civil disputes developed into criminal offenses. This was a shock to the two families. Yigong and Wanjuan admitted their mistakes and made self-criticism. At the same time, the mediators and the family members studied the regulation on land ownership, and understood that urban land belongs to the state.... With the help of the mediators, the two cousins voluntarily made a division of the property. The dispute was finally resolved in 1983, and the two families have kept in good relation since then. "The Procedure of Mediation" (1987) reproduced in R. Folsom and J. Minan (eds.), *Law in the People's Republic of China: Commentary, Readings and Materials*, 114–121 (1989).

Mediation continues to be used in China to resolve most disputes, including economic issues. However as China becomes more technologically developed and the economy more decentralized with individuals and enterprises making contracts with each other and foreigners, China will be faced with increasingly complex legal issues. These could point to the inadequacy of mediation as a dispute resolution mechanism. First, mediation is a relatively slow process susceptible to the influence of personal power and persuasion. In addition, it is generally not undertaken by legally competent personnel. As China's economic system expands, trained legal personnel will be required to cope with increasingly complex problems. This may explain the trend toward legalism among specialized households in rural China. They often want formal, written contracts protecting them against local officials in case of dispute. Successful resolution of such a dispute and the protection of the household's interests would require a fair application of the relevant laws by competent and neutral legal personnel. Mediation in cases such as this may well become increasingly inadequate to deal with greater economic complexity.

INTERNATIONAL CONCILIATION AND MEDIATION

Arbitration is often designated as the method of dispute settlement in China's international business agreements. Nevertheless, a relatively few but increasing number of such transactions actually result in arbitrations. Once again China's striking preference for nonadjudicatory dispute settlement typically prevails and recourse to binding arbitration is limited.

In international transactions, even when arbitration is specified, "friendly consultations" between the parties will almost always commence the dispute settlement process. Quite often the business agreement will stipulate such consultations must occur before mediation or arbitration is "triggered." Furthermore, especially before arbitration takes place abroad, the conciliatory services of China's International Economic and Trade Arbitration Commission (CIETAC), are frequently required or employed. This is the same body that conducts Chinese international arbitrations if designated to do so. Its conciliation services are sometimes undertaken jointly with the American Arbitration Association in cases when U.S. firms are party to the agreement. The high rate of success of conciliation practices in resolving China's international business disputes explains why few arbitrations actually occur. Confucian principles of harmony and Communist ideological distaste for formal adjudications, it may be supposed, carry over into the international arena. Successful international contract conciliations by CIETAC result in the signing of a "mediation document" by the parties setting forth the terms of the settlement. It is not clear whether international mediation documents are enforceable in Chinese courts. Such enforcement is available in domestic contract disputes settled by conciliation or mediation.

One of the critical clauses in commercial contracts with the Chinese is the "trigger clause" authorizing recourse to arbitration. The Chinese often seek to avoid triggering arbitration whenever "there is a prospect of amicable settlement." Foreign attorneys often seek a trigger clause more like the following:

> Any disputes arising from the execution of, or in connection with, this Agreement shall first be settled amicably by negotiation, failing that they shall be submitted to joint conciliation conducted by the American Arbitration Association and the Chinese International Economic and Trade Arbitration Commission. Notwithstanding the foregoing sentence, either party to this Agreement may at any time have recourse to arbitration in Stockholm, Sweden to settle such disputes in accordance with the UNCITRAL Arbitration Rules in effect on the effective date of this agreement.

The inclusion of such a clause, at a minimum, gives the foreign party greater bargaining leverage in settlement negotiations because of the Chinese aversion to foreign arbitrations. In addition, Chinese and foreign enterprises tend to prefer arbitration clauses in contracts to avoid the people's courts. Many foreign executives feel that Chinese courts are too inexperienced and politicized. In general, only cases when arbitration is impossible or inappropriate end up before the courts.

ARBITRATION

Arbitration as a method of resolving disputes has been available for some time in the People's Republic of China. As early as 1954, the Chinese established a Foreign Trade Arbitration Commission (FTAC) within the China Council for the Promotion of International Trade (CCPIT). The FTAC later became known as the Foreign Economic Trade Commission (FETAC). In January of 1989, the FETAC was renamed the Chinese International Economic and Trade Arbitration Commission (CIETAC). It functions in Beijing, Shanghai and Shenzhen under a new, permanent set of Arbitration Rules adopted late in 1988 by the National Congress of the CCPIT. In 1958, the State Council established a Maritime Arbitration Commission within the CCPIT. This Commission has been renamed the Chinese Maritime Arbitration Commission (CMAC) and is quite active as a maritime dispute resolution center.

CIETAC and CMAC continue to be the preferred forums from the Chinese perspective for resolving disputes that arise out of commercial transactions with foreigners. The number of arbitrations undertaken by CIETAC has been rapidly rising and now exceeds 100 annually. It is the second busiest arbitration center in the world. The vast majority of disputes resolved through CIETAC involve import and export contracts, but joint venture disputes with other Chinese persons are also covered. On balance, CIETAC arbitrations appear both fair and impartial. There are, however, drawbacks to employing CIETAC to resolve disputes. Most of the arbitrators are Chinese officials or linked to the government in some way. Although CIETAC is frequently referred to as being "independent," its underlying goals are potentially indistinguishable from those of the Chinese government. Recently, a small number of prominent Hong Kong and foreign attorneys have been admitted to the list of CIETAC arbitrators. Three arbitrators are generally used, one each selected by the parties and the third appointed by those two. The 1988 Arbitration Rules provide for challenges to the selection of CIETAC arbitrators but fail to specify the grounds for such challenges.

The CIETAC Arbitration Rules generally parallel the UNCITRAL Rules but contain less detail. For example, the examination, verification and evaluation of evidence is within the discretion of the CIETAC arbitration tribunal. This includes the power to call witnesses, consult experts and conduct investigations. There are no provisions for cross-examination of witnesses or for the subpoena of documents by the parties. Each side appears before the tribunal in person or through appointed attorneys, who can be any nationality. The place of arbitration typically is Beijing, Shanghai or Shenzhen, although proceedings may be held elsewhere in China if necessary. The proceedings are normally held in Mandarin or Cantonese. CIETAC awards are final, binding and may not be appealed.

Foreigners often seek to utilize international arbitration centers as an alternative to CIETAC. Arbitration specialists have stated that China generally agrees to allow arbitration in Stockholm of foreign trade contracts, notwithstanding the fact that Chinese representatives in the provinces sometimes assert the contrary. To date, the Stockholm Chamber of Commerce in Sweden has emerged as the leading arbitration center designated in United States–China contracts, although other third-country venues include Zurich, Geneva, and London. While custom and practice suggests that a lawyer may successfully obtain such provisions for international arbitration in contracts with Chinese organizations, these organizations strongly resist allowing a dispute to actually be arbitrated abroad. Several arbitrations involving Chinese and U.S. parties have been initiated before the Arbitration Institute of the Stockholm Chamber of Commerce. The first case to reach a final award without being settled or withdrawn was won by the Chinese party. In that award, decided in December 1988, the tribunal ruled against Senitron, an Arizona-based electronics firm, which had initiated arbitration in October 1986 against the China National Machinery and Equipment Import/Export Corp. (MACHIMPEX).

Arbitration has also been increasingly invoked as a method of settling *domestic* commercial disputes. Under regulations issued in 1983, the State Commercial and Industrial Administration Bureau (SCIAB) exclusively performs this role. The SCIAB is an administrative department directly subordinate to the State Council. It has local and regional, as well as national, offices. Domestic arbitrations have been used to settle disputes within and between state enterprises and their respective ministries. SCIAB has generally applied the developing Chinese law of economic contracts in its awards. Its adherence to "neutral principles" has garnered respect from disputants and some outside commentators.

Lester Ross has highlighted the growing use of arbitration and litigation to settle "off-plan" domestic economic disputes. He recounts the following "Timber Sales Case":

> Zouping Mediation Order 87–34 involved a complaint brought by a trading company in Jilin, more than one thousand kilometers away in northeast China, against a Zouping village. The suit actually was directed against the village leader who, in a scenario frequently encountered in the post-Mao era, was doing business for the village and for himself at the same time. The respondent village leader was engaged in furniture manufacturing as an individual household; an extraordinary turnaround from the ethic of revolutionary self-sacrifice that had been the official norm among cadres during the Maoist era. The village leader ordered a carload of Korean

pine, a very valuable northeastern softwood preferred for its durability, workability and appearance. An entire carload is a very large order for an individual household business and probably would have been difficult to arrange under ordinary circumstances. The respondent was only able to make the deal when the original purchaser, a building materials wholesaler, ran short of funds, allowing the respondent to step in as replacement consignee.

Business fell short of expectations, however, and the respondent soon found himself unable to meet his payment obligation. The supplier filed for arbitration, choosing Zouping as the venue presumably because of its closer connection to the case. The supplier also may have expected that a Zouping tribunal could more effectively identify and locate assets belonging to the respondent. The arbitration committee investigated and ruled in favor of the supplier. However, the original claim for 33,150 RMB, based on alleged delivery of sixty-seven cubic meters at 510 RMB per cubic meter, was reduced by a finding that only sixty-five cubic meters had actually been delivered. The respondent was ordered to make payment, although part of his obligation could be met by resale of the forty cubic meters remaining in his inventory. Indeed, it is likely that his original intention was to resell much of the timber to others, reserving only a portion for his own furniture manufacturing business. Ross, "The Changing Profile of

Dispute Resolution in Rural China: The Case of Zouping County, Shandong," 26 *Stanford of International Law* 15 (1989).

ENFORCING ARBITRAL AWARDS

Judicial enforcement of CIETAC or SCIAB arbitral awards is anticipated by Chinese laws. Until recently, there was no authority in PRC law for the enforcement of foreign arbitral awards. After years of debate, China acceded in 1987 to the United Nations Convention on the Recognition and Enforcement of Foreign Arbitral Awards (the New York Convention). This fills an important gap in commercial dispute resolution practices between the Chinese and foreigners. Some foreign arbitral awards may now be recognized and enforced in the people's courts. Accession to the New York Convention also facilitates the recognition and enforcement of CIETAC and CMAC arbitral awards in courts of other nations.

When China agreed to the New York Convention, it attached certain reservations to its instrument of accession. The PRC has adopted the reciprocity and commercial reservations available to all contracting states under the New York Convention. Especially as interpreted in the implementing Notice on the Convention issued by the Supreme People's Court, these reservations place important limitations on the power of Chinese courts to recognize and enforce foreign arbitral awards. The reciprocity reservation means that China will recognize and enforce an arbitral award pursuant to the New York Convention only when it has been made in the territory of another contracting state. Under the commercial reservation, China will implement a foreign arbitral award only when it relates to "commercial legal relationships of a contractual or noncontractual nature," as defined by PRC law. Only if foreign awards satisfy both the reciprocity and commercial reservations, and were rendered on or after April 22, 1987, will they be recognized and enforced in the people's courts.

Parties to international agreements are always free to choose a judicial forum rather than arbitration. However, there is considerable concern at this point about the ability of the people's courts to handle sophisticated commercial law disputes. The Chinese for their part are likely to continue to be reluctant to submit disputes to foreign courts. As a result, litigation of international agreements is not likely to become a primary method of settling PRC disputes. Friendly consultations, conciliation, mediation and arbitration will continue to dominate Chinese international dispute settlement.

PRIVATE LITIGATION AND CIVIL PROCEDURE

Private litigation has been growing steadily since the Cultural Revolution. This trend is especially noticeable in the disposition of civil cases. There are now over a million civil cases being filed annually. While litigation as a method of dispute settlement is statistically dwarfed by mediation procedures, the Chinese are becoming noticeably more litigious.

For many years, civil procedure law in the PRC was not terribly important. Most private disputes were mediated, and longstanding culturally based aversions to litigation kept the courts relatively free of civil lawsuits. This began to break down after the Cultural Revolution as a surge of marriage, family, property and debt collection cases reached the newly restored people's courts. In the 1980s, with the growing deregulation and privatization of China's economy, contract disputes emerged as a common type of civil litigation. Indeed, economic complaints are said to have quadrupled between 1982 and 1990. Torts claims, never widely filed in the people's courts, were formally recognized in the 1986 General Principles of Civil Law. In the late 1980s, the trial of administrative cases developed as individuals and organizations started suing government departments and functionaries. All of these developments have increased the significance of civil procedure law to the Chinese legal system. This significance was acknowledged by the Standing Committee of the National People's Congress when it issued a provisional Law of Civil Procedure in 1982. A finalized version of this law was adopted in 1991.

The emergence of clear rules of civil procedure has contributed to the expansion of civil litigation. These rules amount to a "green light" to private parties to use the courts. Unlike the criminal arena, in civil litigation Chinese courts perform more than ceremonial functions. The people's courts continue, as they must by law, to stress mediation in most private disputes. Increasingly, however, private litigants are going to trial. The courts are being forced to render final judgments upholding private rights and obligations when mediation does not solve the dispute.

It is difficult to obtain a good understanding of how the law of civil procedure actually operates in the PRC. Case law reporting in this area is nearly nonexistent. Generally, it appears that the people's courts and civil litigants (along with their lawyers) are in a stage where all concerned are trying to ascertain just exactly what are the rules of civil procedure. The people's lawyers and other representatives are busy assessing how these rules influence outcomes and affect trial strategies. The people's courts are genuinely attempting to implement this new body of law, but are concerned about producing results which might be ideologically criticized by the Party. The private law context of civil litigation makes this an especially acute concern.

EVIDENCE, JUDGMENT AND REMEDIES

Parties to civil litigation may argue their own cases or be represented by another person. In addition to lawyers, close relatives, worker associates and any citizen approved by the court may represent civil litigants. Powers of attorney are utilized when this occurs. However, parties to divorce suits must ordinarily appear in person before the court. Government organizations, enterprises and other institutions may "support" civil suits by individuals or units injured by acts which have damaged the civil rights or interests of the state, collectives or individuals. This authorization in the Civil Procedure Law is apparently intended to overcome the reluctance of such institutions to release evidence or get involved in civil litigation. Such help is extremely valuable to individual litigants and a duty of evidentiary support has been proclaimed in a 1981 "Joint Notice" issued by the Supreme People's Court, the Ministry of Justice, the Ministry of Public Security and the Supreme People's Procuratorate.

Rules of evidence for civil cases are established in the Law of Civil Procedure. These rules reflect the inquisitorial, not adversarial, style of Chinese judicial proceedings. There is, for example, a duty of all "who know something about the case" to offer testimony. This provision may amount in practice to a subpoena power, especially if the demand for testimony is channeled through the courts. Anyone who refuses to testify at the request of a litigant would breach the Law of Civil Procedure. The people's courts may compel testimony under the authority to issue "coercive measures against hindrance to civil actions." All litigants are obliged to present evidence in support of their assertions. Curiously, however, they are not required to make statements in their own cases. This suggests a right of silence. Indeed, refusals to make statements are not to "affect the establishment of facts" by the court. It is not clear whether litigants who are witnesses to facts at issue may be compelled to testify. If so, their right of silence is qualified.

All evidence offered to prove facts must first be verified. The people's courts have a duty to collect and investigate evidence in civil cases in "an all-round and objective way." They must determine whether documentary evidence is true or false. This is a notable admonition because documentary evidence (especially affidavits) are commonly used in Chinese civil trials. The court, not a litigant, has the power to select and appoint experts in connection with civil litigation. The court also has the power to send an inspector to "the scene," or to have an inspector review material evidence. Litigants or their adult family members have a right to be present at "the scene" but if they are not present this does not affect the results of the inspection. Reports of inspectors and corroborations by experts must be done in writing and submitted to the court. Thus, the people's courts are very much in control of the development of evidence in Chinese civil litigation. The parties and their lawyers or representatives play a secondary role.

In an ordinary civil trial, the professional judge is likewise in command of the proceedings. The judge introduces the evidence, including the testimony of witnesses, and examines the witnesses, the attorneys or representatives of the litigants doing so afterwards only with permission. Once this "court investigation" of the facts is complete, the litigants or their agents are given an opportunity to argue their cases before the professional judge and the two lay assessors who traditionally make up the bench. This tends to be a repeat of the arguments raised during the pretrial judicial mediation with the professional judge. Prejudgment mediation is then attempted and, absent a settlement, a final judgment is rendered.

The Civil Procedure Law does not specify the judicial remedies available to civil litigants. These are, instead, covered by Article 134 of the 1986 General Principles of Civil Law. The principal "forms of civil liability" (remedies) available in private cases are cessation of infringement, elimination of obstructions, elimination of danger, return of property, restoration of original condition, repair, reconstruction or replacement, payment of compensation, elimination of effects and restoration of reputation, and apology. These remedies may be used separately or in combination. The courts may, in addition, issue admonitions, order repentance, impose fines or detention, and confiscate property used for illegal activities or property that was illegally obtained. The general rule as to litigation costs in China is that they "follow the event" and are paid by the losing party. Surprisingly, enforcement of civil judgments and remedies can be a problem because of the low status and lack of political power of the people's courts.

APPEALS

The right of *one* appeal to contest a civil judgment or ruling of a trial court exists. Appeals must be made within 15 days of judgment or within 10 days of a ruling. Appeals may be filed with the trial court or the appellate court. The respondent receives a copy of the appeal from the trial court, and has 15 days to reply. Failure to reply does "not affect the court hearing."

The appellate court undertakes an "overall examination of the ascertainment of facts and the application of law" by the trial court. This amounts to a *de novo* review of the litigation. The court is not restricted to the scope of the issues raised by the appellant. Ordinarily, the court chooses "a collegiate bench" to hear and decide the case. The court may decide an appeal without a formal hearing when unnecessary. It may do this only after "perusing" the files, making an investigation, questioning the litigants, and "checking the facts."

The appellate court affirms the original judgment if it finds that the ascertainment of the facts and the trial court's application of law were correct. If the facts were correctly found, but law incorrectly applied, the appellate court renders a new judgment "according to law." If the initial judgment was based on unclear facts and insufficient evidence, or a violation of legal procedure prejudiced the judgment, the appellate court must reverse. The requirement of a reversal for prejudicial procedural error is very important. This insures the right to take appeals based upon the provisions of the Law of Civil Procedure. More significantly, it sends a message to the people's courts that civil trial procedures matter. Reversal on the basis of prejudicial procedural error might be professionally awkward for trial judges. Upon reversal, the appellate court may order a trial *de novo* or proceed directly to render a new judgment. The courts can also resolve appeals by mediated settlements which are recorded. Judgments and rulings of Chinese appellate courts are final and cannot be further appealed.

The Law of Civil Procedure establishes "judicial supervision procedures," which have no direct parallel in American law. These procedures amount to an alternative appeals route. Civil litigants may initiate supervisory appeals of trial proceedings by alleging "definite error" as to law or fact to the president of the trial court or to the next higher court. The trial court's judicial committee or the superior court hears such supervisory appeals. They can order *de novo* trials or, if a superior court, conduct such trials themselves whenever they find definite error. Supervisory appeals do not stay the execution of civil trial judgments. However, an order of a trial *de novo* has such an effect.

There are advantages and disadvantages to initiating supervisory versus ordinary civil appeals. The supervisory procedures may be faster and may draw immediate attention to a case. This is especially true if the supervisory appeal is initiated before the trial court president. They amount, however, to an outright rebuke of the trial judge. Proving "definite error" in supervisory appeals is presumably more demanding than proving "prejudicial error" in ordinary appeals. Since, in either case, reversal is the objective, the ordinary civil appeals route would seem to maximize the potential for securing this goal.

Lastly, regardless of the appeal route chosen, there is always the possibility of reopening "final" civil judgments via complaints to the procuracy. The procuracy has the power to "protest" any outstanding civil judgment, and has done so on a regular basis. The same case can even be reopened repeatedly. The 1991 version of the Civil Procedure Law seeks to control this practice by detailing the grounds for protest and requiring that requests for such action be filed within two years of finality.

FOREIGNERS AND CIVIL LITIGATION

The Law of Civil Procedure deals with civil litigation involving foreigners (*shewai*). Cases involving "Chinese compatriots" from Hong Kong and Macao are treated as foreign litigation. In general, the Civil Procedure Law provides that foreign and stateless persons commencing civil actions or answering complaints in the people's courts have the same rights and duties as citizens of the PRC. The trial court for most cases involving foreigners is the People's Middle Level Courts, not the Basic Courts. A general rule of reciprocity concerning the rights granted foreigners in the people's courts is followed. Whenever foreign courts would impose limits on the Chinese in civil litigation, the people's courts implement reciprocal limitations. Moreover, the civil litigation status and immunities accorded foreign persons and organizations may be altered by PRC treaties. The treaty provisions prevail if they differ from those found in the Civil Procedure Law.

Foreigners involved in civil litigation in China may encounter a variety of language difficulties. The Law of Civil Procedure requires that trials involving foreign persons or matters be conducted in the local Chinese dialect. Foreign parties may request interpreters, but must be prepared to pay appropriate fees. In addition, foreign persons and enterprises who wish to be represented by attorneys before the people's courts *must* employ licensed PRC attorneys. Once again, language difficulties may be encountered, especially as between local Chinese counsel and foreign attorneys employed as advisors by the litigant.

When the parties to Chinese trade contracts agree to resolve their disputes through China's arbitration centers or before its courts, this "choice of forum" clause must be honored. In the absence of such an agreement, trade disputes can be litigated in the people's courts. Presumably, when the parties have selected a foreign arbitration center (e.g., the Stockholm Chamber of Commerce) or a foreign court to settle their disputes, the people's courts will abstain from hearing the dispute. This is not made explicit by the Civil Procedure Law, however. There are rules for reciprocal enforcement of foreign judgments according to treaties and international conventions to which China is a signatory. However, foreign judgments will not be enforced by the people's courts if they violate basic principles of PRC law or "China's social interests."

In 1991, China acceded to the Hague Convention on Service of Process Abroad. This convention facilitates international service of process, especially writs of summons. For example, United States plaintiffs (acting through requests by U.S. courts) may summon a Chinese defendant resident in the PRC by service upon a "central authority." The PRC has designated the Ministry of Justice as its central authority for such service. The Ministry will then arrange for service upon the defendant through the people's courts. Service of "extra-judicial" documents such as family certificates, bills of exchange and demands for payment can also be done under the Hague Convention. To facilitate this process, the U.S. documents should be translated into Chinese.

Under the Civil Procedure Law, the Ministry of Justice has five service of process options. These are direct personal service, substituted service, agency service, postal service or public announcement. Any rejection by the Ministry of the request for service under the Hague Convention triggers a duty to provide reasons to the applicant for such a rejection. The Convention specifies that only infringements of the national sovereignty or security of the PRC may justify a rejection. Unlike the Civil Procedure Law, there is no authority to reject on public order or public policy grounds. Americans will want to remember that all of this can be done in the reverse with Chinese parties effectively achieving service upon U.S. defendants through the Hague Convention.

A CHANGE IN DISPUTE SETTLEMENT MENTALITY

It is easy to get lost in the complexities of the civil procedure law developed in China since the Cultural Revolution. Its social significance often gets overlooked, especially because it is "merely" procedural law. This excerpt from a 1988 issue of the *Beijing Review* reminds us not to overlook this perspective.

> With the continuous improvement in China's legal system and the efforts to educate in knowledge of the law, a sense of law has gradually taken root in people's minds. Law is no longer something on paper, rather it appears in everyday life.

A construction unit did not refill a ditch they had dug to lay water pipes. Someone fell in and was hurt. He filed a lawsuit and won compensation from the construction unit.

People disabled in the course of public duty appealed to the courts against their employers for no longer showing any concern for their livelihood and welfare. They too won their cases.

Long-distance bus passengers bought tickets and arrived at the bus station on time, but the bus had left early, causing them some financial loss. They had to turn to people's courts to demand compensation.

A construction team from Wuxian County, Jiangsu Province, built a road-side garden in Shanghai's Yangpu District. They put up a trellis for a vine, which, however, was not fixed firmly as required. A 14–year–old boy climbed it for fun, fell off and died. The boy's parents lodged an appeal with the district court against the construction team. According to Article 125 of the General Rules for the Implementation of the Law of Civil Procedure, which stipulates that owners or managers of buildings are responsible for damage or injury caused by those buildings or things dropping from them, the court ruled that the construction team pay the boy's parents a large sum of money.

The feeling used to be that to go to court was a disgrace and decent people are not involved in lawsuits. Today, a noticeable change has taken place in this mentality. Jan. 18–24, 1988 at p. 28.

China is still far from becoming a litigious society. However, there are indications that the traditional reluctance to resolve civil disputes in the courts is diminishing. This is especially true for cases involving debts, economic contracts, residential property rights, divorce, adoption and maintenance.

CHAPTER VI

PEOPLE AND PROPERTY

The family and its hierarchical structure provided a model for key aspects of imperial Chinese life. The bond between the state and its citizens was governed theoretically on the principle that those in positions of power owed a fiduciary-like obligation to those over whom they exercised authority. Citizens owed respect and obedience to the state. In addition, relations between China and foreign peoples, and the organization of some dimensions of commercial life all arguably drew, at least in their idealized forms, upon the structure of the family.

Property was considered to be owned by the entire extended family. Thus, the laws of property and family were tied together. The legal validity of contracts for the sale of land was part of China's early history. Documents involving the sale of land indicate that by the 4th century B.C. some land had come to be fully alienable. By the Han period (206 B.C.–220 A.D.) privately held land could be bought and sold. Because reliable statistics do not exist indicating how much land was privately owned, only the general principle of such transfers can be established. Han writers, such as Tung Chung-shu, often emphasized the widespread phenomenon of alienability. Following the collapse of the Eastern or Later Han Dynasty in 220 A.D., land became much less freely alienable, until commercial development during the Song Dynasty reversed the trend.

The traces of Chinese history are imprinted on the property and family laws in place today. The Chinese Constitution, Civil Law, Marriage Law, and Law of Succession broadly outline the framework for these laws in the People's Republic of China.

PROPERTY RIGHTS: PUBLIC AND PRIVATE OWNERSHIP

The traditional economic features of socialist law are public ownership of the means of production, state ownership of land and the collectivization of its use, central economic planning, and only a grudging tolerance of limited forms of private ownership. Another is the goal of liquidating all capitalist forms of ownership. As seen in this chapter, China has modified its approach to the traditional features of socialist law to accommodate its own needs.

Property rights in China today are based on a mixed system of public and private ownership, although in actuality it is still decidedly more public than private. The concept of "preliminary socialism" gives legitimacy to a mixed private-public economy. This ideological concept, which was pronounced as part of official ideology in 1987, is based on the view that China emerged from a semi-colonial, semi-feudal period in 1949 without having passed through the necessary stage of capitalist economic development. This resulted in China's productive forces being behind those existing in the developed capitalist countries. To offset this deficiency, China first needed to go through the period of "preliminary socialism" when a private economy would coexist with the socialist public economy.

The 1982 Constitution broadly outlines three forms of property ownership: first, ownership by the whole people—state ownership; second, ownership by the working people—collective ownership; and third, ownership by the individual economy—individual ownership. As part of this framework, the right of citizens to own lawfully earned income, savings, houses and other lawful property including such items as bank accounts, vehicles and other everyday articles of personal property is expressly protected. The Chinese concept of property includes both tangible and intangible property.

Private enterprises, officially defined as profit-seeking businesses with eight or more employees whose property is privately owned, began appearing around 1981. Enterprises of this type tend to be service oriented. The Constitution was amended in 1988 to expressly allow the right to transfer the use of land and to permit and protect the private economy. Shortly thereafter, private economy regulations were adopted defining possible business forms and the permissible scope of business activities.

The state has title to all real property in China. In 1990, provisional regulations were promulgated on leasing tracts of land to foreign investors for development and management. Foreign investment enterprises and other entities may secure the right to use urban land and fixtures for a fixed term by contracting with local government. The contract typically requires a lump sum payment of a grant fee and the development of the property in accordance with the zoning law.

The General Principles of Civil Law, which became effective on January 1, 1987, also contain provisions concerning the ownership, possession and disposal of property. These provisions are found in the Civil Law Articles dealing with "Property Ownership and Related Property Rights" and "Intellectual Property Rights." Three generalizations about the operation of the Civil Law in the context of property and ownership are possible. First, the Civil Law broadly defines the property relationship between the state and the state enterprise—the enterprise is given property to operate and manage. The nature and extent of property rights vested in the state enterprise as a result of this transfer is subject to theoretical controversy. The absence of a clear theoretical basis for state enterprise property is an obstacle to additional reforms in the state-owned sector of the economy and to enterprise autonomy. Second, the Civil

Law expressly permits private ownership of the means of production "within the limits of the law." The contours of these limits of the law are not clear, so future administrative intervention and interpretation will be needed. Third, the Civil Law introduced for the first time a uniform rule governing the transfer of property. Transfer of property ownership occurs on delivery, unless the parties agree to the contrary or the law otherwise provides.

The bulk of the means of production in China is publicly owned by "the whole people" (state) or by "collective organizations of the working masses" (collective). The concept of state ownership refers to the holding of property by state enterprises, governmental agencies and certain nonprofit institutions. This is the predominant form of ownership in the Chinese economy, but the nature and extent of this right is still developing.

The predominant view until the late 1970s was that property held by state enterprises and other governmental agencies is "owned" by the state, not by the enterprise or other governmental entity. The enterprise or state entity had the right of operative management (*jingying guanli quan*) of the property. The nature of this right has been described to mean:

1. State organs [and] state-run enterprises have the power according to the provisions of state policy, laws, and decrees to control the

property they manage within the scope of their functional authority;

2. State organs [and] state-run enterprises can participate in civil intercourse in the capacity of legal persons [and] independently assume property liability to third parties;

3. The content of the right of operation and management is, according to the state's intent, to exercise the powers and functions of possession, use [and] disposition over state property in order to fulfill the state plan. Ownership of the property is still vested in the state. State organs and state-run enterprises certainly cannot acquire ownership. Epstein, "The Theoretical System of Property Rights in China's General Principles of Civil Law: Theoretical Controversy in the Drafting Process and Beyond," 52 *Law and Contemporary Problems* 177, 195 (1989).

The term operative management meant the right to possess, use, and dispose of state property according to law and the economic plan.

This conceptual view of property, originally developed by Soviet theorists, was recognized by the Chinese as problematic in the late 1970s. For example under this framework of property relations, the state has the right to reassign property from one state enterprise to another without the necessity of paying compensation because the state plans the operation of the economy and owns the property. In the early 1980s, the policy decision was made that successful economic reforms required giving state enterprises more power and control over their assets. Thus, the Chinese incorporated the idea in the 1982 Constitution that enterprises had the right to operative management autonomy (*jingying guanli zizhu quan*). Chinese theorists have not clearly defined the relationship between "operative management rights" and "operative management autonomy" or the relationship between the state and the state enterprise. Those theorists who argue that operative managements rights do not invest enterprises with any property rights usually also support the principles of central economic planning and rigorous state control of economic activities. Theorists who advocate autonomous property rights in state enterprises take a different view. The absence of agreement on the theoretical nature of state enterprise "property rights" is a serious obstacle to economic reform of the state owned sector of the economy.

Collectively owned property is owned by a group of individuals in the collective, usually workers or peasants, not the state. In this non-private form of ownership the collective itself owns the property. As indicated in the 1983 Urban Collective Regulations, assets collectively owned are not for the individual benefit of the members of the collective: "No department or individual is allowed in any form or under any pretext, to transfer indiscriminately, misuse, retain, or divide for private use the funds, profits, factory buildings, equipment, raw materials, products and supplies of collectively owned enterprises." Enterprises that involve collective ownership tend to be those producing simple items or those performing simple tasks such as bicycle repair. Collective ownership and state ownership are both "socialist public ownership" and thus are distinguishable from private or individual ownership.

Individual ownership, which promotes individual enterprise within the socialist economy, refers to ownership by individuals or households. Enterprises of this type tend to be service oriented such as restaurants or tailoring. This form of ownership which permits individual entrepreneurs has received widespread attention in the West in recent years since it resembles and is based on notions of capitalism. The Constitution makes clear, however, that this form of ownership is guided, assisted and supervised by the administrative controls of the state, including licensing of individual enterprises. Regulations adopted in 1988 provide administrative sanctions, including the revocation of the private enterprise's business license, for such violations as exceeding the registered scope of the business or engaging in illegal business activities. Tax, labor or other violations may also result in penalties. Although the private sector of the economy is declared a "supplement to the socialist public ownership economy" by both the Regulations and the 1982 Constitution, it was undoubtedly the most dynamic sector of the Chinese economy through the 1980s. Private enterprises came under heavy criticism in late 1989 for consuming scarce resources, contributing to an unfair distribution of wealth, and for promoting exploitative behavior. However, articles appearing in the *People's Daily* in early 1992 implied that the Chinese leadership may again be placing greater emphasis on private enterprise to spur economic development.

The Civil Law defines property ownership as including the "owner's rights to lawfully possess, utilize, profit from and dispose of his property." Ownership is not restricted to individuals. Co-ownership by share or joint ownership is allowed under the Civil Law. Under co-ownership by share, each of the co-owners has rights and obligations in proportion to his or her share. Co-owners by share may transfer their share to third parties. When a share is sold, however, the other co-owners have priority in purchasing the share. In contrast, under joint ownership each of the co-owners rights and obligations extends to the property in its entirety. Joint ownership is similar to the concept of community property that has been adopted by some states in the U.S. because disposal requires the agreement of all of the joint owners.

AGRICULTURAL PROPERTY

China's land mass is about the size of the United States, but only about ten percent of the PRC is arable land. Yet, China is still a country where agriculture is the primary occupation of its citizens. About 900 million of China's population are engaged in farming. The classic movement of large numbers of persons from the countryside to the cities as part of the process of industrial development has only marginally occurred in China. To a large extent, the lack of rural to urban migration can be attributed to stringent government control. For example, housing and food coupons are allocated only to residents in a specified area. Individuals moving to a new area without official permission would not have access to these coupons. This allocation system has acted as a brake on unauthorized migration. The introduction of limited private enterprise within the cities has changed this situation slightly. Individuals may sell and purchase certain goods in the free market, thus avoiding the need to rely on government coupons. However, individuals still depend upon friends or relatives to share their meager living accommodations.

Prior to 1949 peasants were by and large tenant farmers, frequently barely subsisting after giving the major portion of their farm produce to the landowner as rent. Land reform was thus a central issue in the political thinking of the Chinese Communists from an early stage. As early as 1927, Mao proposed that peasants refuse to pay rent to their landlords as part of a national revolutionary strategy. Mao relied on peasant grievances against the landlord to recruit his rank-and-file revolutionaries, just as revolutionaries had done earlier in Mexico. The prospect of land reform had the effect of drawing many peasants to the revolutionary cause.

One of the first actions of the new, post–1949, government was land reform. Individual tracts were initially distributed to the Chinese peasants based on the family's classification. For example, poor peasants gained more than middle or rich peasants. Land reform, however, was merely the first step in a lengthy process aimed at increasing agricultural production. In the short term, land reform was also designed to break the power of the landlord class. The redistribution of land resulted in a situation where the average landholdings by a single family were relatively small and fragmented.

In order to increase production and facilitate centralized planning, the CCP began a process of agricultural reorganization. While the exact timing of each stage varied depending on local conditions, in general the first step began in 1952 with the formation of mutual aid teams. Families assisted each other with agricultural activities such as planting and harvesting. The goal was to get the peasants used to cooperating with individuals outside their immediate family. Agricultural cooperatives followed mutual aid teams beginning generally in 1953. Under the cooperatives, peasants pooled their land with neighboring families and farmed the land as a whole. Each family, however, retained ownership of their land and compensation was based on the amount and quality of land contributed to the pool as well as the amount of labor expended. Starting around 1955, the next stage in agricultural reorganization, collectives were implemented. With the formation of collectives, land became the property of the collective and private land ownership was abolished. Individuals were paid on the basis of their labor. Peasants were allowed to keep a small private plot of land for produce, such as chickens and vegetables. Finally, communes began to appear in 1958 as part of the Great Leap Forward.

Communes, usually including 4,000–5,000 peasant households, were created essentially on the same lands the peasants had previously cultivated, thus maintaining local community integrity. This process of organizing the peasants into communes or large production units was seen by the Chinese leaders as creating "peasant land ownership." This term did not mean that the peasants owned the lands of the former landowners, but that the peasants collectively had a proprietary right to the produce extracted from the land. From the earliest days of the Communist regime, except for a brief time during the Great Leap Forward (1958 to 1960), peasants have had absolute ownership of the produce from small private plots of land not pledged to the commune production quotas. As to the products collectively produced by the commune, the individual has a beneficial use, a usufruct, in the product.

Since the founding of the PRC in 1949, Chinese agricultural policy has fluctuated between two different approaches to rural development. One approach attempted to impose an ideological vision on agriculture where moral incentives and rewards—the love of Mao and socialism—were the mechanism for mobilizing the countryside. Private property and private markets were suppressed. The other approach was exactly the reverse. It stressed material incentives, free markets, and allowed for economic inequality. A number of policy changes dominated the period 1978–89. These included de-collectivization and family farming, sharp increases in prices paid by the State for agricultural products, and market vitalization. All of these changes were aimed at reinvigorating the slumping rural economy. However, in response to continuing economic problems, especially inflation, Jiang Zemin, the General Secretary of the Communist Party, called for "strengthening rural controls" in December 1989, a policy that portends an increased emphasis on the use of collectivized production units.

In 1978 the communist leadership laid down the broad policy that has resulted in the abolition of collective agriculture. The new "household responsibility" or "production responsibility" system began to sweep the country in 1981, and by 1986 virtually all of China's agriculture was implementing the new responsibility system. The lowest organizational unit in the agricultural system, the production team (typically composed of 20–40 households), was gradually replaced. Under this new system, agricultural workers are allowed to contract for the use of collectively owned land. Although legal title remains in the collective, extensive use rights, often for fifteen to twenty years, are created by the contract.

The Land Administration Law states that all land in the PRC is publicly-owned. Individuals may not own land. The only requirement to use the land as a contract farmer under this responsibility system is to supply the State at a fixed low price, an agreed-on quota of a specified commodity, which typically occupies one-sixth of the household's land. Rent is paid by the delivery of this set quantity of produce to the State. While the State technically still owns the land, the position of the household is distinctly owner-like. Apart from the quota requirement, the contract-workers are free to plant whatever crops they choose and to consume them, sell them to the State at a higher non-quota, negotiated price, or sell them on the free market. Certain sideline products, such as pigs, fish, fruit and fowl can be sold on the free market without restrictions.

A Real Estate Administration imposes fees on land used for private purposes such as farming or housing sites. The land use fees vary widely, depending on the area of the country and normal use, and are calculated on a square meter of land basis. A property tax also is levied on the value of buildings and residences.

From the establishment of the contract system through the mid–1980s, judicial resolution of production responsibility contract disputes increased. By 1985 this type of dispute accounted for over 10 percent of the approximately 225,000 economic disputes tried by Chinese courts. After 1985, the number of production responsibility disputes that were litigated decreased as collectives and peasants gained experience in drafting contracts and establishing appropriate contract fees. In resolving production responsibility contract disputes, the courts have resorted to Party policies, legal norms (among which the most important has been the Economic Contract Law), basic principles of fairness, and the opinions of local government or administrative offices. Because economic contracts differ in certain ways from production responsibility contracts, the Economic Contract Law generally has been used by the courts for guidance in establishing general principles of contract law.

The results of the production responsibility system in terms of agricultural output were impressive through the mid-1980s. Nevertheless, of all the problems in rural China today, the one causing the most concern stems from the production responsibility system. In 1990, it was reported that "problems with implementation, regulation, and corruption have turned the contract system—initially well-accepted—into an organizational quagmire." In many instances, the process of dividing up the land was defective, often the plots were too small, too scattered, and not rationally distributed among families. As a result, errors were made in setting up the initial land contracts.

The ultimate social and political consequences of the success of this production responsibility system to traditional communist thought are significant. It underscores the need to empower individuals with an owner-like interest in land as a means of stimulating initiative. Notwithstanding problems in implementing this system, it was effective in fostering individual initiative, and the State's unwillingness to protect it in the future would have serious political, environmental, and economic consequences.

URBAN PROPERTY

In urban areas, which are home to about 40 percent of the country's 1.133 billion people, houses and apartments are generally owned by the state or by a collective unit. Since 1949 housing has been heavily subsidized. Rents traditionally are fixed at a low rate and account for about 3 percent of a person's income.

In the mid–1980s, China began an experimental housing reform program in an attempt to correct a serious housing shortage by channeling people's money into the country's infrastructure. Statistics in 1986 showed that about one quarter of the urban residents, or 10.54 million families, had inadequate or no housing. In response, Yantai and three other cities were selected as pilot cities in 1986 for an urban housing reform program designed to privatize state-owned housing. The housing reform program is aimed at turning the cost of housing into a market commodity to be bought, sold or rented at prices reflecting its true cost, and is based on the principle of changing from the administrative allocation of housing to individual choice. As a corollary, both rents and wages are to be raised so that individuals will eventually pay prices high enough to cover the cost of new construction. In 1990, the reform program was reported to have spread to 250 cities and counties throughout China.

Tenants of public housing generally are not allowed to sublease their units. Leasing is allowed when housing is privately owned. Only the building or dwelling house may be leased by its owner, however, because the land is owned by the state. Under Chinese law, buildings and dwelling places are considered "personalty." Private property may be mortgaged or pledged as security for debts.

Since 1979, Special Economic Zones have been instituted where foreign investors may lease or construct buildings and use land without acquiring title. Use certificates must be obtained from the appropriate state agency. The term or period of land use depends on the enterprise. For example, the maximum land use period that may be contracted for by the tourist industry or for industrial purposes is thirty years; scientific, educational and technological uses may be certified up to fifty years.

THE FAMILY

The laws of property have been closely associated with those relating to the family in China. The feudal marriage system is the legacy and backdrop for family law in the People's Republic of China today. In many ways, the current laws and attitudes of the Chinese concerning marriage, the family, children, and divorce are influenced by past feudal practices.

A feudal marriage system was in effect in China for over two thousand years. Its principal features were the compulsory arrangement of marriage by the parents designed to maximize the social and economic benefits to the families, the supremacy of men over women in a patriarchal system in which the family was "ruled" by the senior male, the severance of a woman's links with her blood relatives when she became a member of her husband's household, and the subordination of the younger generations to the older generations. A happy marriage for a woman depended on two factors: her ability to bear sons and her establishing a harmonious relationship with her mother-in-law. Concubinage and polygamy were practiced, especially among the wealthy. Women often committed suicide to avoid arranged or mercenary marriages.

Chinese law traditionally recognized three types of divorce. First, divorce was possible by mutual consent, including the consent of the husband's parents. Second, the standard method of ending a marriage was by repudiation: There were seven grounds by which a husband could repudiate his wife most of which related to offenses against the husband's authority or the wife's failure to produce an heir. There were only three grounds by which the wife could prevent the repudiation: "She could not be sent away if she had mourned her husband's parents' death for three years, if her husband's family had become rich after their marriage, or if she had no family to take her in." The third basis of ending a marriage was "in the case of intolerable acts against the principle of conjugality." As a practical matter, the wife often had only two choices, to commit suicide or to run away. A widow could not remarry after the death of her husband. The inferiority of women was based on custom and belief, and included such practices as footbinding where girls between the ages of five and seven had their feet bent back so that the bones of the instep were broken to reduce the size of their feet. A third century poet captured the traditional view of women—"How sad it is to be a woman! Nothing on earth is held so cheap."

The establishment of socialism in China changed the feudal family system and attempted to alter the relationship between family members in order to replace the traditional sense of loyalty to the family with loyalty to the state. The major structural change was the shifting of the family power axis, which moved from father-son to father-mother. Since 1949, the Chinese leadership has adopted many new policies and programs redefining the status of men and women, with an emphasis on equality in both the home and workplace. The 1980 Marriage Law is the fundamental declaration governing marriage, family relations, and the status of children in the PRC today. This law runs counter to the feudal marriage system that existed in China for several thousand years.

MARRIAGE

The importance to the Communist Party of changing the traditional family relationship is evident in the fact that one of the first laws promulgated by the new government in May 1950 was the Marriage Law. The new law abrogated the feudal practices of arranged and mercenary marriages, and substituted the concept of freedom of marriage based on the willingness of the two parties. Polygamy was outlawed. The absolute authority of the father over the family was replaced with "equality between the sexes" in order to normalize the relationship between parents and children and between husband and wife.

In essence, the Marriage Law attempted to change the Chinese people's traditional attitude toward marriage and the family. It also placed a significant emphasis on duty. The parties to the marriage, for example, were duty bound to love, respect, assist and look after each other, to care for their children, and to strive jointly for the welfare of the family. In order to assist in the implementation and, more importantly perhaps, the enforcement of the law, the All China Women's Federation was established. Its primary task was to explain the law and to ensure its enforcement in rural areas of China.

The Marriage Law of 1980 became effective on January 1, 1981. Compared to the 1950 Law, the 1980 Law has two significant features: One deals with the obligation to follow family planning and the other deals with the reassertion of a woman's right to obtain divorce. The Constitution also declares that women enjoy equal rights with men and that the State protects marriage, the family, and the mother and child. A variety of other laws contain provisions affecting family law. The Civil Law of 1986, for example, stipulates that "a citizen enjoys the right to freedom of marriage; mercenary marriages, arranged marriages and all other conduct that infringes freedom of marriage is prohibited." Another illustration is found in the Criminal Law of 1979 that prohibits "crimes of interrupting marriage and the family."

The legal formalities for a marriage are contained in the 1980 Marriage Law and the Marriage Registration Regulations of 1986. Marriage registration is an important mechanism for promoting the interests of the State and of the parties to the marriage. Registering the marriage at the marriage registration office of the locality where either party is domiciled is an indispensable procedure to the issuance of a marriage license and the establishment of a valid marriage. A marriage license is issued when the registration office finds the proposed marriage to be in conformity with the

Marriage Law. In 1988, 9.46 million couples applied for registration of their marriages and 8.99 million couples received approval. Those who did not receive approval were denied for a variety of reasons, such as being under age, some were "near" relatives, and others had certain diseases.

According to a sample survey by the State Family Planning Commission, 2.5 million couples entered into unlawful marriages in 1988. A nonregistered marriage is technically "void" even though there is parental consent to marry and a wedding ceremony has been held. Nevertheless, certain *de facto* marriage arrangements, such as cohabitation without registration, may create certain limited rights. Thus, for example, although children of a void marriage are considered born out of wedlock, such children have the same rights as those born to a valid marriage, including the right to take either their father's or mother's family name. An unregistered marriage does not create the legal right to support, alimony or inheritance, however.

According to Chinese tradition, a woman ordinarily became a member of her husband's family upon marriage. Her new family had a claim to her labor and the children she bore carried on her husband's line. In this context, it is understandable why daughters were viewed of secondary importance. The 1950 and 1980 Marriage Laws changed this practice by allowing the married woman to become a member of either family, according to the agreed wishes of the two parties to the marriage. Similarly, the Marriage Law also gave children the choice of adopting either their father's or their mother's family name.

The 1980 Marriage Law stipulates that both sexes should be at least two years older than the age for marriage set in the 1950 law. Article 5 of the 1980 Marriage Law provides that no marriage shall be contracted before the man has reached 22 years of age and the woman 20 years of age. A marriage is not permitted, even with parental consent, if one party is below the legal age. Furthermore, no court order or administrative license can waive the mandatory legal age requirements. Due to governmental urging, the actual marriage ages for men and women have tended to be higher than the levels set in 1980. The intent of the 1980 change was to formalize the rules and to prevent earlier marriages in order to discourage population growth. Specifically, the 1980 Law's recommended guidelines for women were first marriage at twenty-four and first (and ideally last) childbirth at twenty-five.

The proclaimed equality between men and women contained in the Constitution and 1980 Marriage Law has proved to be a mixed blessing for women. In practice, this equality frequently has meant that women are expected to undertake the same duties as men in addition to their traditional household duties. Tiring household chores and work outside the home have placed a heavy and remorseless burden on many Chinese women, especially those living in the more remote and rural areas. According to a 1982 survey of 4,660 married women, 82 percent of them had a job outside the home. Those women whose children were born around 1949 have gotten the worst of both worlds: subjugation to their parents and mothers-in-law while they were young; subordination to their jobs outside the home in their later years.

Both the 1980 Marriage Law and the Constitution contain provisions designed to protect the rights of children. The Marriage Law obligates parents to educate their children irrespective of gender. In addition the Marriage Law also expressly protects illegitimate children, adopted children, and stepchildren. The father of an illegitimate child is required to furnish support until the child is self-sufficient. Adoption terminates the rights and relationship between the adopted child and the natural parents, and gives the adopting parents the rights and relationship of natural parents.

Attitudes and traditions are difficult to change. Despite significant progress in enacting new laws affecting the family, changing traditional attitudes continues to be a problem. Arranged and mercenary marriages have made significant comebacks in some remote rural places. Reports of parents arranging marriages for their children frequently for their own financial gain and of abductions and trafficking in women also exist. For example, *Reuters News* reported that 323 women were sold in

Sichuan province in 1986 and 132 in one county in Hubei province in 1986 and 1987. Other reports indicate various other provisions of the 1980 Marriage Law are not being followed. In the Qinghai area, the provincial Higher People's Court recently reported that over one-fifth of all marriages were between cousins, and as a result violated the established degree of kinship for marriage eligibility set out in the 1980 Marriage Law. The current law is not followed in other respects. Some recent reports, for example, indicate an increased tendency of adult children to obstruct the remarriage of their parents because they see remarriage as potentially interfering with their inheritance rights.

FAMILY PLANNING

China's goal is to limit its population to around 1.25 billion people by the year 2000. According to official accounts, China's population went from 540 million in 1949 to 1.133 billion based on the July 1990 census. The population is now increasing by about 17 million people a year. This means that China will have to sustain over 100 million additional people in the next six years. China will confront a profound population control problem because more and more women will reach their peak period for child-bearing. According to the State Family Planning Commission from 1989 to 1994, each year will see about 100 million Chinese women in their peak period for child-bearing (ages 20 to 29), and the figure will not drop until the year 1995.

The history of family planning in the PRC can be divided into four general periods: from 1949 through the first public promotion of birth control in 1954; from 1954 through 1966 when the Party and the State ceased all efforts to implement family planning; from 1971 until 1979 when the State policy was "later, longer, fewer;" and from 1979 through the present One–Child Policy. The legacy of China's present population explosion can in large measure be traced to Mao's decree in the early 1960s that women should have as many children as possible. He was convinced that China could meet the double threat of war with the United States and the Soviet Union with a large army and a vast population to support it.

The principle of family planning is included in the current Marriage Law and is one of the most remarkable features of the state's attempt to remold the traditional Chinese family. The 1982 Constitution states that "both husband and wife have the duty to practice family planning." The 1980 Marriage Law encourages late marriage, late childbirth, and family planning. These national laws have been supplemented by provincial policies and regulations. For example, the 1987 Sichuan Provincial Planned Birth Regulations provide that couples who have given birth to two children "should adopt sterilization measures." The Marriage Law provides that a marriage is not permitted between a man and a woman "where one party is suffering from leprosy, a cure not having been effected, or from any other disease which is regarded by medical science as rendering a person unfit for marriage." Nevertheless, the Provincial Regulations go even further to provide that "couples who have serious hereditary diseases, including psychosis, mental deficiencies, and physical malformation must not be allowed to bear children. Those who are already pregnant must terminate the pregnancy." These regulations would apply, for example, when the disability existed but was not discovered prior to the marriage or when the disability only became apparent after the marriage.

The distinctive features of family planning have been crystallized into the following general rules: Each couple should have only one child; in exceptional circumstance a couple may be allowed two children; and in no circumstances is a third child allowed. These general rules have been modified in rural areas and for ethnic minorities.

State family planning goals are pursued through a mixture of positive and negative sanctions and educational persuasion. Economic penalties and social pressures are used to motivate adherence to the State declared policy against large families. Families who sign a certificate stating they will have only one child receive economic benefits both for the child and for themselves. As a practical matter, families are required to sign such a certificate. The economic benefits are withdrawn, however, if parents have two children, and increasingly severe penalties follow for every additional child.

For example, following the birth of a second child, a 15 percent salary reduction is imposed on the parents until the child is seven.

Late marriages and late childbirth are also "encouraged" as a means of family planning. The actual benefits of adhering to this suggestion vary between provinces or other political-administrative subdivisions. For example, in Beijing those who marry after the age of 24 are given more days off from their jobs than those who marry sooner. In order to have a child, the couple must be authorized by the state to do so. Those couples who delay having a child until after the age of 26 have a priority in securing authorization to have a child. In addition, the couple may receive other benefits. Those who have an unplanned second, third or fourth child are fined for each unplanned child. However, as domestic economic reforms have brought new prosperity to many Chinese, the threat of fines for not complying with state family planning policy has lost some of its deterrent force.

The importance of family planning is constantly being reinforced. Consider, for example, the family planning program in Hengdong County of Hunan province, as outlined in a Beijing University professional journal. The numerous family planning visits were constantly and regularly made:

> A visit is paid to youths at marriageable age for-heart-to-heart talks persuading them of late marriage. . . .

A visit is paid to newlyweds who are greeted with congratulations and who are mobilized for late childbearing . . . to inform them about contraception, to examine their contraceptive measures and to persuade their practice of late childbearing. . . .

A visit is made to single child families to mobilize the couples to get single child certificates. For example, Yand Renjun was reluctant to pledge to have a single child after having a daughter. His wife had an unplanned pregnancy in 1984. Yand's case was talked about among the local people. Learning the story, deputy township party secretary Guo Shangchi paid a visit to Yand and had heart-to-heart talks with him. Like Yand, Guo had also had only a daughter, but he not only pledged to have a single child, but also underwent sterilization. Immediately after the talks, Yand Renjun said, "Though I become well-off now, I should do what the Party calls for. I am ready to get the single child certificate." Moreover, he accompanied his wife, on that very afternoon, to the hospital for the surgical operation. . . .

A visit is made to persuade married women "by thorough and painstaking ideological work," to practice birth control. . . .

A visit is paid to the employees who are on home leave for family reunion, and they are reminded of contraception.

The Chinese policy and law on abortion has been linked to China's policy on population growth. From 1949 through 1953, abortion was illegal in the PRC. From 1953 through 1965, abortion was legal under certain specified conditions. During the period 1965 through 1978, "induced abortion was a lesser element of fertility control." Finally, from 1978 through the present, the Party and the State formulated the law of abortion as positive law.

Special State agencies exist to publicize and implement family planning. Contraceptives are free of charge. Abortion is legal and readily available upon demand, and it is free of charge to those women who have not yet had a child. Pressure for abortion can be intense, even if the pregnancy is in an advanced stage. The Criminal Law of 1979 contains no reference to abortion—either to the woman or to the person performing it—and thus is no impediment to the use of abortions. No medical fees are charged for sterilization, and in 1988 it was reported that sterilization receives the most emphasis as a method for "avoiding pregnancy contrary to policy."

In 1986, the Vice Minister in Charge of the State Family Planning Commission stated that when the One–Child Policy was introduced, it "was enforced to the extent that forced abortion and sterilization became common." Guangdong Province, for instance, passed a local ordinance enjoining women from giving birth in specified circumstances. It does not expressly require abortion or "remedial measures" in instances of "unplanned births." However, in such circumstances, abortion would be the only means of enforcing the Ordinance. The provincial official in charge of family planning in Guangdong acknowledged such use of abortion in 1983:

> Those women who have already given birth to one child must be fitted with IUDs, and couples who already have two children must undergo sterilization of either the husband or the wife. Women with unplanned pregnancies must adopt remedial measures [abortions] as soon as possible. This is based on the directives of the CCP Central Committee and the State Council and on the summation of family planning practices of many years....

In a 1988 article appearing in the *Stanford Law Review,* it was reported that "sometimes the local government compelled the pregnant woman to have an abortion by issuing an arrest warrant for her, listing the crime as 'pregnancy,' and removing her ... to a place where someone performed an abortion." Savage, "The Law of Abortion in the Union of Soviet Socialist Republics and the People's Republic of China: Women's Rights in Two Socialist Countries," 40 *Stanford Law Review* 1027, 1085 (1989). This report is not an isolated one. Steven Moser, an anthropologist, reports having seen local officials in Guangdong Province arresting, imprisoning and browbeating village women into abortions and sterilizations. Medical workers were under standing orders not to let "illegal" children live. Infants who arrived prematurely—that is, before their mothers had agreed to an abortion—were killed at birth by lethal injections.

The current One–Child Policy is inconsistent with the Chinese cultural tradition of large families. Enforcing this policy is difficult, especially when the first child is a daughter because sons have always been favored in China since it was through them that the family line was continued. Much time is consumed in urging sterilization or abortion on those who already have had one child, and in trying to convince parents and, with greater difficulty, grandparents that a girl baby is as "good" today as a boy. It is a constant struggle by all accounts. While officially condemned, female infanticide continues in some rural areas of China. In addition, the birth rates suggest widespread disregard for the One–Child Policy. For example, in 1985, the average woman in China had 2.1 children. In 1986, the figure had risen to 2.4, and most demographers were predicting continuing increases. Urban women have been more willing to limit births because of "inadequate housing and busy lives." In addition, surveillance and hence enforcement is easier in the cities. This has not been the case in the countryside, however. By all recent reports, China's 900 million strong peasant population is essentially disregarding the state's family planning policy, and since 1988, rural families have been allowed to have a second child if the first is a female. In some measure, changes in economic policy, such as allowing peasants to sell products above quota levels at market prices, have reenforced the Chinese tradition for large families in order to take advantage of economic reforms. In the short run, the government may not press family planning issues in the countryside in order to avoid antagonizing the peasantry and threatening economic production, not out of a sense of human rights.

The current policy of limiting the size of families in China will have a profound future effect on the family support structure between generations. If the One–Child Policy ultimately succeeds, two-fifths of the population would be over the age of 65 by the year 2050. Under the One–Child Policy, there will be fewer children to support the same number of parents. Song Yuhua, an official of China's National Committee on Aging, recently said: "The trend of the future will be what we call the ratio of 4:2:1. That means one child will have to take care of two parents and four grandparents, and this could result in a series of problems." Western demographers have observed that no country has yet had more than 18 percent of its population in the over 65 category. Thus, the implications of the success of the One–Child Policy are daunting.

Except for a retirement system that benefits part of the urban population, financial support for China's elderly continues to depend almost entirely on their families. The law tries to deal with the problem of having fewer able-bodied individuals to care for elderly relatives. The Marriage Law provides that parents who have lost the ability to work or have difficulties in providing for themselves have the right to demand that their children pay for their support. This parental right is stipulated to make sure children support and assist their parents in old age. Notwithstanding this legal protection, recent reports have discussed the difficulties faced by the elderly who are dependent on their children for support. Although grandparents who have the capacity to bear the costs have the express duty to rear their orphaned grandchildren to the age of majority, such grandchildren, or grandchildren generally, do not have the expressed reciprocal duty to support their grandparents. Although the Marriage Law includes provisions for the care of the elderly, more protection is needed.

DIVORCE

The 1980 Marriage Law permits a marriage to be terminated administratively by mutual consent when both desire or by court-ordered divorce when one of the parties objects to the termination. If the parties to the marriage mutually agree to the termination, the marriage registration office issues the divorce certificate provided that the registrar determines that the parties want the divorce and that property matters and any custody issues are settled. The courts are not involved in this administrative procedure. According to statistics from the Ministry of Civil Affairs, mutual consent divorces increased in Beijing from 2,203 in 1986 to 5,181 in 1989, constituting 30.3 percent and 41.2 percent of the total of the respective years.

When one party seeks a divorce without the other party's agreement, he or she may apply directly to the people's court. This has now become the most common way to end a marriage. In this case, the divorce occurs through "court mediation." When the mediation is "successful" and both parties agree, the divorce request is withdrawn. When a mutual reconciliation between the parties does not occur, the court has the power to grant the divorce, which legally ends the marriage, or refuse to grant it. When both parties agree to end their marriage through mediation, the court is required to grant the divorce.

The Marriage Law is designed to build up and strengthen marriage relations. It deliberately avoids stating the grounds needed to secure a contested divorce. As a result, adultery, cruelty, and other objectionable acts are not in and of themselves stated grounds to end a marriage. The errant party is first given the opportunity to recognize the mistake(s), to reform and to work at mending the marital relationship. Only as a last resort will the court terminate the marriage. The court generally must be satisfied that there is a "complete alienation of affection"—or as Marx said, "internal collapse"—between the parties before granting a divorce. The courts seem to construe the "complete alienation of affection" in very narrow terms.

The reasons cited in divorce cases are varied. One recent study cited "family rows over the division of household duties" as the primary cause in 28 percent of the cases. Another major cause was extramarital relationships, which accounted for 20 percent. This reason is often described by the terminology "intrusion of a third party in marital relationships." Other reasons included the imprisonment of one of the spouses, conflicting interests and personalities, economic family disputes, lack of love, troubles with a stepmother, medical conditions, sexual incompatibility, in-law problems and an inferiority complex of one of the spouses. Hasty marriage is another reason frequently cited. This reason is undoubtedly influenced by the fact that Chinese couples do not normally date for a prolonged period before getting married.

The ancient social code of *li* can be seen in the 1980 Marriage Law requirement that makes mediation a compulsory first step requirement in any dissolution case. Mediation is tried for divorce applications filed jointly by husband and wife and for those filed by one spouse. When one or both parties seek a divorce, a concerted effort is made through mediation to try to effect a reconciliation between the parties.

Today in China, about 70 percent of the petitions for divorce are filed by women. Because divorce is more readily available under the 1980 Law, the divorce rate has been steadily increasing since the law was enacted. Nevertheless, the divorce rate is relatively low by Western standards because divorce is still condemned by public opinion. For example, in 1988, 1.05 million couples applied for divorce, but only 650,000 divorces were granted. Moreover, the patient in-depth work of education, mediation and reconciliation that precedes the granting of permission to divorce erects a practical barrier to securing a divorce when it is contested. In the words of a presiding judge of the Beijing Supreme People's Court—"divorce, as a social phenomenon, will continue to exist. But it will be kept at a relatively low level."

Unless the court finds that it is essential to act on a husband's divorce application, the 1980 Marriage Law prohibits a husband from applying for a divorce when his wife is pregnant or within one year after his wife has given birth to a child. In addition to applying to the usual type of case, this restriction also applies to situations where the pregnancy or childbirth results from an extramarital relationship. The theory of this provision is that the protection of the health of the mother and child is paramount, even in those instances when the wife is at "fault." This prohibition on applying for divorce does not apply when the wife petitions for the divorce.

As to custody, the Marriage Law gives the mother custody of a baby still being breast-fed. Thereafter, the question of custody is a matter for agreement between the parties. In situations where the couple has adhered to the One–Child Policy, for example through sterilization, child custody disputes can be exceptionally bitter. When an agreement cannot be reached, the court should make a judgment in accordance with the rights and interests of the child and the circumstances of both parties. Apart from the breast-fed infant exception, the 1980 Marriage Law gives only general guidelines on this determination. The financial position of each party, his or her moral qualities, the affection for the child, and the ability to raise the child properly are circumstances that typically will affect the court's judgment on custody. Recent reports indicate that in rural areas courts are influenced by continuing patriarchal social values to favor the father in custody disputes, especially when male children are involved. As a matter of judicial practice, when the child is old enough to express a preference as to which parent should be granted custody, the child is consulted and the stated preference is considered.

Regardless of who has custody of the child, both parties retain the right and duty to rear and educate their children. When one party is given custody of a child, the other party is responsible for part or all of the necessary costs of the maintenance and education of the child. The former spouses should reach an agreement regarding the amount of the cost and the duration of its payment. Absent an agreement, the people's court makes this determination. An agreement reached between parents or a judgment made by the people's court in connection with the cost does not prevent the child from making a reasonable request to increase the amount decided upon by agreement or judicial decision.

Although not explicitly stated in the Marriage Law, an equal division of property acquired during marriage seems to be a guiding general principle. This general principle is tempered by the express requirement that "special consideration should be given to the rights and interests of the wife and children." Consequently, when the parties do not agree on the division, the court will order the property divided after taking into consideration the actual state of the family property and the rights and interests of the wife and child or children. Property in joint possession is divided by agreement between the parties. Debts incurred jointly during the marriage are paid out of the joint property, whereas debts incurred separately are the responsibility of the party incurring the debt. Divorcing couples who had jointly contracted with the government for farmland under the rural responsibility system must divide their interests in such a way so their obligations to the state are not adversely affected.

When one party has maintenance difficulties, the former spouse is obligated to render appropriate financial assistance. Both parties are expected to reach an agreement on the details of maintenance. When an agreement cannot be reached, the people's court determines the matter. A former spouse incapable of working because of age or poor health and who is in need of maintenance can obtain a court judgment for support. Although the marriage law contains no express requirement that the other ex-spouse be capable of paying the spouse in need, this requirement of being capable would seem to be implicit in the actual administration of the Marriage Law.

DEATH AND SUCCESSION

In ancient China, property was considered owned by the family, not the individual. Under Confucianism, the traditional ideal was for the entire clan to live together, thus pooling all family property. As a result, property remained undivided and in the family when the head of the clan died. Only when the family itself was partitioned did succession occur. When this happened, all sons enjoyed the first right of inheritance. Daughters had a secondary right of succession. They could inherit family property only if there were no male successors or heirs. Testate transfers by will existed, but were generally the exception to intestate distribution.

Inheritance runs counter to the general ideological tenets of communism because it facilitates the private accumulation and distribution of wealth. This perpetuates the social inequities characteristic of bourgeois capitalism criticized by

Marx, Lenin, and Mao. Notwithstanding this ideological criticism, the leadership of the PRC initially allowed the right to succession, including testate and intestate transfers, as early as the 1950 Marriage Law.

The justification for inheritance is grounded in the practical policy of encouraging individual initiative to spur economic growth. The Communist Party journal *Red Flag* articulated the rationale: "Practice has proven that [the Law of Succession] is beneficial to the accumulation of social wealth, conforms with the demands of developing our nation's productive forces, accords with the nature and characteristics of our nation's productive relations and with popular will." Focusing on the adverse consequences of not permitting the right of inheritance, the Journal continued, "if we only allow the peasants to have and use the means of production during their lifetime, allocating them elsewhere on their death, these people's enthusiasm will be dampened and there will be no way for the individual economy and individual operations to continue to exist." See Schwartz, "The Inheritance Law of the People's Republic of China," 28 *Harvard International Law Journal* 433 (1987).

Today, the right of inheritance is constitutionally protected. The 1982 Constitution provides: "The State protects by law the right of citizens to inherit private property." The 1980 Marriage Law also protects this right. The Law of Succession (LS), which is the first comprehensive inheritance law in the history of the PRC, became effective in 1985. Prior to 1985, only provisional regulations on inheritance existed. The Civil Law also contains some provisions affecting succession, but they apply only to cases of intestacy.

The Law of Succession (LS) is the main source of law on inheritance. As a general matter, it reflects the government's policy of encouraging economic development by permitting citizens the right to dispose of property. It also reflects the tension found in much of the law in the PRC between state control and individual freedom. There are certain noteworthy provisions to the LS that aptly reflect the government's policy.

The LS lists the types of property that may be inherited. Included within the list are the "means of production which the law permits a citizen to own," property rights in copyrights and patents, and "other lawful property." The right to use and to possess land pursuant to a land contract is inheritable property. In permitting this right to be inherited, the government is providing a strong incentive to make productive investments in the land subject to the right. The reference to other lawful property in the LS is calculated to permit new categories of property to be treated as being disposable as the government policy of defining "property" changes.

Testate and intestate succession are both allowed. Both forms of succession are limited by the principle that a share of the decedent's estate must be reserved for those individuals who are dependent on the decedent or cannot support themselves because they are minors, aged, or infirm. This requirement of reserving a portion of the estate embodies the Chinese tradition of supporting the aged and providing for the young. By placing the obligation on the decedent's estate, the LS relieves the state of bearing this obligation.

Statutory heirs are grouped into two categories under the law. The surviving spouse, children, and parents of the decedent are in the first category, and they have the right to inherit all of the estate in equal shares. The right of representation is expressly allowed. Should no person in the first category exist, the estate is distributed to those persons in the second category, siblings and grandparents of the decedent.

In administering this succession regime, certain common principles apply. Males and females have equal rights of inheritance. Legitimate, illegitimate, and adopted issue of the deceased are defined as "children" and generally have equal succession rights. Adopted children generally are unable to inherit from their natural parents. Stepchildren are treated as children provided they were supported by the decedent prior to his or her death. Otherwise, they have the right to inherit only from their natural parents, unless all relations with their natural parents have been terminated. Adoptive parents are treated as natural parents and inherit equally with the surviving spouse and children. The courts have consistently assigned to the first category of takers, parents who lived with the deceased at the time of death. Although this approach of equal sharing by parents when there is a spouse or issue has been sharply criticized by Chinese commentators and is contrary to most United States law on descent and distribution, it is consistent with the traditional Chinese view of property being owned by the family, not the individual.

All prospective heirs, including surviving spouses, are required as a condition of inheritance to fulfill their duty of support to the decedent. Heirs may also forfeit their right to inherit from a decedent for a variety of reasons other than for nonsupport. The provisions on forfeiture reenforce the traditional Chinese value of providing support for one another within the family. However, it may in practice work to the advantage of sons and to the disadvantage of daughters. Traditionally, daughters "marry out" of the family. Consequently, they may be considered by either the decedent or the courts to have breached their duty of support more easily than sons.

United States community property principles provide a useful analog to understanding the Chinese concept of joint marital property. A decedent cannot dispose of the entire portion of joint marital property, but only his or her half portion. Houses or movable property purchased from the income of several family members are regarded as joint family property and only the specific share belonging to the deceased can be inherited. Moreover, the LS encourages heirs to keep the decedent's estate intact until the death of the surviving spouse. The law expressly permits heirs to decide through consultation the time, method, and shares of the estate. Thus, the law distinguishes between when the right to participate in the estate accrues and when that right is exercised.

The LS allows an individual to dispose of property by testamentary instrument. Both holographic wills and witnessed wills are permitted. The latter type is valid when witnessed by two or more persons with legal capacity and who are neither successors or legatees, or "persons whose interests are related to those of the successors and legatees." Oral wills before a notary, who then creates a record of the individual's directions, are also allowed. This provision would seem to be of primary benefit to illiterate individuals who wished to avail themselves of the benefit of a will.

There has been a steadily increasing number of civil cases dealing with succession in China. In 1987, for example, the courts handled over 24,000 cases involving inheritance. The main problem has been the continued practice of depriving widows and married daughters of their right to inherit property. The government is attempting to reverse this practice through propaganda and education. However, this action may not be strong enough to reverse traditional practices and customs.

CHAPTER VII

BUSINESS AND LABOR

According to the 1982 Constitution, the state sector is the leading force in the economy of the People's Republic of China. Starting in the early 1980s, there was a quiet retreat from this position. The amount of China's industrial output produced by state enterprises steadily dropped. Correspondingly, during the 1980s, there was rapid growth in the number and economic significance of individual, private and collective enterprises. These enterprises accounted for nearly half of the gross national product (GNP) of the People's Republic by the late 1980s. They were an engine of economic growth and jobs. In April of 1988, the Constitution was amended to affirm the development of a private sector as a supplement to the state economy. This amendment provides that the State will protect the legitimate rights and interests of the private sector while supervising, guiding and managing it.

From late 1988 until the spring of 1991, the Party implemented a retrenchment policy aimed at recentralizing the economy and increasing support for state enterprises. China's aging leadership saw a link between economic and political liberalization, and they felt threatened by this connection.

In addition, the leadership concluded that the economic problems emerging since 1988 (such as high inflation, increasing wage inequalities, and a broad decline in the standard of living) had contributed to the general sense of dissatisfaction that fueled the 1989 Democracy Movement demonstrations. Therefore, in order to reassert their political control and to stabilize the economy, the Party implemented a program aimed at expanding state control over the economy and reversing earlier market oriented reforms. As a result, hundreds of thousands of private sector businesses disappeared between 1989–1991 for want of government licensure, credit or other support. In early 1992, there have been indications that the economic pendulum is once again swinging towards decentralization and promotion of collective and private enterprise.

STATE ENTERPRISES

The Chinese character for state enterprises translates literally as enterprises "owned by the whole people." A significant feature of business entity law in the PRC since the Cultural Revolution has been the revision of state enterprise law. These revisions have not been supported by the whole of China's leadership or people.

State enterprises can be sued, bring suit and enter into contracts. The assets of state enterprises come from allocations of government funds or earnings. Although the State is not legally responsible for their debts and liabilities, most state enterprises are heavily subsidized. Some subsidies result from bad management or featherbedding of workers; others simply reflect price controls or government policies which in essence mandate revenue deficits. China's state enterprises are not really businesses. Rather they are welfare societies that provide their workers with education, housing, medical care and only incidentally, a wage. In the past, management bonuses often depended upon output, regardless of its marketability. The costs to the government of state enterprises have driven much of the reform movement in Chinese business entity law. This reform movement has focused generally on diminishing centralized state planning, increasing enterprise autonomy, enhancing business competition, and providing material incentives as a means to improve the performance of management and individual workers.

this may be a little strong.

The Bankruptcy Law has been one component of these reforms. After heated debates and an unprecedented rejection of the first draft, a Bankruptcy Law was promulgated in 1986 by the Standing Committee of the National People's Congress. The Bankruptcy Law did not become effective until three months after the 1988 State Enterprise Law was adopted. Both laws are designed to make state enterprises responsible for their economic performance and as a result more efficient and productive. Previously, there had been little linkage between the economic rewards received by an enterprise or its workers and their performance.

If it suffered, the enterprise was subsidized by the government. There was little negative impact on those directly involved in the operation of the enterprise. An additional goal of the Bankruptcy Law and the State Enterprise Law is to integrate state enterprises into China's fledgling market system.

Bankruptcy is the ultimate penalty ("the stick") behind the drive to reform state enterprises. The Bankruptcy Law acts as a deterrent to inadequate economic performance and as a reminder of the power of the State in the Chinese economy. It seems reasonable to conclude that the threat of bankruptcy may have some positive effect on economic performance. A signal of increased responsibility and accountability was sent to all state enterprises with the first bankruptcy since the founding of the PRC, the 1986 Shenyang Explosion–Proof Equipment Factory proceeding.

In China, as part of the normal process of developing a new policy or law, the government first experiments with various aspects in selected target regions of the country. During the experimentation stage, details are tested and revisions occur before a law is enacted nationally. This stage in the development of the Bankruptcy Law began in 1985 and included the 1986 Shenyang bankruptcy proceeding. This proceeding was designed to set an example for delinquent management and labor. Initially, city authorities placed the Explosion–Proof Equipment enterprise "on probation."

When it failed to meet various economic goals established by the authorities, the city initiated bankruptcy proceedings at the request of the firm's creditors. The factory was eventually auctioned off to a local company and the bankrupt estate distributed to the creditors. Some seventy workers received unemployment benefits for six months. Most of them obtained new jobs through the local labor bureau. One director, Shi Yongjie, was in effect held responsible for the bankruptcy. He was publicly humiliated and denied a variety of employment benefits. Even so, the message from the authorities was mixed. Six other Shenyang industries placed on probation at about the same time were not thrown into bankruptcy. They survived with tax relief, cheap loans and technical aid. City officers realized if bankruptcy was overused, unemployment would result.

The State Enterprise Law of 1988 defines various Party-government-enterprise relationships. Its primary objective is the elimination of CCP and government interference with state enterprises. The Law introduced "director responsibility" principles into state enterprise management. It expressly gives factory managers (acting "democratically" in consultation with workers' congresses and a management committee with worker representatives) the power to decide on production, the hiring and dismissal of personnel, and the performance of the enterprise. Prior to 1988, the Chinese leadership had alternated between giving state enterprise officers total control over management and allowing a CCP committee within the enterprise to have key decisionmaking powers. The State Enterprise Law seeks to isolate Party committees within state enterprises by directing them not to interfere with managerial decisions. However, these committees must "guarantee and supervise" Party policies and principles in state enterprise affairs. The State Enterprise Law does not indicate how to resolve conflicts resulting from these potentially divergent instructions to Party committees.

Similarly, the State Enterprise Law prohibits the government from interfering with management decisions. Instead the government is to regulate the market, letting the market in turn guide the enterprise. The 1988 Law, for example, gives state enterprises the right to arrange production (guided naturally by state plans), to request adjustment of mandatory plans, to reject additional non-essential assignments outside the plan, to sell production above plan quotas on the free market, to choose their own suppliers (which are, of course, planned) and to set its own prices (if not subject to State Council price controls). In addition, state enterprises are guaranteed the right to deal directly with foreigners, to control their retained earnings and fixed assets, to hire, fire and redeploy staff, to set wages and bonuses, and the right *not* to be subject to state exactions of manpower, materials or money.

The State Enterprise Law is thus a major attempt at deregulation of state enterprises from

Party and government controls. This is a monumental undertaking. The results to date are not particularly encouraging. Local Party officials and bureaucrats (nicknamed "popos" or "mothers-in-law") resent their loss of power and continually inject themselves into basic management decisions. Beginning in 1989, an active role for Party bosses in the management of state enterprises was officially supported as part of the return to ideological controls. Self-criticism and presentation of the official version of events at Tiananmen Square are recurrent themes in mandatory political study groups held on company time. Notwithstanding the State Enterprise Law, promotions, bonuses and benefits are the levers exercised by Party leaders within state enterprises. However, there were some preliminary signals in early 1992 that ideological constraints may be loosening once again.

Some successful reforms of state enterprises have been accomplished by using industrial responsibility or leasing contracts, a policy reaffirmed by the conservative Party leadership in November 1989 in anticipation of the renewal of many contracts during 1990. This approach is modeled on the success with agricultural responsibility contracts. A state enterprise may, for example, contract to pay a percentage of its revenues to the government. Commercial and retail state enterprises have been leased to individuals or collectives in return for rent or a share of the revenues. The balance of the revenues after taxation ("the carrot") may be retained. Such monies are used for expansion, capital equipment, employee benefits and bonuses. The last two expenditures are included to serve as material incentives for increased worker productivity. At the same time, the state enterprise may be weaned of government subsidies. The result is a wider economic gap between effectively and poorly managed state enterprises.

A showcase example of an industrial responsibility contract is the Shoudu Iron and Steel Company. Under its initial 1982 contract, the company was obliged to increase the amount of money it returned to the state by 72 percent annually. Its base year was 1981. Retained revenues were allocated as follows: 60 percent to expansion funds, 20 percent to collective welfare funds and 20 percent to employee bonuses. The firm's payroll was also linked to its revenues: Every 1 percent increase generated a 0.8 percent rise in the payroll. The company also agreed to absorb depreciation costs on its assets without state financial assistance. Shoudu Iron and Steel reportedly prospered under this and succeeding contracts. Production increased dramatically, revenues and wages rose, equipment was upgraded, employee housing built and environmental pollution decreased. The controversy surrounding this success story came from those who felt that the state was not receiving a large enough share of the revenues and that company employees were unduly benefiting. Nevertheless, the Shoudu Iron and Steel story has been widely publicized by supporters of the effort to reform state enterprises. Its record is thought to indicate what can happen when Party and state officials stand firmly behind this goal and the laws intended to implement it.

DEVELOPMENT OF THE PRIVATE AND COLLECTIVE SECTORS

The private and collective sectors of China's economy have undergone phenomenal growth since the Cultural Revolution. From a base line of almost zero, millions of businesses have emerged to help develop the nation. Indeed, the private and collective sectors have been responsible for much of China's economic growth since the Cultural Revolution. Until 1989, they were nurtured by various Party and government policies. Privatization of state enterprises had even begun. Shares in some state enterprises were sold to workers and, in a very few instances, local governments auctioned state enterprises such as restaurants to collectives or individuals. Chinese law distinguishes between collective, individual, and private enterprises. Many township collective enterprises exist in rural areas where there has been a notable movement of labor from the farm to the factory. Some collectives operate their own manufacturing or assembly plants, especially for canned goods, textiles and handicrafts. Though of less economic importance, private individual enterprises number in the millions. Many involve curbside businesses, such as tailors, shoe repairers, and vendors. Tax evasion is widespread among China's individual enterprises, and this was one reason cited by government authorities in their 1989–91 crackdown against the private sector. Private enterprise is also seen as the source of prodemocracy ideas and funds. There is some reality to this perception. During the protests of 1989 in Beijing, a group of private businessmen supported the "Flying Tiger Brigade"—approximately 400 motorcyclists who acted as couriers for the student protesters.

The legal status of China's private sector was formally acknowledged in the 1986 General Principles of Civil Law. This Law recognizes partnerships, "industrial/commercial households" and "rural contract operation households" as lawful business entities. Rural contract operation households play an important role in China's agricultural contract system. They include members of rural collectives who contract to farm land and pay a portion of their yield to the state as "rent." The rest of their harvest may be sold in the market. Industrial/commercial households, such as street vendors, function mostly in urban areas and are either individually or family run. They may have their own trade name, but must be registered and approved to do business by the State. The Civil Law provides that the legitimate rights and interests of all types of households are protected by law. Their legal obligations are borne either individually or by the family. Officially, no industrial or commercial household business is supposed to have more than two helpers and five apprentices. The relationship between the employer (the household) and the laborer is regulated by the government in order to prevent exploitation. Some businesses are nominally run as collective entities to avoid these limits.

Partnerships are recognized by the 1986 Civil Law. They are comprised of "citizens" who by written agreement jointly run a business. According to the Civil Law, the partnership agreement must provide for capital shares, a distribution of profits, responsibility for liabilities, and termination. Partnerships may register trade names. All partners are jointly and severally liable for partnership debts, unless otherwise provided by law. Partners paying a disproportionate share of partnership debts may seek reimbursement from other partners. The partnership law established by the 1986 Civil Law has provided greater legal security for China's private sector. Laborers' coops are said to be the most prevalent form of partnership business.

The line between individual or family businesses (*getihu*) and private enterprises employing others for hire (*siying qiye*) is blurred in practice and in law. Rumors exist of private enterprises employing hundreds of persons, though most seem to employ fewer than twenty. Many are involved in the industrial, transport, building or communications sectors. Interim Regulations on Private Enterprises in the PRC went into effect in 1988. These regulations govern sole proprietorships (households), partnerships and limited liability companies employing at least eight people. The regulations concern the establishment, dissolution, rights, duties, labor management, financing, taxation, supervision and punishment of such enterprises. Some of the most interesting features of these regulations are the recognition of the proprietary rights of investors in private enterprises and the call for greater supervision by government bureaus. As with many revisions in the field of Chinese business entity law, they reveal internal policy conflicts about the wisdom of promoting independent enterprise in a socialist state. Their very existence, however, signals forward momentum in the development of a body of Chinese law for which there is little precedent under Communist Party rule.

BUSINESS ENTITY LAW

Business entities recognized under PRC law as legal persons enjoy limited liability. Thus the provisions of the 1986 Civil Law governing such recognition are critical to most enterprises. State and collective enterprises, foreign equity and contractual joint ventures, and wholly foreign-owned enterprises may be recognized as legal persons. To do so, they must fulfill the requirements of the Civil Law on capitalization, structure, offices, civil obligations and registration. Individual household and partnership enterprises cannot be recognized as legal persons and therefore cannot obtain limited liability. In other words, the domestic private sector is largely excluded from limited liability. The legal personality of an enterprise terminates on dissolution, bankruptcy or cancellation in accordance with law. In general, a business that is not a legal person does not have legal capacity and therefore may not enter into certain contracts or conduct other legal acts. In addition, various types of business practices can only be undertaken by business organizations that are legal persons.

China's business registration law is administered by the State Administration for Industry and Commerce. Most enterprises in China must be registered with this government office. Basic information concerning the nature of the business conducted and its capitalization are contained in the registration. The 1986 Civil Law requires enterprises to adopt and register articles of association. Registration is a condition to obtaining Chinese trademarks. Failure to do so can result in criticism, fines, frozen bank deposits, mandatory liquidation, and revocation of construction permits or business licenses. Limited liability extends only to business conducted within the scope of registration. Registered enterprises used for illegal purposes that harm state or public interests can have their income confiscated. The 1986 Civil Law also provides for administrative and criminal fines when an enterprise conducts business activities beyond the scope of its registration, willfully deceives tax or registration authorities, conceals funds to avoid debts, or disposes of property after termination.

"Joint operations" among domestic Chinese enterprises located in different geographic areas of China are being encouraged to increase industrial output. They are supported by recognition in the 1986 Civil Law which allows such operations to become legal persons or to operate as contractual partners. Previously, economic decentralization was favored by Mao for military defense purposes. An attacker would find it difficult to destroy China's industrial base if it was scattered across the vastness of the nation. However, many regional monopolies serviced by local state enterprises were sheltered by this approach. This pattern is slowly changing as government barriers to a national marketplace are removed. The Shanghai Bicycle Company, for example, has established a joint operation with six producers in other provinces. They are licensed to make its famous "Forever" model. The Jin Xing Electrical Group, which produces televisions in numerous cities, may become the nation's first national manufacturer. They already make about a quarter of all the TVs in China.

PRICES AND MARKETS

A broad trend towards free market economics (taking goods off "the plan") was apparent during most of the 1980s. The number of products allocated through central planners dropped from 250 to 20 by 1988. The share of industrial output and retail sales subject to state planning dropped to 30 percent. Nevertheless, China's economy remains heavily regulated. The government's central administration fixes prices for most important consumer and producer goods whereas local economic bureaucrats set prices and control the supplies of locally distributed goods. The price of a commodity is fixed generally on the basis of whether the government sees the good as a "necessity" and on the consumption pattern that the government is encouraging at a given time. The fixed price has little to do with actual costs. (While there have been some hints of change in early 1992, reregulation of previously deregulated areas has been the prevailing trend since 1988.)

Price controls go to the heart of government regulation of the Chinese economy. No other area has provoked more controversy in the drive for economic reform. Price controls are a litmus test on the progression or regression of the economic reform movement.

China administers agricultural commodity prices through regulations issued by the State Council. Commodity prices are regulated on a national basis, in rural markets and by enterprise. Specific prices are proposed by the National Price Bureau and adopted by the State Council. Provincial price departments carry out national plans and enforce price standards within their jurisdictions. There are price differentials for various types of commodities depending upon the season, quality and other factors. Some commodity prices fluctuate within administratively established ranges.

The commodity price regulations combine the conflicting principles of a planned economy with those of a market economy. Maintaining a balance between these principles has not been easy. At present, commodity price controls are still in place for agricultural products sold in the state (as opposed to private) sector. Market pricing on commodity sales in excess of state contract quotas was one of the first of the agricultural reforms adopted after the Cultural Revolution. Since ever increasing quantities of China's agricultural produce have been sold in privately supplied marketplaces, the significance of price controls in this area has decreased dramatically. Even in the state sector, since the mid–1980s, some regulated retail prices have been allowed to rise in response to market forces. At the same time, China's consumers have frequently benefitted from subsidies which have partially offset price increases. Nevertheless, many urban dwellers in China perceive that their incomes have not risen as fast as food costs. Dual-pricing has led to considerable profiteering by persons (mainly Party and state officials) who obtain goods in the state sector and resell them in private markets. This corruption has caused some leaders to call for reregulation of all agricultural prices. Among the citizenry, it contributed to the frustration that led to the 1989 spring demonstrations in China.

Price controls in the industrial sector are also administered through State Council regulations. Deregulation of the prices of industrial goods has come much more slowly than in agriculture. Regulations in this area are often adopted on a trial basis. A representative trial regulation issued in 1984 set the prices of machinery goods according to their qualities and grades. This regulation permits enterprises manufacturing machinery of "top quality" to increase their prices by 20 percent. "Quality" goods may be raised from 8 to 12 percent above the prices ordinarily allowed. Energy-saving products may be sold at a 15 percent premium. Products technologically out of date may gradually be lowered in price. This kind of pricing flexibility provides incentives for industrial reform. There are also sanctions which apply to the production of consistently inferior industrial goods. These include reductions in salary and suspensions of bonuses for workers and managers. Such sanctions are authorized under general quality control regulations adopted by the State Council.

Free market pricing of industrial goods sometimes occurs by contract. In this respect, Chinese law attempts to transfer the two-track pricing reforms of the agricultural field to the industrial sector. State enterprises are now permitted by contract to produce goods in excess of mandatory quotas and outside state price controls. In practice, it pays enterprises to minimize the proportion of goods turned over to the State while maximizing the amount of raw materials and other inputs

PROBLEMS

supplied at low, state prices. Managers contract with suppliers, decide on production levels and sell at market prices. This is done with considerably more entrepreneurial risk and reward than when producing goods for the State, which is why state quotas often have not been met. While state enterprises are taxed at 55 percent on their "outside revenues," they may keep the rest for reinvestment, bonuses, worker housing, medical care and recreation. Managers compete for loans from state banks to develop their free market capacity and they pay interest on such loans. Problems of crossover sales and profiteering have also arisen in the industrial sector, so much so that wholesale abandonment of dual track pricing of industrial goods may follow. In the short-term, state enterprises can participate in a "double-guarantee" system designed to insure the availability of energy, raw materials, transport services and the like in return for firm commitments by them to meet state supply quotas and tax payments.

Broad price reforms have been tested in the city of Guangzhou (Canton). The *Beijing Review* reported in 1987 on some of the problems encountered with Guangzhou's price controls:

> Under China's old price structure, prices reflected neither the true value of the goods nor the relationship between their supply and demand....
>
> —The purchasing prices for farm and sideline products were unduly low, and selling prices

were still lower than the purchasing prices. The state had to subsidize them.

—The prices of manufactured goods were high, but the prices of minerals, energy and raw materials were too low. For example, the 1978 profit rate for state-owned industrial enterprises was 21 percent, 43.19 percent for light industry, 47.68 percent for the textile industry and only 0.46 percent for coal. Due to their low prices and meager profits, household goods like soap, matches and toilet paper were often out of stock.

—The price of commodities bore no relation to quality. For a long time the state set a unified price for every kind of commodity.

—Charges for transport, urban public utilities and services were unduly low. For example, it cost just five to 20 *fen* to ride a bus. Every year the municipal transportation and communications company lost 1 million yuan. Sept. 24, 1987 at pp. 14–15.

The Guangzhou reforms involve far fewer fixed prices on agricultural and industrial goods than previously. There are, instead, more prices floating within limits and more free market prices. Indeed, the overall proportion of goods subject to fixed prices decreased dramatically. Only key commodities such as grain, oil, fuel and medicines, along with transport fares, rent, water rates, electricity, tuition and postage, are subject to fixed prices. Floating prices are allowed for services and recreational activities such as hotel rooms, concerts and the theatre. Free market prices govern more than half of all prices, including most food items. However, the State still buys some foodstuffs and subsidizes their retail price in off-seasons. The total amount of subsidization has been declining.

The Guangzhou experiment in broad price deregulation provides a model which, under the present PRC administration, seems unlikely to spread throughout China. In 1988, former Communist Party Chief Zhao Ziyang formulated a "New Order for the Socialist Commodity Economy" which proposed ending state control of prices within 4 to 5 years. Gradual wage and labor decontrols would also have been implemented in favor of merit pay and competitive markets for labor, money and raw materials. In the fall of 1988, Zhao Ziyang came under heavy criticism within the CCP leadership for his economic proposals. This criticism, combined with Zhao's support for the demonstrators in 1989, led to his removal from the Party's leadership (including his post as General Secretary of the CCP) after the suppression of the Democracy Movement. At this point, in the spring of 1992, it appears that Guangzhou will be allowed to continue its price reforms. They are being tolerated by the central government, although some leaders have openly encouraged their continuance along with even more radical experiments in Guangdong Province such as privitization of state enterprises.

The tensions inherent in moving China's planned economy into the marketplace are evident in its regulatory law. China has, for example, an unusual collection of laws supporting competition and encouraging collaboration. Regulations Concerning the Promotion of Economic Combinations were adopted on a provisional basis in 1980. These regulations encourage state enterprises to voluntarily participate in economic combines by signing a contract. Producers and processors of raw materials might, for example, execute such a cartel agreement. The regulations provide that combines can enjoy incentives in the marketing and supply of products.

Regulations Concerning Development of Socialist Competition were also provisionally issued in 1980. Under these regulations, state enterprises are given more power to decide on production, marketing, finance, and the like without interference from local authorities. No monopoly of any commodity is allowed other than those (such as the state tobacco monopoly) designated by the government. Although these regulations give priority to the government's economic plans, state enterprises may produce in excess of plan quotas. In addition, authorities cannot create local monopolies, or forbid the sale locally of products that are made elsewhere.

The government is thus in a legal position which allows it to choose between economic combines or socialist competition. Prior to 1989, as the deregulation campaign aimed at China's aviation market illustrates, the trend was clearly in the direction of more competition and fewer state authorized cartels. Indeed, as market forces increasingly came into play the capitalist phenomenon of "multifarious monopolies" reared its head. The *Beijing Review* reported in 1988 that price fixing by cartels taking advantage of supply shortages was an important source of inflation:

> Enterprises in the same line of business usurp the pricing organs by together fixing the prices of their products. Last year, directors of 18 printing and dyeing factories decided to raise the prices of over 50 dyestuffs; ten pharmaceutical plants, which produce raw materials for the production of *Xinnumin,* an anti-biotic, raised the price of their products; representatives of the vinyl factories in Shanghai, Beijing and four provinces raised the price of polyvinyl alcohol; 108 low-voltage electrical goods enterprises in March 1987 issued a 'joint letter to consumers,' in which they announced price rises for 260 products; in November, nine enterprises in Beijing, Chongqing, Shenyang and five other cities called a meeting and decided jointly to raise the price of a certain kind of refractory material they produce. Feb. 8–14, 1988 at p. 24.

New regulations were adopted by the State Council to combat these practices. No enterprises or trade associations may establish a "monopoly price," regardless of whether the State has set a ceiling price for the relevant product or decreed that it is subject to a floating or free market price. The

State will punish offenders and replace monopoly prices with "reasonable" ones. China's answer to monopoly pricing is thus reregulation of markets, not a greater promotion of competitive alternatives. This is a step backwards from the development of a market economy, one which the Chinese explain by reference to the infant state of their economic system. There may be some legitimacy to this explanation, but monopoly pricing controls could undercut the progress toward deregulation of prices.

ADVERTISING REGULATION

The State Council has issued a series of regulations on the distribution of periodicals and advertising in China. Advertising is broadly defined to include all activity designed to sell products or generate income from services. Public, private and foreign investment enterprises are subject to these regulations. There are also entry controls. Advertising companies and agents must register and be licensed. In practice, this licensing system is used to control advertising content. There are, for example, rules aimed at truth in advertising. Fraud, deception or misleading advertising is prohibited and all advertising content must be clear, factual and presumably politically correct.

The regulations on advertising completely prohibit certain advertisements. For example, advertisements which violate state law or policy are prohibited. On this basis, cigarette advertising is widely prohibited in the PRC. So too are ads that damage the dignity of any Chinese nationality or have a reactionary, superstitious, obscene or repulsive content. Libelous ads or those which violate national secrets are illegal. The prohibition against use of superstitious advertisements is especially significant because this kind of advertising is potentially powerful in Chinese culture. Various colors, for example, convey different superstitions. Advertising formats are also controlled. For example, billboard advertising must not injure the "tasteful surroundings of local appearance and scenery."

Violation of the advertising regulations can result in legal liability. Sanctions include administrative censure, fines, and suspension or revocation of licenses. Furthermore, consumers or users of products or services have a right to compensation for losses which result from advertisements that violate these regulations. This creates an important private cause of action remediable in the people's courts. There have been, for example, numerous successful cases filed by persons whose portraits have been used in advertising without their consent.

CURRENCY CONTROLS

Banking is a state monopoly in China. There are essentially two banking systems. The People's Bank of China handles most, but no longer all, foreign currency and international transactions.

The People's Bank acts as China's central bank and oversees various specialized banks such as the Industrial and Commercial Bank, the Agricultural Bank, and the People's Construction Bank. These banks service most of China's domestic banking needs. The China Investment Bank, the China International Trade and Investment Commission (CITIC) Industrial Bank, and the Shanghai Bank of Communications are special banks that mostly serve foreign transactions. A rapidly increasing number of foreign banks (particularly those from Hong Kong and Britain) maintain representative offices or branches in Shanghai, Beijing, Guangzhou and other leading cities. The banking activities of foreigners are basically limited to international financing.

Currency controls are a topic of major interest to foreign investors and traders in China. They always want to be paid in hard currency, not *renminbi* of the PRC, and they resent being forced to exchange at less than the official rate (which is itself much less than unofficial market rates). Foreign Exchange Control Regulations issued by the State Council govern such payments and exchanges. Foreign exchange, for these regulatory purposes, includes not only notes and coins, but also securities and instruments payable in foreign currencies. This includes, for example, bills of lading, bank drafts and checks.

The State Administration of Foreign Exchange supervises all foreign exchange in the PRC. It has authorized the Bank of China and a few other banks to engage in foreign transactions. Since the regulations generally prohibit the use of foreign currency anywhere in China (one exception is the Shenzhen special economic zone where Hong Kong dollars are allowed), the Bank of China is the primary key to unlocking China's limited hard currency reserves. However, for the most part, foreign exchange credits accumulated with the Bank by foreign or domestic enterprises may only be withdrawn with the approval of the State Administration of Foreign Exchange. Obtaining this permission is difficult and often said to be the most troublesome feature of doing business in the PRC. Currency swaps and import substitution strategies are just some of the creative devices used to avoid the impact of China's stringent exchange controls.

The foreign currency earnings of Chinese citizens on inventions, writings, lectures, and artistic performances can be retained in foreign currency accounts. Accessing these accounts is once again very difficult. However, Chinese citizens frequently obtain foreign currency and its equivalent, Foreign Exchange Certificates (F.E.C.), in a thriving illegal market which the government ignored until late 1989. The F.E.C. market is mostly a byproduct of China's tourist trade where F.E.C. are issued upon exchange of hard currencies. Foreigners pay for various goods and services using F.E.C. while in China. Some of these certificates inevitably find their way into private hands. Since F.E.C. can be spent at hard currency shops intended for foreigners throughout the country, and have been used in private commercial dealings as a form of "hard currency," they have substantial value to Chinese citizens. Regulations issued by the State Administration of Foreign Exchange Control now strictly limit the convertibility and use of F.E.C. by PRC persons or entities.

INSURANCE AND SECURITIES

The insurance business has rapidly expanded in the last decade. Property, investment, product liability, personal accident, social welfare and unemployment insurance are some of the most common policies being written. The chief insurer is the People's Insurance Company of China, a state enterprise. It has created a number of standardized policy contracts. The law of individual insurance contracts is governed by China's Economic Contract Law and State Council regulations.

The insurance industry, like most in the PRC, is heavily regulated. The Interim Regulations of the Administration of the Insurance Enterprises issued in 1985 by the State Council are probably the most important. These regulations govern the establishment of insurance businesses and their administration. Various reserve, investment and reinsurance requirements have been created with the goal of protecting the interests of the insured. These requirements are especially strict when regional or local governments establish insurance companies.

Financing Chinese enterprises or government expenditures through securities offerings is a practice which has returned since the Cultural Revolution. The treasury, for example, undertook a major domestic bond issue in 1981, the first since 1966. Bonds with a value of 5,000,000,000 yuan were issued. Treasury bond issues normally offer two-tiered interest rates. State and collective bondholders receive a rate that is lower than that paid individual bondholders. The extra interest is apparently required to attract individual investors. The Bank of China has also floated government bond issues abroad payable in Japanese yen or German marks.

The State Council issued Interim Regulations for the Control of Bonds Issued by Enterprises in 1987. These regulations authorize the issuance of bonds by state enterprises, but generally prohibit the issuance of stock. This allows state enterprises to raise capital without loss of state ownership. Collective enterprises are allowed to issue shares of stock, but not bonds. This allows collective enterprises to be owned by individual shareholders, but effectively limits their ability to raise capital. Even though the sale of stock to the public by collective enterprises is theoretically inconsistent with various laws which provide that such enterprises are owned exclusively by collective workers, thousands of such stock offerings have been made. Foreign joint ventures may issue stock on an experimental basis. In all cases, the People's Bank of China must approve the issuance of Chinese stocks and bonds. It has adopted a "merit" approach to granting securities approvals. "Fair, just and equitable" issues will be approved under the 1987 regulations.

Communist ideology notwithstanding, Shanghai stock trading resumed in 1986 for the first time since the 1949 revolution. Two stocks were traded. They quickly "sold out," despite mandatory ceilings on stock dividends and restraints on alienation (resale) of the shares. Shares in other state and collective enterprises have been traded on experimental exchanges established in Guangzhou, Beijing, Shenyang and elsewhere. In December of 1990, a national stock market was opened in Shanghai and shares in a few enterprises have even been sold to foreigners. In Shenzhen, across from Hong Kong, a fledgling stock market has taken to the streets. Trading outside the market has become rampant as share prices have risen. As with the many experiments in capitalism undertaken in recent years in China, all stock offerings have been highly controlled events. Nevertheless, they are symbolic of the revision and reform of Chinese securities law, indeed of all of PRC regulatory law, since the Cultural Revolution. The future of these reforms is uncertain and likely to be influenced by political developments.

CHANGING LABOR POLICIES

Just as the regulations regarding enterprises and business practices have undergone changes since the founding of the PRC, so has Chinese labor law been through several stages of development. The government's policy toward labor-management relations, including trade unions, incentives, worker input in management, labor discipline, and welfare programs has been driven for the most part by national economic developments. These developments have resulted in the emergence of two distinct systems of labor law. One system of labor laws applies to domestic enterprises and the other governs foreign enterprises doing business in China.

In examining Chinese labor law and the various economic reforms that affect labor, it is important to realize that the PRC continues to adhere to the Communist Party's traditional political goals and ideals, including that of a predominantly state-run economy. It is also important to recognize that the need for labor laws in a state-run economy is fundamentally different from that found in a market economy. Wages and working conditions are largely determined by the State, and thus the process of collective bargaining between labor and management does not exist.

In the mid–1950s, China's economic policy was based on nationalization of industrial and commercial enterprises and assignment of the work force to specific jobs to meet the dictates of state planning. Neither the employer nor employee had much formal control over the allocation of jobs or the assignment of labor within various industries or geographic areas. Consistent with this approach to regulating the labor system through administrative orders, China adopted the "iron rice bowl" policy. It dictated that permanent employees were assured lifetime employment, and state enterprises were prohibited from discharging permanent employees, except for egregious misconduct. In addition, workers and their families enjoyed a wide range of fringe benefits, such as subsidized medical care, housing and educational facilities. According to the iron rice bowl policy, workers could also look forward to a pension on retirement.

The State's approach toward the role of the worker and management changed during the 1980s as a result of two policies. The first was the desire to attract foreign investment and the necessity of adapting the labor laws to make this possible, and the second was the decision to introduce certain reforms in the domestic economy as a means to increase production. These domestic reforms included greater use of wage and profit incentives, more tolerance of small scale private enterprise, a reduced role for central planning and greater reliance on market forces to determine prices, and a change in the relationship between managers and workers. The impetus for domestic reform was influenced in part by the successes of the production responsibility system in the agricultural sector of the economy.

CONSTITUTIONAL PROVISIONS AFFECTING LABOR

The 1982 Constitution contains the most significant statements on the government's general policies concerning labor. Important constitutional provisions include labor discipline, the duty and right to work, labor incentives, labor insurance and worker participation.

Until the mid–1980s, wages, working conditions, and benefits were all established by the State, and collective bargaining as it is known in the United States was almost nonexistent. This situation has undergone significant change in the past few years as a result of the political decision to open China to foreign investment. The introduction of foreign investment has necessitated the development of a new legal framework to regulate labor relations between management, which often is represented either wholly or partially by foreign investors, and the labor force, which is generally Chinese. The fundamental aim of the new regulations is to protect the Chinese worker from what the leadership sees as a major problem facing Third World countries: the exploitation of indigenous workers by foreign companies. The foreign investment labor force is hired primarily on the basis of a contract employment system, whereas the domestic labor system is regulated primarily through administrative orders and economic planning.

The gap between the labor system governing foreign investment enterprises and domestic state-owned enterprises narrowed during the 1980s. The reforms implemented with the approval of the Party brought labor relations in state-owned enterprises more into line with the contract-based pattern applicable to foreign investment enterprises. This change to a contract-based system is significant because it is the first major attempt to use the legal system to solve the problems associated with labor.

The general principles of Chinese contract law apply to the contract-based system of employment. These include the principles of equality, voluntariness and mutual benefit. Using a contract-based system of labor in the domestic economy necessitates the development of mechanisms to guarantee employee rights under their contracts and ways to prevent enterprises from abusing their considerable regulatory powers. After a decade of progressive labor reforms, which included the employment contract system, in 1988 China lurched back in the direction of orthodox communist principles that stress centralized planning and greater administrative control. This shift in policy will undoubtedly affect the future contours of labor law in the PRC.

Changes in the domestic labor system that either permit or mandate contract employment will eventually require an examination of labor's right to strike. Both the 1975 and 1978 Constitutions contained provisions that gave workers the right to "strike," although the term was not defined nor were procedures set out for the exercise of the right by workers. Significantly, this right is not contained in the 1982 Constitution, although there have been reports of strikes and work slowdowns in recent years.

According to the 1982 Constitution, the socialist economy of the PRC is "under the ownership by the whole people." This provision is premised on the principle that the workers' interests are parallel to the government's interests and will never run counter to them. As the collapse of communism in Europe attests, the workers' interests do not always correspond to the government's interests in socialist countries. In the view of some Chinese legal scholars, the right to strike was deleted from the 1982 Constitution because of the Chinese leadership's adverse reaction to the Solidarity Movement's influence in Poland, and the concern that the exercise of this right could disrupt economic and political stability. The contract-based system of employment in the PRC will inevitably force a reconsideration of the theoretical premise that the economy is under the ownership of the people.

Three provisions in the 1982 Constitution deal with labor discipline. Article 15 provides that "disturbance of the orderly functioning of the social economy or disruption of the State economic plan by any organization or individual is prohibited." This provision is reinforced by Article 28—the state penalizes actions that disrupt the socialist economy—and Article 53—citizens must observe labor discipline. Strikes, work stoppages or slowdowns would arguably be in violation of these constitutional provisions. Thus, a legal basis exists to thwart any claim of the right to strike by workers.

The 1982 PRC Constitution also states that citizens have the right and the duty to work. It commits the government to creating conditions for employment, improving working conditions, and providing vocational training to citizens before they are employed. This challenge is no small task. China's labor force, both in urban and rural areas, is characterized by an oversupply of unskilled labor and an undersupply of skilled and professional workers. Its size is staggering. China's workforce numbers over 450 million people and is larger than the entire population of every country except India. The Chinese leadership faces the formidable task of creating at least 16 million additional jobs a year to accommodate normal growth in the labor force. By 2000, it has been estimated that there will be 250 million excess workers in a country that has as yet no general unemployment benefits system and where, for ideological reasons, the mere recognition of unemployment is a sensitive issue. Part of the impetus behind the government's policy advocating the formation of collective and private enterprises was to create employment opportunities.

The concept of labor incentives is contained in Article 42 of the Constitution. Increased remuneration and social benefits are keyed to expanded production. Unlike some earlier periods in the development of the PRC, such as during the Great Leap Forward, the focus on increasing production also was accompanied by attempts to improve the quality of output. There is a clear programmatic goal in the Constitution that if labor as a whole cooperates with the tasks set before it by the State, then wages, conditions and benefits will gradually improve and the material conditions of life will become better. The other side of this goal is that if production does not improve, neither will conditions nor wages. Material incentives are stressed, but the characteristic Chinese use of moral persuasion also is present: "The state encourages citizens to take part in voluntary labor" and "promotes socialist labor emulation."

The 1982 Constitution includes provisions on labor insurance similar to those found in the 1978 Constitution. The 1982 version guarantees that citizens "have the right to material assistance from the state and society when they are old, ill, or disabled." The state is also constitutionally committed to developing "social insurance, social relief and medical and health services" as the means of enabling citizens to obtain this right.

The provisions on worker participation in management decision-making are outlined in Articles 16 and 17. Workers are given the right to elect and remove managerial personnel and to decide major issues concerning the operation and management of state and collective enterprises. These provisions are consistent with the responsibility system in domestic labor policy and principles of economic decentralization. In practice, there has been a clear departure from earlier patterns of labor-management relations in which managers were essentially dominated by the workers. Managers frequently failed to take any disciplinary action against lax labor practices out of fear of being criticized for "suppressing the masses." Today, there has been a return to a stricter system of managerial inspection of labor and enforcement of rules as a means to increase production. This system has been portrayed as one that will benefit managers as well as workers through increased earnings for both the enterprise and the individual.

ADDITIONAL LAWS AFFECTING LABOR

In addition to the Constitution, there are other important laws and regulations that affect labor in the PRC. Although China does not yet have a coordinated labor code, a substantial body of law dealing with labor administration exists, including the 1988 Labor Protection Law. Between 1949 and 1985, for example, the State Council and Ministry of Labor and Personnel (and its organizational predecessors) issued 1,629 regulations on labor and personnel matters, a figure that does not include regulations issued by local labor bureaus. One local labor bureau in the early 1970s, for example, issued regulations on the subject of wages and fringe benefits over 700 pages in length.

The development and implementation of labor laws governing foreign investment enterprises preceded the current labor law changes applicable to state-owned enterprises. In 1980, the State Council issued the Provisions on Labor Management in Sino–Foreign Joint Ventures, and in 1984 additional guidance was provided by more detailed regulations. Additional laws governing foreign investment enterprises were promulgated in 1986 and in the years following. The Chinese government sees these laws as contributing to the creation of a predictable economic climate crucial for attracting foreign investment.

In 1986, the State Council implemented a contract employment system in state-owned enterprises through a series of regulations, the most important being the Interim Regulations on the Implementation of Labor Contracts in State–Owned Enterprises (Labor Contract Provisions). The Labor Contract Provisions do not apply to collectives or foreign investment enterprises.

The Labor Contract Provisions mandate the use of contract employment and provide a variety of employment standards on such topics as termination, unemployment, and benefits. They also establish a three-step process for labor dispute resolution: consultation, arbitration, and final resort to the administrative tribunal within the local people's court. The guiding principle contained in the Provisions is the allocation of the labor force according to the economic forces of supply and demand. It differs significantly from the iron rice bowl policy which essentially guaranteed lifetime employment. Part of the reason for the change was the government's effort to cut the costs of subsidizing the wages of unnecessary workers in state enterprises.

Under the contract system, once an employment contract expires, either party can discontinue the employment relationship without penalty. During the term of the employment contract, the relationship also can be ended by an employer, but generally only on the payment of damages. The Labor Contract Provisions establish what appears to be the only mechanism to resolve a worker's breach of contract claim. If one side violates the labor contract and causes the other side economic losses, compensation should be paid according to the seriousness of the consequences. Because the terms "compensate" and "seriousness of the consequences" are subject to differing interpretations, their meanings cannot be conclusively determined until they are further defined by implementing procedures or practice.

According to recent reports, about 5 percent of the workers in all state-owned enterprises are employed under labor contracts. This relatively small percentage can be explained partially by the fact that the Labor Contract Provisions apply only to newly hired employees. Those individuals working under the old system that applied before the introduction of the contract system are guaranteed lifetime employment. At the present rate of introduction, it will take about thirty years before all workers in state enterprises are covered by the contract system.

Another provision of the Interim Regulations concerns unemployment relief, which is interesting because unemployment is not supposed to exist, at least theoretically, in communist countries. Article 25 states that a contract worker waiting for employment will receive "an unemployment relief allowance and a medical allowance according to state regulations." The state regulations referred to would appear to be the Interim Provisions Governing Unemployment Insurance for State Enterprise Employees, which also became effective in 1986.

LABOR INSURANCE BENEFITS

Closely tied to the labor laws are regulations dealing with labor insurance. The first labor insurance regulations were passed in 1951 and 1953. Like the 1950 Trade Union Law, which required management of state enterprises to provide building, staff and funding for the union of their factory, labor regulations provide that management must pay the full cost of labor insurance for state enterprise employees. The Labor Contract Provisions, which apply to contract workers, cover employee sickness, disability, and retirement. Article

20 specifies that a contract employee who becomes sick or disabled while on duty, or a pregnant employee, should be entitled to the same benefits as a regular employee. A contract employee who becomes sick or disabled while not on duty receives three to twelve months leave with pay and medical benefits. In addition, the employee receives a medical subsidy equal to three to six months wages of a regular worker if unable to return to work and the employment contract is terminated. The length of the employee's leave with pay and benefits, and presumably medical subsidy, is determined by length of service in the enterprise.

The Chinese government provides pensions for many workers, but not by means of a nationwide scheme like the U.S. Social Security system. Instead, each state-owned enterprise is responsible for providing a pension to its own employees. This system has created two different kinds of problems. First, older state-owned enterprises have many more retirees to support than those established more recently. In some of the older enterprises, one worker now has to cover the retirement fund for one and a half pensioners, while some new plants have next to no pensioners. Second, economic reforms in China prior to 1989 opened the way for the creation of many small-group enterprises (collectives) and private businesses. Many of these ventures are not financially able to set up their own pension systems. Some of these ventures purchase retirement plans from the state-owned People's Insurance Company. Nevertheless, some workers' livelihoods are not secure upon retirement. A draft of the 1986–1990 economic plan approved by the Communist Party calls for research and experimentation with different kinds of social security systems. Thus the solution to these problems may be some type of national social security system.

Under the current system, state enterprise workers are entitled to roughly 50 to 70 percent of their full-time wage scale when they retire. Pension eligibility is gender based. Men can retire at age sixty if they have worked both a total of twenty-five years and at least five years at the enterprise from which they retire. Women also have the five-year last enterprise requirement, but they are required to have worked only a total of twenty years and may retire as early as age fifty.

As with many other areas, the Labor Contract Provisions provide guidance on the direction of labor policy development. Article 26 of the Labor Contract Provisions establishes a pension system for retired employees. It uses contributions from both state enterprises and workers. The enterprise contributes "about 15 percent of the total amount of a contract worker's wages" into a pension fund on a monthly basis, while the contract employee's contribution "should not exceed three percent" of wages, deducted on a monthly basis. This provision presumably reflects a policy decision that pension plans are to be fully funded, so they do not cause payment problems for future generations, which, as noted above, is a problem with the current system.

Labor Insurance Regulations cover all employees of foreign investment, state-owned and other specified enterprises. Pursuant to the regulations, enterprises are responsible for providing benefits to employees who have been injured or disabled in the course of employment and to their beneficiaries in the event of death. Benefits are also provided to workers who are injured or disabled when they are "off duty," but the benefits are substantially lower than "on duty" benefits.

The right to compensatory benefits is not dependent on the finding of employer fault. In addition, contributory negligence and assumption of the risk are not defenses to a claim for benefits. Thus, even when an employee's injury is caused by his or her own lack of skill or care in carrying out assigned duties, compensation benefits are still available at levels prescribed in the regulations.

Management must provide for all the injured worker's expenses including hospital, and to and from transportation costs, as well as full pay during the time of the worker's incapacitation. Often the worker will be treated in a clinic operated by the factory where the injury occurred or in a hospital chosen by the enterprise. When a partial disability results from illness or job-related injury, the worker receives 10 to 30 percent of his or her previous wages. Where disability is total, the worker receives 75 percent of the former wage on a permanent basis.

The worker's enterprise is financially responsible for worker sickness, injury or disability even though it may occur outside the workplace. The total cost of treatment is borne by the enterprise, although the worker-patient is responsible for such items as special and expensive medicines and incidental travel expenses. For the first six months a worker is absent from work, the enterprise pays from 60 to 100 percent of the worker's wage. After that, the expense is borne by the labor insurance fund at the same operative rules. Dependents of the worker are also entitled to benefits under the labor insurance fund and the enterprise responsibility system. The cost for one-half of hospital expenses and ordinary medicines is paid for worker dependents.

Domestic economic reforms and foreign investment are the engines of reform for Chinese labor law. In many respects, the laws affecting labor, both domestic and foreign, are moving closer to the Western model. Nevertheless, the Chinese labor system is and probably will remain substantially different from the Western model. The Chinese leadership will have to contend with increasing numbers of unemployed and workers' concerns about actual and potential job security. These are the types of issues that the government needs to address in order to prevent them from contributing to the growing dissatisfaction, especially by the urban population, toward the CCP and Chinese government.

TRADE UNIONS

Chinese trade unions are considered to be the "representatives of the working class." Yet, the role and function of Chinese trade unions is radically different from trade unions found within the United States. The difference is primarily attributable to the special relationship between the unions and the government. The Trade Union Law requires unions to "defend the laws and orders of the People's Government and promote and implement the policies of the People's Government in order to strengthen the people's authority under the leadership of the working class." In such a role, it is difficult for unions to have an identity separate and apart from the government. Rather, the tendency exists for Chinese trade unions to simply become instruments of the State.

The Trade Union Law, which was adopted in 1950, gives legal status, organization and responsibility to trade unions in the PRC. The right to organize trade unions is held by all wage-earners, which includes almost all working people. Party control of trade unions was established early in the Chinese labor movement. Trade union activities came under heavy attack and suppression, first during the Great Leap Forward (1958–1960) and again during the Cultural Revolution (1966–1976). Twenty years elapsed between the Eighth Trade

Union Congress (1958) and the Ninth National Trade Union Congress (1978). During the 1978 Congress, the All China Federation of Trade Unions (ACFTU) formally reactivated trade union organizations in the PRC. The ACFTU, which has quasi-legislative power, heads the trade unions of the PRC and local trade unions report to it. At the 1978 Congress, Deng Xiaoping enunciated a policy of greater trade union support for worker welfare and participation in enterprise management within the context of the policies, regulations and laws of the State.

Under Article 7 of the Trade Union Law, the duties of the trade union fall in three main categories: protection of wages, benefits and welfare of members; education of workers to carry out government policies; and the inculcation of labor discipline to meet state promulgated production plans. In the post-Mao era, the first of these aims has been stressed, though not to the exclusion of the other two. The return in 1989 to more orthodox communist principles is likely to shift this emphasis.

Trade unions operate at the national, regional and enterprise levels. Since the late 1970s, trade unions have been organized into trade union committees, called trade union congresses. These committees or congresses exist at various levels of each enterprise—interindustry, city, workshop, management and factory. The congresses, which have existed for several decades in various forms, are an institutional system for worker participation. They are usually staffed by a number of full-time union officials recruited from the ranks of the workers. The trade union congresses have a distinctive organizational identity and are primarily accountable to the employees or workers. As such, they are the principal mechanisms through which employees can make their views known to management.

In theory, workers have the right to dismiss members of the trade union congress with whom they are displeased. The trade union congress must submit work reports to the union membership and has the right to make demands on management, such as requiring reports, participating on work committees and inspecting work places. Trade unions must be consulted when management seeks to terminate an employee, and management is not allowed to interfere with their functions. The overall impact of trade union congresses is somewhat benign and their effectiveness tends to vary from state enterprise to state enterprise.

Trade unions act as a link between the state and the working masses. As previously noted, collective bargaining between labor and management as it is known in the U.S. does not exist in China. Trade union professionals are state appointees. There is no such thing as representative elections or an administrative agency like the National Labor Relations Board (NLRB) to render decisions pertaining to elections or other labor-management disputes. Labor itself, through its trade union, has no independent power and any power or input by trade union officials upon management decisions is state imposed and state regulated.

Beginning in the 1970s the PRC began to experiment with self-management in industrial enterprises. This trend, giving greater authority to general managers, continued into the 1980s. In 1984 it culminated with a call by the Central Committee for a widespread opening up of the Chinese economy by the use of local on-site planning instead of centralized development, labor incentives through wage increases and greater profits, and a greater acceptance of the role of market forces. Even with self-management, the revitalization of bonus award incentives and piece-work pay, the central government and its ideological and policy priorities still rule in China. However, the economic reforms of the Chinese economy have brought unions greater independence from government and Party supervision.

Material incentives for labor have followed the rise and fall and rise again of the trade unions. Such incentives were present in China from the beginning of the PRC in 1949 in an attempt to put the infant State on its feet. But material incentives were reduced or all but eliminated during the Great Leap Forward and again during the Cultural Revolution in favor of such abstractions as moral rewards and the selfless new socialist citizen.

With the leadership of Deng Xiaoping, worker incentives in the form of bonuses, wage increases, better housing and profits were reintroduced. However, whether the amount of government support for them will continue at current levels is somewhat in doubt.

CHAPTER VIII

CONTRACT AND TORT

The current Chinese conception of contractual obligations reflects socialist ideas, but at a more fundamental level, the conception is the product of historical evolution over the millennia. During the Han period (206 B.C.–220 A.D.), written contracts acquired both legal and moral significance. Contract enforcement was conceptualized in terms of upholding the general moral obligation of truthfulness and of depriving dishonest persons of ill-gotten gains. Contractual obligations were part of an undifferentiated moral sense of Confucian values, and thus no separate body of contract theory existed. During the millennia following the Han period, the concepts and precedents from this period played a continuing role. Thus, the legacy of Han contract practices can be seen in the format of Chinese contracts appearing in the late nineteenth century.

Documents from the Han period are revealing. Most of the contracts contain detailed subject-matter descriptions, indicating that contracts were used for a variety of purposes. The contracts collected from different locations show a consistency in format, suggesting a common body of contract custom or law. They included the names of the parties, their places of residence, and their legal or social status. Contracts were dated and witnessed by those who "have knowledge of the contents of the contract document."

The general absence of references to contracts in the imperial codes suggests that contract matters were left principally to the realm of custom. Nevertheless, there is evidence demonstrating that contracts were enforced by state judicial officials following the collapse of the Qin Dynasty (207 B.C.). For transactions that affected taxable items, the parties were required to use a broker who would draft the contract, collect the applicable tax and remit it to the state, and record the transaction.

Traditionally, socialist law distinguishes between "civil law" and "economic law." Civil law regulates the non-state-related areas of economic activity, such as agreements between private individuals and succession to family property. Economic law governs relationships between the state and other parties and the relationships between state enterprises.

The PRC follows the general socialist distinction between civil law and economic law. The latter regulates the relationships arising from the management of the national economy and the economic activities of socialist organizations. Economic contracts are made primarily between socialist organizations, such as the plants and enterprises managed under the system of ownership by the people and the system of collective ownership. In contrast, the civil law regulates primarily the rights and responsibilities which emerge among citizens as individuals in the course of their civil activities. The economic law relationships are collective, planned and hierarchical, whereas civil law relations are individualistic, unplanned and horizontal. Included within the province of civil law, under the rubric "Obligations Arising From Acts that Infringe on Rights [Delicts]," is the law of torts. This chapter is devoted to an examination of both the law of contracts and torts.

The 1982 Constitution declares: "The basis of the socialist economic system of the People's Republic of China is socialist public ownership of the means of production...." The state, as the leading force in the national economy, is directly involved in the administration and operation of commercial and industrial enterprises. In addition to the "public" sector of the economy, there is a "private" sector. The Constitution provides that "the state protects the lawful rights and interests of the individual economy" as a complement to the socialist public economy. The overall objective of the legislation and regulations implementing these constitutional declarations has been to create a mixed economy in which market mechanisms function side-by-side with a sector directly controlled by state planning.

CONTRACT LAW

Under the responsibility system found in the agricultural sector of the Chinese economy, individual farmers or farm families contract with the state or collective. Although state quotas of specified commodities must be met, there is substantial freedom to use the land and to dispose of its produce. The individual responsibility system has been extended to the industrial and commercial sectors of the economy, but many of the ideological and practical details have not yet been worked out. Nevertheless, the conceptual framework for managing the Chinese system of independent entities is "obligation" law. As Professor William Jones has observed: "Once the decisionmaking function is shifted from the planning authority to the individual entity, the basic legal device will be a contract, not an order. When a tire factory needs rubber, it has to arrange to buy it from the best available source. It does not get a directive to the rubber factory that it has been designated to supply this particular need." Jones, "Sources of Chinese Obligation Law," 52 *Law and Contemporary Problems* 69, 73 (1989).

The Chinese statutory law on contracts is found in the 1986 Civil Law, the 1982 Law of Economic Contracts (LEC), and various other statutes and regulations. In a formal sense, this makes the task of ascertaining the law difficult, a matter that is complicated by the fact that the Civil Law provisions on contract law are admittedly incomplete.

The task is further complicated because the law is composed of two somewhat inconsistent theoretical approaches. On the one hand, the Law of Economic Contracts is based on the concept that the parties can only enter into contracts that are directed or permitted by the state. On the other hand, the Civil Law provisions are generally based on the concept of freedom of contract and private autonomy, notwithstanding numerous references to the primacy of socialist or public ownership.

THE LAW OF ECONOMIC CONTRACTS

At the theoretical level, Chinese scholars disagree on whether economic contract law is within the scope of economic law or civil law. Those who contend that contract law is part of the civil law base their argument on the proposition that contract law cannot operate without the assistance of such basic civil law concepts as competence, legal persons and agencies, which are civil law concepts. Those who oppose this view stress the fact that economic contract law is primarily a legal instrument to carry out state plans. This debate is relevant as a legislative-process matter in order to avoid conflicts and duplication. It is also relevant in determining whether an economic tribunal or a civil tribunal has jurisdiction over a disputed matter. The people's courts typically allow their economic rather than civil divisions to exercise jurisdiction over foreign economic contracts, and thus at least in this context the matter has been resolved. As a practical matter, whether a statute or regulation is treated as an economic law or civil law should not affect its application.

The Law of Economic Contracts (LEC), which applies to contractual relations among domestic enterprises, is the most important law affecting this type of contract. More than 90 percent of China's industrial capacity, for example, is governed by the LEC. The organizational arrangement of the Law, which became effective on July 1, 1982, is reminiscent of the German-style code. After setting out certain general principles, contracts are then divided into various types of business-related agreements, such as sales, leases, contracts for the use and supply of electricity, and so on.

The LEC is primarily designed to regulate contracts between "legal entities". The term "legal entity" generally refers to one of five Chinese entities: (1) an organization with independent autonomy, separately owned assets, a budget, and the capacity to engage in economic activities; (2) agricultural bodies; (3) government departments; (4) business units; and (5) social organizations. Thus, the LEC regulates the economic contract relations between such state entities as enterprises, state organs, institutions, and social organizations. To a large extent, the LEC is a tool used to carry out the state plan. Although the Law of Economic Contracts primarily regulates contracts between state enterprises, it also covers contracts between private individuals and legal entities. Contract relations between individual households on the one hand and legal entities on the other hand are subject to its provisions. Since 1982, the LEC has been supplemented by numerous regulations governing specific contract areas.

In 1985, the National People's Congress promulgated the Foreign Economic Contract Law. It governs contracts between Chinese enterprises or businesses and foreign businesses or individuals, but does not apply to international transport contracts because of their unique characteristics. With this exception, virtually all contractual transactions between foreign and Chinese entities are affected by the Foreign Economic Contract Law.

Because China does not accord binding precedential value to judicial decisions, the general principles stated in the Law of Economic Contracts are important to understanding both it and the Foreign Economic Contract Law. Three general principles are common to both these laws: (1) the principle of equality and mutual benefit; (2) the principle of achieving unanimity through consultations; and (3) the principle that contracts are to be made in accordance with Chinese law. The Economic Contract Law also includes the principle of "equal rewards." Parity is required in contracts formed between domestic enterprises subject to the law. This principle of "equal rewards" or parity is distinct from the common law concept of consideration or a bargained-for change in legal position. A guiding principle applicable only to the Foreign

Economic Contract Law is that of following international trade practices.

The stated purpose of the LEC is to protect the legitimate rights and interests of the parties concerned in economic contracts, maintain social and economic order, attain better economic results, ensure the fulfillment of state plans and promote the development of modernization. An economic contract is defined as an agreement between legal persons specifying their rights and obligations under the agreement in order to achieve a given economic objective. Although the LEC does not further define what constitutes an economic objective, any activity that involves monetary or commercial matters presumably satisfies this requirement.

The Law of Economic Contracts contains the requirements concerning contract formation and the consequences of breach. An economic contract must be in writing, unless it can be immediately performed. The LEC does not explicitly authorize the use of oral contracts, but they are implicitly recognized and are given the same legal effect if they can be immediately performed.

The LEC does not provide express rules on offer and acceptance. The Law of Economic Contracts provides: "An economic contract is made when both parties reach agreement through consultation on the principal clauses of the contract." This provision has been interpreted in *Principles of Civil Law Jurisprudence,* a textbook on Chinese contract law, as establishing the requirement of offer and acceptance.

The principal terms of the contract "offer" must include the subject matter, the quantity and quality, the price or compensation, the time, place and manner of performance, responsibility for breach, and other provisions that the law requires or become necessary because of the nature of the transaction. According to Henry Zheng, a scholar on Chinese law, "if a contract fails to contain these major provisions, the court is likely to apply the rules of interpretation in the Civil Code and the established business practice to supplement these provisions and enforce them." H. Zheng, *China's Civil and Commercial Law* 71 (1988). Thus, the courts have considerable latitude to complete the open terms of certain contracts.

Two requirements exist for a valid "acceptance" of an economic contract. First, the offeree must unconditionally accept the terms of the offer. Second, the acceptance must be communicated to the offeror within the time period stated in the offer. Modification of the contract offer by the offeree will turn the acceptance into a new or counter offer. The counter offer would have to be accepted by the original offeror before the economic contract would be formed.

In addition to these general requirements of "offer" and "acceptance," an economic contract must generally conform to state policies and mandatory plan requirements before it is legally effective.

Thus, contract provisions governing product quality, quantity, and price must meet existing state plans and standards. If the contract does not meet state policies and mandatory plan requirements, it is deemed void *ab initio.* The many statutes dealing with price controls, both national and local, that are supported by severe penalties for the crime of "speculation" constitute perhaps the most significant limitation on freedom of contract.

The common-law concepts of unjust enrichment and restitutionary damages are not expressed in Chinese contract law. Nevertheless, the LEC does provide a similar remedy. Property that has been acquired under a void contract should be returned, which is restitutionary in nature. The law also imposes liability on a party whose fault causes the contract to become void.

The formal rules governing breach of contract differ rather strikingly from their common law counterparts. The LEC considers fault as an essential factor in determining liability for breach, whereas the common law generally is not concerned with fault. Under Chinese law, a party is at fault when the breach occurs either intentionally or from negligence. Chinese contract theory does not include the concept of anticipatory repudiation.

The general approach to remedies also has distinguishable features. A breaching party may be subject to administrative or criminal penalties. If major accidents or serious losses occur as a result of wrongdoing, or illicit contracts are entered into, criminal responsibility may be imposed. The LEC divides damages into two categories: liquidated damages and compensatory damages. Liquidated damages, which should be specified in the contract, are payable on breach irrespective of whether there is an actual loss. Compensatory damages are payable when the liquidated damages are not sufficient to compensate the actual loss suffered by the non-breaching party.

The common law of contract remedies ordinarily allow a breaching party to pay money damages equal to the value of performance. In contrast, Chinese contract law is based on the principle that the payment of damages does not release the breaching party from the obligation to perform. Thus, if a nonbreaching party demands fulfillment of the contract, performance should be continued and the payment of a penalty cannot be a substitute for specific performance. This provision is calculated to ensure implementation of state plans. Because large numbers of economic contracts in China are signed according to state plans, failure to fully perform such contracts would adversely affect the realization of state goals. Since most economic contracts are entered into pursuant to state policies and plans, liability rules are generally designed to prevent nonperformance.

Specific performance is one of the fundamental characteristics of Chinese contract law. Whenever the nonbreaching party demands specific performance, the demand must be satisfied unless the circumstances clearly indicate that performance has become impossible or unnecessary. The breaching party's obligation to specifically perform is not obviated by the payment of damages or penalties.

The general preference for specific performance, rather than damages, finds its roots in Confucian philosophy and the concept of *li.* It is the preferred remedy under socialist contract principles for a number of reasons. First, purchasing substitute goods with a damages award is not generally possible in China because the planned "market" is characterized by chronic shortages and sellers' market conditions. The remedy of cover for breach of contract, which is widely applied in the United States through the Uniform Commercial Code, is not available in China. Thus, substitution is not a practical alternative. Second, no reliable mechanism exists for measuring money damages. The prices set by the central authorities are not a reliable way of valuing the goods or services. The formidable task of both calculating and then proving damages makes the preference for specific performance understandable. Finally, economic contracts are often used to implement state planning policies, and specific performance is essential to carry out those policies.

Breach of contract occurs upon unilateral termination, alteration of contract terms, or failure to perform either in whole or in part. The responsibility for breaching a contract is borne by the breaching party. The obligation to make penalty payments is an important part of the regime designed to insure contract performance. There are several aspects of penalty payments that are noteworthy. The obligation is similar to the American concept of punitive damages insofar as a penalty is exacted. However, the penalty payment provisions are dissimilar in that application of the obligation to pay is not subject to judicial discretion. Rather, they are governed by special regulations. In addition, the non-breaching party is entitled to a penalty payment as a matter of right, irrespective of the breaching party's state of mind or intent.

The Economic Contract Law has extensive provisions on the remedies available for breaching various kinds of economic contracts. Generally, remedies for breach of economic contracts include, compensation for the loss, penalties as specified by the contract or by law such as fines for illegal contracts, and specific performance. When a breach does not result in any loss, the breaching party still must pay the prescribed penalty. When the breach causes a loss which is less than the prescribed penalty, the penalty must be paid, rather than compensatory damages. However, if the loss exceeds the penalty, the breaching party must pay compensatory damages within ten days after quantum of breach is determined.

The LEC imposes economic penalties when deposits are used to guarantee performance. A deposit often conceptually functions as a down payment or partial payment for a fully performed contract. When a contract is breached, the deposit may be used as a penalty to punish the breach. A breaching party who has made a deposit is not entitled to return of the deposit. It is forfeited. If the deposit-receiver breaches the contract, the receiver must return twice the amount of the deposit. Thus, a nonbreaching buyer is entitled to a repayment of the deposit plus an equal amount. In both instances, a penalty is imposed on the breaching party.

Changes in state economic policy and the state economic plan create special problems. One problem that arises is whether a contract that violates economic policy or the state economic plan at the time of signing is enforceable. For transactions between Chinese domestic enterprises, the LEC provides that such a contract is null and void. A related problem is whether a fully or partially executed contract may be affected by a subsequent change in a state plan or policy. In contracts between Chinese enterprises, the contract may be amended or terminated, but such amendment or termination must be reported to the relevant business department handing down the plan for prior approval.

Force majeure is a separate ground permitting the amendment or termination of an economic contract. It is defined as an "event which is caused by forces outside of the control of the parties and could not be avoided by exercise of due care, such as natural disasters, earthquake, war." While natural disasters are included within the concept of *force majeure,* it is not clear whether the term would be broadly read to include more sensitive events, such as civil insurrection, strikes, slowdowns or other labor disturbances. The LEC does not treat a revision or cancellation of the state plan as a case of *force majeure.*

A variety of nonjudicial means are available to the parties to settle disputes involving economic contracts. Such disputes are not normally enforced through the courts. The Economic Contract Law provides: "If disputes over an economic contract arise, the parties concerned shall promptly resolve them through consultation. If consultation is not successful, any party may apply to the contract administration authorities specified by the State for mediation or arbitration, and it may also directly bring a lawsuit in the people's courts." In 1980, the economic divisions of the people's courts, which have jurisdiction over such disputes, handled a total of 4,400 cases. More than 4,300 of the cases were eventually resolved through judicial mediation, the rest by court order.

THE GENERAL PROVISIONS OF CIVIL LAW

Prior to the adoption of the General Provisions of Civil Law (Civil Law), which became effective on January 1, 1987, no statute existed that regulated the contractual relations between individuals. The absence of a statutory body of law is understandable because private transactions between citizens in the PRC were limited by the socialist nature of the economy. Consequently, the need for contract law and associated contract norms as a means of settling disputes between private citizens did not exist. Increased private ownership and market privatization have changed this phenomenon, however.

The Civil Law is not a complete or comprehensive code. In the civil law tradition, it would be classified as a "General Part" because it lacks the special parts normally found in a civil code that deal with specific situations. For example, in order to resolve a warranty issue associated with the sale of goods, one has to look to the general principles for guidance. At one level, this may not be particularly helpful since those principles are general in nature and admittedly incomplete. At another level, the adoption of the general principle can be regarded as a confirmation of China's adherence to the principles of continental European law, rather than the common law tradition. In a narrower sense, it gives Chinese economic law a conceptual basis that it had previously lacked.

The approach of adopting only general principles was not an oversight. When the Civil Law was introduced to the National People's Congress, it had been decided to adopt the Civil Law in stages rather than as a comprehensive code. It was anticipated that the detail normally found in special parts of a civil code would be added later. This pattern of beginning with general principles and adding elaborative detail only after some experimentation and experience with implementing the law is characteristic of the general process of policy formulation in China. In this way, the Chinese leadership believes it can be responsive to concerns raised by those affected by the new law. At some point, it is anticipated that a comprehensive Civil Code will be adopted.

The General Principles of the Civil Law are intended to be supplemented. The Supreme People's Court Judicial Committee significantly augmented the existing general principles in a lengthy opinion issued in 1988. One important statute that supplements the Civil Law is the Economic Contract Law, which preceded the adoption of the Civil Law. Thus, in a formal sense the General Principles operate in conjunction with the Economic Contract Law and the various regulations that affect economic contracts.

The Civil Law permits two types of private economic endeavors: the private industrial and commercial household and the rural contractual household business. The former are small-scale activities, administratively licensed to operate in both the rural and urban sectors of the economy, that provide goods and services outside of state planning directives. They can be operated on an individual, household or cooperative basis, and they have legal rights to their "means of production." Rural contractual household businesses engage in agricultural production on collectively-owned land pursuant to contracts with collective economic entities. These production responsibility contracts for land do not confer ownership of the land, but rather create rights (and obligations to the collective) in using the land and gaining income from it. The predominant legal framework for this production responsibility system, notwithstanding the existence of numerous regulations, is contractual, not statutory. The contractual right to exploit the land for a fixed term of years may be transferred by inheritance, but clearly falls short of being ownership of the land.

The Civil Law does not contain a separate chapter that deals with contract law. Rather, the Civil Law furnishes rules for situations not covered by separate contract statutes and provides general guidelines for coordinating the application of these other statutes. Contract law principles are generally interspersed throughout it. The one exception is Section 2 of Chapter VI dealing with civil liability for breach of contract.

The failure to segregate the various provisions dealing with contract law, combined with the absence of an index, makes the Civil Law difficult to use. Moreover, the Civil Law is not integrated with the other laws, statutes, and regulations dealing with contract law. The need to coordinate among the various laws affecting contracts creates difficulties. Thus, for example, the Civil Law provides that written or oral contracts between citizens are valid. In contrast, the Economic Contract Law generally requires a writing, whereas the Foreign Economic Contract Law always requires a writing.

The Civil Law defines a civil legal act as the lawful act of a citizen or legal person to establish, change or terminate civil rights and obligations. Henry Zheng's analysis of civil legal acts and their relation to contract law clarifies the matter:

> A unilateral (civil) legal act is the (civil) legal act that can be established through the expression of mind by one party. These legal acts are legally binding without the need of consent by the other party. Execution of wills, renunciation of inheritance rights, revocation of appointment of an agent, ratification of the acts of an unauthorized agent, etc., all fall within this category. Bilateral (civil) legal acts are (civil) legal acts which become legally binding only upon the meeting of minds by both parties. Bilateral (civil) legal acts are also called contractual acts. Contractual acts include: (1) both parties pursuing an identical objective, such as acts to form a partnership or joint venture with common goal; (2) both parties not pursuing an identical objective. For instance, under a sales contract, the seller seeks payment, the buyer seeks the goods. Contractual acts represent a majority of (civil) legal acts and in importance far outweigh unilateral (civil)

legal acts. H. Zheng, *China's Civil and Commercial Law* 81 (1988).

The Civil Law contains the basic provisions for a valid contract. The requirements for a valid legal act or contract include: (1) capacity or competence; (2) expression of genuine intent; and (3) consistency with law and public interest. In the area of contract formation, the principle of the exchange of equal values is the Chinese Civil Law equivalent of the common-law concept of consideration. Conditional civil legal acts, which create obligations when the conditions occur, are permitted and correspond to the common law concept of condition precedents. As a general matter, contracts may be in writing or oral, unless the law provides otherwise.

Certain types of civil acts are declared null and void. They include civil acts by those without capacity for civil conduct; civil acts executed under duress or fraud; and civil acts executed in malicious collusion to infringe the interest of the state, of a collective or of a third person. Contracts in conflict with mandatory state plans and civil acts disguised in a legal form to achieve an illegitimate purpose are also invalid.

Voidable contracts include those that are obviously unfair and those made by persons having a significant misconception as to the contract's content. The Civil Law provisions are similar to the common-law rules on unconscionability and mistake as grounds for rescission of contracts. The court or "the arbitration agency" has the power to modify or rescind such contracts. The 1988 opinion of the Supreme People's Court provided significant detail on the subject of void and voidable contracts and provided authoritative definitions of wrongful acts which nullify civil obligations under Chinese law. These definitions include the basic elements for a *prima facie* case for each of the identified wrongful acts.

Under common-law principles, a material mutual mistake prevents the formation of a contract. Unilateral mistakes, which are more common than the mutual mistake situation, do not prevent formation of an executory contract. Unilateral mistakes may constitute a defense when the party not making the mistake was or should have been aware of the mistake. The Chinese have taken a different approach to the problem of unilateral mistake. According to the 1988 opinion of the Supreme People's Court, it is not necessary to show that the other party knew or should have known of the mistake. All that is required is that the misunderstanding conflict with his or her own intention and that the misunderstanding result in a major loss. The misunderstanding can be with respect to the other party, the subject matter of the contract, quality, specifications or quantity.

Under Chinese law, when a contract contains ambiguous terms regarding quality, place of performance, or price, and the meaning cannot be determined from the context of the contract, the following four principles apply if party consultation does not result in an agreement. First, if quality requirements are unclear, state quality standards shall apply; if there are no state quality standards, generally held standards shall apply. The reference to "generally held standards" appears conceptually similar to the American Uniform Commercial Code's provisions on implied warranties of fitness and merchantability. Second, if the time limit for performance is unclear, the debtor may at his or her convenience fulfill the obligations towards the creditor; the creditor may also demand at any time that the debtor perform those obligations, but sufficient notice shall be given to the debtor. Third, if the place of performance is unclear, and the payment is money, the performance shall be effected at the seat or place of residence of the party receiving the payment; if the payment is other than money, the performance shall be effected at the seat or place of residence of the party fulfilling the obligations. Finally, if the price agreed by the parties is unclear, the state-fixed price shall apply. If there is no state-fixed price, the price shall be based on market price or the price of a similar article or remuneration for a similar service.

The Civil Law covers the use of deposits to assure contract performance. If the depositor fails to meet the terms of the contract, the other party may retain the deposit. If the party accepting the deposit defaults, the deposit is required to be repaid in double. Similar provisions on the posting of deposits can be found in both the Economic Contract Law (Article 14) and the Foreign Economic Contract Law (Article 20).

The Civil Law specifies the consequences relating to breach of contract. A nondefaulting party to a contract is entitled to demand specific performance or take remedial measures and also to claim compensation for losses suffered. In a 1989 case involving a restaurant that failed to provide satisfactory services for a wedding reception, the court ordered the restaurant to return the entire price paid by the plaintiff: "failure to provide satisfactory food defeated the purpose of the entire reception." Although the court did not employ the doctrine of consideration in its analysis, the basic idea that the plaintiff effectively had received nothing of value justified the return of the contract price on the theory that there was no exchange of equal value. Liability for compensatory damages is limited to the actual loss suffered.

Parties are permitted to agree in advance on the contract damages and penalties in the event of breach. When the penalties (*weiyujin*) exceed the loss or when no loss occurs, the party in breach shall pay the penalties in accordance with the contractual provisions. When the penalties are not enough to compensate for the loss, the party in breach is required to make up the deficit. This approach is apparently different from Article 20 of the Foreign Economic Contract Law, which allows the parties to petition the courts or arbitrators to make adjustment if the penalties (*weiyujin*) far exceed or are far less than the damages.

Finally, the injured party is under an obligation to mitigate the loss. The provisions on liability for breach incorporate the concept of mitigation of damages. As would be expected, the principle of mitigation requires timely or prompt action by the party suffering the loss. The failure to mitigate damages forecloses a party's right to claim compensation for any additional losses resulting from the failure.

The economic problems surfacing in the summer of 1988 and the political decision to suppress the Democracy Movement in 1989 did not bode well for the development and refinement of the Civil Law provisions dealing with private contracts, at least in the short run. The reform of China's economy, which was partially blamed for the economic and political instability, was one of the forces that led to the adoption of the Civil Law. The movement toward a freer economy where quasi-private companies were to provide economic dynamism was reversed in mid 1989 in favor of greater centralized planning. In early 1992, reports from China suggest that future economic reforms relating either to the continuation of centralization or possibly a return to more decentralization are under consideration. However, extensive privatization of the economy is not likely to be advocated in the near term. As a result, there will be a more limited role for private contracts in the Chinese economy.

The Law of Economic Contracts is likely to be increasingly important since it is predicated largely on planned economic principles.

In addition to the difficulties of predicting the consequences of political decisions as they pertain to the economy, determining the real impact of the LEC on domestic practices is also difficult, and perhaps impossible. Attempting to assess the actual operation and impact of the Civil Law is similarly problematic. In 1989, Professor William Jones observed that "it is impossible to know exactly what is, in fact, going on in China in connection with the formation and performance of economic contracts. No Westerner is in a position to make a study of actual practice, and the Chinese do not seem to be very interested in law-in-action studies." Jones, "Sources of Chinese Obligation Law," 52 *Law and Contemporary Problems* 69, 86 (1989). Unfortunately, scholars studying China are in large measure left with analyzing the letter of contract law, rather than the law in operation.

TORT LAW

The origins of China's tort law can be traced back to the Qin Dynasty (221–207 B.C.). Two features of the ancient Chinese tort law are especially noteworthy. First, the rules defining liability were narrowly categorized. No general principles were established concerning liability, and thus no regularized system of liability developed. Second, tort liability was generally conceptualized as an adjunct to criminal proceedings. The laws were designed primarily to protect the interests of society. As a result, torts—such as those involving personal injury—were considered crimes. The right to damages or compensation, if any, was recognized only after the criminal proceeding.

The ancient pattern of establishing narrow rules on a wide range of subjects concerning compensation for tort damages was continued when the PRC was founded. Moreover, until recently, there was no single act or code that delineated the liabilities associated with tortious conduct. Thus, the law of torts could be found in customary law and various selected statutes, such as the Patent Law and the Environmental Protection Law. Scattered and rudimentary bases of tort law were swept aside during the Cultural Revolution, and as a practical matter the system of Chinese tort law ceased to exist during this ten year period.

The 1982 Constitution contains an outline of basic rights and freedoms. Nevertheless, these rights are worded broadly and accord little by way of concrete legal protection. In 1987, the Civil Law was adopted. Chapter VI of the Civil Law is subdivided into General Provisions, Civil Liability for Breach of Contract, Civil Liability for Torts, and Forms of Civil Liability. Among other things, the Civil Law clarified and systematized the principles of civil liability for torts. By American standards, the provisions on tort law contained in the Civil Law are not very extensive. As a result, substantial room for refinement and development exists. Given its relatively recent adoption, modifications and improvements in this area are likely in the future.

THEORIES OF LIABILITY

The theory of liability under Chinese tort law is similar, but not identical, to that found in the United States. Chinese tort law is essentially fault-based, notwithstanding the existence of some applications of strict liability. Damage awards are far more limited than in the United States. In general terms, a tortious act under the Chinese Civil Law is an act or omission that unlawfully invades the property right or person of another. The act must be unlawful. To be unlawful, it must invade an individual's rights that are given or approved of by the Constitution, other laws or social values. If the conduct is lawful, no liability exists notwithstanding the fact that injury may occur.

Unlike the ancient system of tort law, civil liability for tortious conduct under the Civil Law is conceptualized as being independent of criminal liability or administrative sanctions. Thus, for example, a driver of an automobile who hits and injures a pedestrian today may be charged either with a crime, or subject to administrative sanctions, such as revocation of his or her driver's license, or be liable in tort.

The Civil Law provides two types of tort liability, one based on fault and the other on strict liability independent of fault. The Law provides the fault based condition for liability in the following terms: "Citizens and legal persons who through their fault encroach upon state or collective property or the property or person of other people shall bear civil liability." Unlawful conduct can create liability as long as the actor caused the damage to occur. The law requires a causal connection between the tortious conduct and the damage suffered. For example, in one recent case, the plaintiff's husband was riding a bicycle that had no brakes. He collided with the defendant who was bicycling in the opposite direction. Following the accident, a quarrel ensued, during which the husband fainted and fell to the ground. He was rushed to the hospital, where he then died. The court held that the plaintiff's husband died as a result of a cerebral hemorrhage. The plaintiff's claim for damages was denied because there was no causal connection between his death and either the collision or quarrel.

In addition to causing the injury, the actor must also be at fault. The term "fault" requires a determination of a person's state of mind. Although the Civil Law does not define fault, it seems clear that tort liability under general principles of Chinese jurisprudence may be based on either intentional conduct or negligent behavior. An individual can be liable for intentional conduct if he or she knows that the conduct might cause injury to another and the actor either expects the injury or takes a reckless attitude towards the injurious result. Liability for negligence exists when the actor fails to foresee the injurious consequences—which should or could have been foreseen—or when the actor foresees the consequences, but does not think they will occur.

The provision on strict liability states: "Civil liability shall still be borne even in the absence of fault, if the law so stipulates." There are several articles in the Civil Law that reference "no fault" liability, including situations involving product liability, environmental pollution, and dangerous activities. The Law does not clearly indicate all the circumstances under which the principles of strict liability or liability without fault apply, however.

"No fault" liability was recognized by the Supreme People's Court in 1988 for individual injuries suffered while safeguarding the legitimate rights of the State, a collective or another party and when there is either no tortfeasor or the tortfeasor is unable to pay compensation. Under these circumstances the injured party may receive compensation from the person or entity whose interests were protected. Liability without fault has been imposed in other instances too. For example, those who engage in extra hazardous activities (which include "work involving high pressure, flammables, explosives, strong poisons, radioactive substances, or high speed transportation vehicles"), those who violate environmental protection legislation, and those who furnish substandard products have been held liable regardless of fault.

The Civil Law fails to define substandard product. Presumably, a plaintiff would have to show a defect that rendered the product dangerous, injury, and a causal connection in order to establish strict liability for a substandard product. Under a recent Supreme People's Court interpretation of the Civil Law, the potential class of plaintiffs includes consumers, users and third parties injured by the substandard product. Some Chinese jurists have argued that imposing strict liability on domestic producers at China's present state of economic development is likely to adversely affect future economic growth. Notwithstanding this argument, the law imposes strict liability.

The relative liabilities of manufacturers and sellers for defective products are covered in the Liability for the Quality of Industrial Products Regulations. They provide that a seller has the duty to verify the quality of products and to compensate for damage caused by them. They also provide that a manufacturer is liable to both the seller and the end user for economic losses caused by substandard products.

There are administrative mechanisms for dealing with substandard products that exist outside the Civil Law. The State Council has granted administrative organs the power to handle disputes about product quality. Given the traditional reluctance on the part of the Chinese to use the courts to resolve their disputes, these administrative mechanisms are likely to play an important practical role in settling disputes concerning product quality.

Because of China's interest in increased foreign trade, the potential application of strict liability rules to foreigners is of special concern. The Civil Law applies to foreigners, except as otherwise stipulated by law. Consequently, if an American substandard product is sold or used in China causing injury and liability is established, a judgment is likely to follow. The statute of limitations is one year from the date when the injured party knew or should have known of the injury if there is physical injury, otherwise it is generally two years, but this can be extended by the court when special circumstances exist.

The Civil Law expressly imposes liability on those persons who infringe upon the following: rights of authorship (copyright), patent rights, rights to exclusive use of trademarks, rights of discovery, rights of invention or rights for scientific and technical research. In any such case, the available remedy includes the right to demand that the infringement stop, its effects be eliminated, and damages be paid.

The Civil Law addresses the joint liability of tortfeasors. If an infringement of an individual's rights occurs as a result of the actions of more than one person, joint and several liability is imposed under Article 130. Thus, if one tortfeasor is unable to pay his or her share of the damages, the plaintiff may recover the entire amount from the other tortfeasor and the solvent tortfeasor bears the burden of the entire judgment. In a recent strict liability case involving a defective refrigerator, the seller of the defective product was held solely liable to the purchaser under the Civil Law provisions on several liability. The manufacturer of the product was not named as a defendant. Had the manufacturer been named, it would have also have been liable under the principle of joint liability, and damages would have been apportioned according to the degree of their respective fault.

If a person without capacity or with a limited capacity causes the injury, his or her guardian is legally responsible. Thus, if a ward causes damage to another, the guardian is liable for the damage. This civil liability may be reduced, however, if the guardian has done his or her duty under the guardianship.

Chinese tort law rejects the doctrine of contributory negligence as an absolute bar to recovery. Rather, Chinese law adopts comparative negligence principles wherein fault on the plaintiff's part reduces the recovery: "If a victim is also at fault for causing the damage, the civil liability of the infringer may be reduced." The reduction of liability in this manner is a characteristic feature of comparative negligence.

DEFENSES TO LIABILITY

The Civil Law also provides defenses from liability even when there is injury to person or property. Citizens and legal persons are excused from liability when the damage to a party is caused by *force majeure,* which is defined as an unforeseeable, unavoidable and unsurmountable objective condition. The defense of *force majeure* is not available, however, if the law provides otherwise.

Self-defense is considered lawful conduct even though injury may occur. Protecting the public interest and the personal safety of oneself and of others is within the scope of this defense. An individual who causes harm in exercising justifiable defense is not civilly liable. However, if the self-defense is excessive and undue harm results, an "appropriate amount" of civil liability can be assessed. In other words, self-defense that goes beyond the limits of what is necessary becomes unlawful conduct.

The defense of "emergency" also exists. Like self-defense, the avoidance of danger to protect the public interest, personal safety, and other interests in emergency situations is permitted. Damage or injury occurring as a result of attempts to avoid dangerous emergencies will not result in liability under certain circumstances. If the actor has not caused the danger and the actions taken are not improper or excessive, then the actor will not be liable. Nevertheless, if the danger was created by "natural causes" the actor may be potentially liable—in the language of this Law "bear appropriate liability." This provision may be operationally dysfunctional. As a possible consequence of this provision, those individuals confronted with dangerous situations may choose not to act in order to avoid possible liability, and such inaction may actually increase the loss, to the further detriment of society.

The doctrine of sovereign immunity has been limited by the Civil Law and the Administrative Litigation Law, which became effective in late 1990. Liability can be imposed on a state organ or its personnel under certain conditions. If a person, acting in the course of his or her official duties, infringes on the lawful rights of a citizen or legal person and causes damage, recovery of damages against the State is available. Under the Administrative Litigation Law, "after an administrative authority has paid damages, it shall order personnel who intentionally [caused damage] or who were grossly negligent to indemnify part or all of the damages [awarded by the court]." The State is not liable for damages caused by state agency employees acting outside of the scope of their employment.

REMEDIES

The law of who is entitled to tort remedies is generally clear. Nevertheless, it may be complicated in certain instances, especially in the employer-employee context. For example, it is common for a work unit to treat an employee as its "property." The unit has strict administrative control over the employee, and often supplies housing, training, medical care and other subsidies. In a 1989 case, *China Foreign Vessel Tally Co. and Huang Fugen vs. First Marine Service Ltd.,* an employer filed suit as a plaintiff against the tortfeasor. The employee-decedent's personal representative also filed suit. Although the court indicated that the employer could not sue on behalf of the employee-decedent without permission of the personal representative, the court did order the successful personal representative to reimburse the employer for the emergency medical care and other expenditures that were made on the decedent's behalf. The employer's recovery was based on the theory of reimbursement. See Force and Chen, "An Introduction to Personal Injury and Death Claims in the People's Republic of China," 15 *Tulane Maritime Law Journal* 245 (1991).

The case is instructive because it conceptually recognizes the protected interest of the employer for its own distinct economic losses. The decision is consistent with common practice of a tortfeasor paying compensation to an employer for causing the injury or death of one of its employees on the theory that the work unit is injured. However, double recovery for the same loss is not permitted.

To most American lawyers, civil liability generally is synonymous with the payment of monetary damages since it is the most frequently used type of relief. With some exceptions, such as whether mental or emotional distress is monetarily compensable, the rules on damages under the Chinese Civil Law seem to be as extensive as those applied in the United States. The general principle is that there must be actual economic loss to property or person that is reasonably calculable. Emphasis is put on the actual existence of such damage, to the exclusion of any probable or speculative damages.

The general rules contained in the Civil Law provide for restoration of damaged property to its original condition or for the payment of compensatory damages. Although there are no specific references to consequential damages, the language of the law is sufficiently broad to require them. The Law also allows for compensation for other serious injuries. Physical injury requires payment of medical expenses, lost earnings or wages, and contribution to the necessary living expenses of the deceased's dependents when the victim dies. In the event of the victim's death, contributions for maintenance of dependents are assessed in light of the average living standard in the area where the deceased lived.

The law provides remedies other than the payment of compensation. These include, for example, return of property, replacement of property, elimination of danger, and so on. It also provides that in cases involving civil responsibility, if it is necessary "to investigate and affix administrative or criminal responsibility, then this will be done."

In such a case, if the party causing the injury is a juristic person, it is the representative or agent who would be criminally responsible.

Finally, although the Civil Law does recognize for the first time damages for emotional distress, compensation for noneconomic injuries is almost never granted. For example, libel and slander may be crimes, but they are not privately compensable torts unless there is injury to property. Damages based on injury to personal rights are limited to property damages. These principles are consistent with general socialist legal theory.

CHAPTER IX

FOREIGN TRADE, INVESTMENT AND TECHNOLOGY

Under Mao Zedong, China followed trade and investment policies of economic isolation and self-sufficiency. These policies were partly a response to past economic exploitation of the country by foreigners. They also reflected communist ideology and a rejection of the economic tenets of modern capitalism. Since the Cultural Revolution, the People's Republic has opened its doors to world trade and investment as part of its modernization and development strategy. This reversal is most evident in its relations with Hong Kong, Japan and the United States, China's three leading trade partners. Roughly one-third of China's GNP is now involved in import or export trade.

Even after the 1989 resurgence in the power of economic traditionalists, the PRC has continued to be receptive to world trade and investment. In the period following Tiananmen Square, however, once enthusiastic foreign investors became cautious and were constrained by their banks and governments. Recentralization, austerity and contractions in China's economy hurt their existing investments. Most China traders found less to buy and sales more difficult. Defaults by the Chinese under import-export contracts rose. Though the doors remained open, many though not all foreigners hesitated to enter. The Taiwanese, South Koreans and (more deliberately) Japanese have led the return to trading and investing in China. Broadly speaking, this reflects a growing trend, the Asianization of China's international economic relations.

FOREIGN TRADE

Prior to 1972, according to United States' policy, trading with the PRC was treated as trading with the enemy. Trade relations between the U.S. and the PRC began to improve following the signing of the Joint Communiqué (Shanghai Communiqué) by President Richard Nixon and Premier Zhou Enlai on February 28, 1972 in Beijing. The Communiqué focused primarily on a summary of the American and Chinese points of view on global politics (e.g., the war in Vietnam, the situation in Korea, and the status of Taiwan) without attempting to reconcile them. In addition, it suggested the desirability of increasing people-to-people contacts, trade between the PRC and the U.S., and exchanges in "science, technology, culture, sports and journalism." However, the United States continued to enforce numerous restrictions on trade with the People's Republic after 1972. Export controls limited the shipment to the PRC of most American goods. High tariffs (known as "Column Two" or "Smoot–Hawley" tariffs) prevented substantial import of Chinese products into the U.S. Trade relations changed dramatically, however, in 1979 with the resumption of formal diplomatic relations between the U.S. and the PRC and the adoption of the United States–People's Republic of China Agreement on Trade Relations.

Under the 1979 Agreement, the United States granted most-favored-nation tariff status ("Column One" tariffs) to goods of PRC origin. Tariffs on Chinese goods dropped dramatically and American imports quickly rose. The U.S. also removed most of its export controls over nonstrategic trade to China. American export control regulations were amended to create a unique category ("Group P") for the PRC which permitted more exports to China than to many other communist nations. A further loosening of controls occurred in 1983, just before President Reagan visited the PRC, when export trade with China was shifted to "Group V." This shift allowed exports to the PRC on a basis comparable to most other noncommunist nations with which the United States trades. Indeed, the Departments of Commerce and Defense, which principally administer U.S. export controls, even authorized the export of substantial quantities of military products to China. Transfers of strategic technology also expanded. Much of the liberalization in trade, especially that relating to military equipment, can be attributed to the desire of the U.S. government to sway the PRC towards its side in what it saw as a triangular power relationship involving the U.S., China and the former Soviet Union. In June of 1989, however, the Bush administration suspended military cooperation with the PRC in response to events surrounding the 1989 Democracy Movement. Goods on the munitions control list were banned from China trade. These limitations also affected nonmilitary sales, such as Boeing 757s, because any product with a component on the munitions control list could not be sold to the PRC.

Since 1980, Chinese imports and exports have benefited from U.S. Export–Import Bank financial support, although this has been slow in forthcoming after Tiananmen Square. Because the United States and China exchanged diplomatic notes in 1980 on investment guarantees, U.S. Overseas Private Investment Corporation (OPIC) loans, insurance and guarantees have also been extended to China. Should OPIC make payment to any American investor or trader in China, the PRC will recognize OPIC's rights to the claims of that person. There are gaps, however, in China's foreign investment relations. One notable omission is the absence of a bilateral investment treaty with the United States. A breakthrough investment treaty signed with Japan in 1988 may presage the filling of this gap. In sum, but for recent Democracy Movement sanctions, U.S. law as now applied to the PRC much more closely resembles trading and investing with an ally than with an enemy.

Nevertheless, trade and investment disputes between the United States and the People's Republic regularly emerge. For example, private American investors owning property in prerevolutionary China or holding imperial government bonds commenced litigation in the early 1980s against the PRC in the U.S. federal courts. This litigation threatened to undermine the lump-sum claims settlement agreed upon in 1979 by the U.S. and the PRC. That settlement released assets frozen by both governments since 1949 for the purpose of paying claimants; however, the American litigants were disgruntled with their return of only 40 cents on each investment dollar. One default judgment was actually entered against the PRC which has always disclaimed liability for the "odious debts" of prerevolutionary China. The lump-sum claims settlement was eventually upheld by the U.S. federal courts, but not before economic relations were frayed. See *Jackson v. People's Republic of China,* 550 F.Supp. 869 (N.D.Ala.1982), 596 F.Supp. 386 (N.D.Ala.1984) (setting aside default judgment), *aff'd* 794 F.2d 1490 (11th Cir.1986) and *Shanghai Power Co. v. United States,* 4 Cl.Ct. 237 (1983), *aff'd* 765 F.2d 159 (Fed.Cir.1985) (no cause of action for recovery in excess of claims settlement).

In recent years, disagreements have arisen about the volume of Chinese imports of American grain, the export of Chinese textiles and goods produced by prison labor to the U.S., Chinese shipment and purchase of military goods and technology in the Middle East (particularly since the Gulf War), and the possible subsidization and dumping of Chinese goods in the United States. In addition, the United States, after goods shipped through Hong Kong are considered, finds itself with a mounting trade deficit with the PRC (second only to Japan). China ameliorated some of these concerns by signing the Nuclear Nonproliferation Treaty in 1991 and by agreeing to multilateral controls over the shipment of missiles in 1992.

Another divisive trade-related issue involves the application of the "Jackson–Vanik Amendment," part of the 1974 Trade Act, to China's tariff status. See 19 U.S.C. § 2432. This provision requires the President in most cases to annually review the emigration policies of communist nations granted most-favored-nation (MFN) tariff status. Such status can be denied if the communist nation's emigration policies do not pass muster. For example, this happened in 1988 with Romania under President Nicolae Ceausescu, causing U.S. tariffs on its goods to skyrocket. Questions surrounding China's emigration policies, and its general human rights record, were downplayed by U.S. authorities for many years prior to Tiananmen Square. Recent events in Tibet and those in connection with the 1989 Democracy Movement have moved the Jackson–Vanik Amendment to the forefront of Sino–American trade relations. President Bush's renewal of the waiver of Chinese compliance with Jackson–Vanik and the resulting continuation of China's most favored nation status in June of 1990 and 1991 was heavily criticized on human rights, arms control and trade deficit grounds. The breadth of this criticism suggests that Jackson–Vanik has moved beyond a mere examination of emigration questions and has become the political fulcrum of Sino–American trade relations.

Early in 1992, Congress agreed upon a conference committee version of the United States–China Act of 1991. This legislation was initiated in August of 1991 as a rebuke of the President's extension of the PRC's MFN tariff benefits in June of 1991. The conference committee version prohibits the President from further extending China's MFN status unless he reports that the PRC has accounted for citizens criminally detained or accused in connection with the 1989 Democracy Movement and that the PRC has made significant progress in achieving Congressionally specified objectives on human rights, trade and weapons proliferation. President Bush vetoed this legislation in March of 1992. As predicted, the House of Representatives mustered the two-thirds votes needed to override, whereas the Senate did not. The political battle over China's MFN trade status is likely to begin anew in June of 1992 when President Bush is once again expected to renew China's Jackson–Vanik waiver.

In the fall of 1991, the United States Trade Representative (USTR) initiated a prominent investigation into the restrictive trade practices of the People's Republic of China under Section 301 of the Trade Act of 1974. See 19 U.S.C. § 2411. This investigation was undertaken in part to mitigate Congressional frustration over President Bush's continued willingness to grant most-favored-nation tariff status to Chinese goods. The Section 301 investigation focuses upon PRC import quotas, prohibitions and licensing procedures, and PRC technical barriers to trade (e.g., standards, testing and certification requirements). It also challenges the failure to publish PRC laws, regulations, judicial decisions and administrative rulings relating to import restraints. Additional issues concern PRC tariffs ranging up to 200 percent and PRC import taxes. The main thrust of the proceeding is to open up China's markets to U.S. exports. It has caused the United States and the PRC to undertake intensive trade negotiations. In the absence of a negotiated settlement, the United States may unilaterally apply tariffs, quotas and other trade sanctions to Chinese exports to the U.S.

While the Chinese are concerned about their future bilateral trading relations with the U.S., they have also taken steps to integrate their trade law into that of the world community. The PRC has, for example, applied to join the General Agreement on Tariffs and Trade (GATT). This agreement now has over 100 member states and customs territories (including Hong Kong) and is the core of the world trading system. The GATT, for example, is the source of many trade rules on tariffs, quotas and nontariff trade barriers. The GATT is responsible for the levels of tariffs applied to trade in goods among its members. The benchmark GATT level is most-favored-nation (MFN) tariffs. This is applied automatically among the

GATT signatories. Thus, when the United States debates MFN tariffs for China, it is considering a special application of that tariff level because the PRC is not a member in good standing of the GATT.

Prior to Mao's assumption of power in 1949, China was a signatory to the GATT. There is a sense, therefore, that its present application is merely a question of reactivation of its membership. China will have to pay "a price" to join the GATT; it may have to pledge certain import levels and rejuvenate its market reforms. Joining the GATT is an important step in the development of PRC trade law and trade relations. Full participation in world tariff and nontariff trade barrier negotiations will come with GATT membership. It will also likely affect a vast range of PRC laws (as yet unpromulgated) on dumping practices, subsidies and countervailing duties, import injury ("escape clause") proceedings and the like. Similarly, GATT membership will influence the applicability of the laws of many nations trading with the PRC. For example, although the United States presently grants most-favored-nation tariff status to the PRC, it does not give Chinese products the benefit of duty-free entry under its generalized system of tariff preferences (GSP) for selected goods from the developing world. Since the GSP is a result of GATT negotiations, accession by the PRC would probably open up the American GSP program to Chinese goods.

In order to make trading with China more attractive to foreigners and to help facilitate China's entrance into the GATT, the PRC recently began a series of trade reforms. In January 1991, for example, subsidies from the central government compensating foreign trade enterprises for losses suffered from exports were stopped. While the removal of subsidies helps the cash-strapped central government and may convince China's trading partners that it will abide by the free-trade rules associated with the GATT, it has caused economic problems for many of China's trading enterprises. In some instances, provincial governments have begun to subsidize selected businesses in order to meet state export targets.

In addition to pressures from the U.S. and other trading partners regarding its trade practices, there has also been debate within the Chinese leadership on the extent to which the country should remain open to foreign trade and investment. The position of Deng Xiaoping and the Chinese government in the spring of 1992 is to continue to open up to the outside world in order to absorb ideas, money and technology that will help the PRC grow. However, a more conservative minority element within the Chinese leadership advocates greater caution in dealing with foreigners in order to protect the PRC from "spiritual pollution" and possible exploitation.

FOREIGN ECONOMIC CONTRACTS

Contracts between foreign companies and PRC foreign trade enterprises are the source of most Chinese trading. Until recently, there were significant moves away from centralization of Chinese trading through selected national and regional state enterprises. Local officials and local trading companies were given foreign trading authority. Exports and imports grew rapidly. However, this trend has been reversed since 1989 as the central government has reasserted control over China's trade.

The Chinese are shrewd trade negotiators, as many a foreign executive has learned the hard way. They deal from a fundamentally different perspective on time and its value. To them, quite literally, time is not money and they exploit the advantages of delay in negotiations. In addition, the Chinese often deliberately cultivate a sense of friendship and obligation in their negotiating opposites, relationships which can promote guilt or dependence to their advantage. Many a foreign trader has been "shamed" into a contract term it later regrets.

Fundamental cultural clashes about the meaning of a contract can also serve to undermine the significance of concluding a China trade agreement. To many foreigners, the signing of a contract culminates the negotiations—they have a deal. The terms of the deal are to be found strictly within the four corners of the agreement. To many Chinese, the same event merely signals that the two parties have established "a relationship," one which allows either to call upon the other for tolerance, flexibility and favors. Much to the surprise of foreign parties, these calls often run counter to the very heart of their hard-won agreement. They find themselves involved in endless rounds of frustrating negotiations. They get worn down, tired of losing money and skeptical of the wisdom of doing business in China. Some pull out, but many hang on—waiting for that pot of gold that surely must be at the end of their Chinese rainbow.

Many Chinese trading companies have developed standardized international contracts with which they usually commence negotiations and from which they are often unwilling to deviate significantly. Use of standard form contracts provides uniformity of terms, and perhaps more importantly, security for the Chinese negotiators. Deviations from the standard form run the risk of sanctions later on should the deal turn sour. As might be suspected, there are major differences between standard contracts depending on whether China is the seller or purchaser. In purchase contracts, for example, a strict penalty clause applies to foreigners for failing to deliver on time. The Chinese find it commercially advantageous to omit such clauses from their international sales contracts.

The law applicable to international trade contracts is of major concern to both parties. For political reasons, the Chinese always insist that contracts with Hong Kong companies be governed by PRC law. This is consistent with the PRC view that Hong Kong is part of China. Hong Kong firms have, largely for economic reasons, acquiesced in this choice of law. Many other Chinese trade agreements, however, omit any designation of applicable law because neither party wants the other's law to govern. When an American entity is involved, this omission is now generally covered by U.S. and PRC accession to the United Nations Convention on the International Sale of Goods (1980) (CISG). Since 1988, most trade contracts between American and Chinese parties omitting a choice-of-law clause are governed by the CISG. It becomes the law of the contract.

One of the most important developments in PRC international trade law since the Cultural Revolution has been the enactment of the Foreign Economic Contract Law of 1985 (FECL). This law governs procedures for drafting international contracts for goods and services (excluding transport contracts). The FECL allows the parties to choose the substantive law governing their trade contracts, and this choice can be made by mutual agreement after concluding the contract. In the absence of such a choice, the FECL provides that the law of the country "most closely related to the contract" applies.

The FECL permits any choice of controlling language. It also covers the enforceability of foreign economic contracts, including *force majeure.* An exemption from liability for damages flowing from the fact of *force majeure* is created and the contract is not void or terminated. The duty to mitigate damages, the enforceability of liquidated damages, and the right to recover damages in the people's courts for breach or invalidity of a contract are part of the FECL. This emphasis on damages as the primary remedy for breach of foreign economic contracts differs from the focus of domestic contract remedies which stress specific performance. The different contexts and PRC interests at stake in domestic versus foreign economic contracts may explain this dichotomy.

The FECL mandates that foreign economic contracts contradicting the laws or social or public welfare of the PRC are invalid. Although consultation by the parties can remove the effects of any such invalidity before judicial remedies are pursued, this provision is so broad that nearly all Chinese contracts are at risk. The FECL further provides that in the absence of relevant Chinese law and regulations, "international norms" apply to foreign economic contracts. Indeed, when the FECL conflicts with PRC treaty obligations, the latter prevails. This is an especially significant provision because of China's ratification in 1987 of the United Nations Convention on the International Sale of Goods. Although the 1985 FECL and the 1980 CISG are quite similar in many respects, they are not identical. The CISG, for example, favors specific performance remedies in ways that are absent from the FECL. Nevertheless, the FECL's preference for damages does not undermine China's commitment to participation in world trade law since the CISG provisions prevail in the event of a conflict.

The relationship between the Foreign Economic Contract Law of 1985 and the General Principles of Civil Law adopted in 1986 is not especially clear. The Civil Law establishes basic contract law doctrines. However, it gives no indication whether these doctrines prevail in the event of a conflict with the FECL. Perhaps the best interpretation is that the Civil Law was intended to expand upon the FECL, not limit its terms or applicability. Civil Law rules on void and voidable contracts and secured transactions, for example, fill gaps in the FECL. Another important issue, the applicability of the FECL to foreign investment enterprises located in China, is not resolved. Arguably, the FECL does *not* apply to equity or contractual joint ventures and wholly-owned foreign enterprises since the contracts of these entities may be governed by the domestic Law of Economic Contracts of the PRC.

The Supreme People's Court issued a 1987 Notice entitled "Responses to Certain Questions Concerning The Application of The Foreign Economic Contract Law." All lower courts are instructed to follow this Notice in resolving FECL cases. The Notice covers six legal questions: (1) Which contracts are governed by the FECL; (2) What are the applicable conflict of law rules; (3) When may certain foreign economic contracts be voided; (4) When may such contracts be rescinded and cancelled; (5) What are the consequences of the voiding or rescinding of foreign economic contracts; and, (6) What relief is available for breach of contract?

The 1987 Notice supplements the FECL in a number of ways, drawing particularly on the contract principles enunciated in the 1986 Civil Law and the CISG. It was one of the Supreme Court's first attempts at broad judicial control over the "interpretation" of Chinese laws. This interpretation clearly involves judicial lawmaking in areas not covered by the FECL. The Notice clarifies the meaning and considerably expands the scope of the law on foreign economic contracts and it provides an immediate and useful supplement to publication of individual decisions of the Supreme Court.

PREFERENTIAL TRADE AND DEVELOPMENT ZONES

Businesses are treated preferentially in China's Special Economic Zones (SEZs), Economic and Technological Development Zones (ETDZs) and selected "open" coastal cities. In these zones and cities, enterprises are granted preferences and subsidies for employment of workers, taxation, utilities, land use, export permits and such. Four rural SEZs were created in 1979. Fourteen coastal cities the government hopes to industrialize with foreign capital were "opened" in 1984. In addition, thirteen ETDZs were authorized in 1985 and an additional SEZ, Hainan Island, was established in 1987. The most important of these areas is the Shenzhen SEZ in Guangdong Province located directly across the border from Hong Kong. This is where much of the growth and development within China's enterprise zones has taken place. Considerable investment and trading in Shenzhen comes from Hong Kong sources. The Hong Kong dollar is accepted as currency there. More recently, there has been a substantial surge in Taiwanese investment in the Xiamen SEZ in Fujian Province on the mainland just across from Quemoy. Smaller sums are being invested in the Zhuhai SEZ adjacent to Macao and the Shantou SEZ in Guangdong Province. Shenzhen and Zhuhai were set up as multipurpose zones incorporating a variety of economic activities such as industry, commerce, housing, agriculture and tourism. Shantou and Xiamen were to focus on the processing of exports.

Some of the commerce in the SEZs is compensation trade. As applied to the PRC, compensation trade refers principally to a contract whereby a foreigner supplies capital equipment (e.g., textile machinery) which is paid for in installments with goods produced by that equipment. The great advantage of such contracts is their avoidance of foreign exchange and debt problems flowing from China's shortage of hard currency. A variation on the compensation trade theme involves "assembly operations." Here the foreigner supplies component parts (e.g., electronics) processed or assembled in China for a fee. Compensation trade is a growth area in China's economic zones and open cities.

In theory, the PRC's preferential economic zones are to be used principally to attract foreign commerce and to serve as "bridges" for introducing foreign capital and advanced technology into the rest of China. In addition, they are seen as classrooms for training Chinese personnel in management techniques and in the use of advanced technology. Deng Xiaoping has referred to the Shenzhen SEZ as a "bold experiment" which he hoped would succeed but "if it fails, we can draw lessons from it." These words reflect the negative side of Shenzhen and other SEZs as they have become shopping and employment centers for well-connected Chinese. For example, about three-fourths of all Shenzhen SEZ production is sold to Chinese buyers, leading to a net outflow of money from the rest of the country to the SEZ. Thus Shenzhen has mostly succeeded in attracting scarce domestic capital. A fence has actually been constructed to isolate Shenzhen from the rest of Guangdong Province. In 1985, Hainan Island was so consumed with illegal trading of foreign goods and illegal currency exchanges that the Party leadership released details of multimillion dollar scandals involving local officials, including the People's Army and Navy. Crackdowns followed, but the general pattern of opportunistic abuse of the SEZs by those with connections (*guanxi*) continues. In spite of these and other problems with China's preferential zones, in October 1991 the Chinese government reendorsed its support for their continuation.

Investment, licensing and trading in SEZs and ETDZs are subject to zone regulations. An early example was the Shenzhen SEZ Regulations for Foreign Economic Contracts (1984) issued by Guangdong Province. These regulations govern joint ventures, cooperative ventures, compensation trade, and assembly agreements in Shenzhen. The regulations require certain clauses for each type of SEZ contract, including dispute settlement clauses. The Guangdong government has also adopted Importation of Technology, Bankruptcy, and Shareholding Company Regulations for Shenzhen. Regulations of this type have often preceded national laws covering the same subjects. Thus, the SEZs and ETDZs are not only economic experiments, they are also legal experiments. Some of the lessons drawn from such experiments found their way into the Foreign Economic Contract Law of 1985 (FECL). For example, the Shenzhen contract regulations emphasize formalities, whereas the FECL does not. The Shenzhen regulations mandate that the Chinese language version of the contract govern. The FECL leaves that issue to the parties' choice.

The economic and legal futures of Hong Kong and Macao under Chinese rule may be forecasted from China's preferential economic zones. Some persons fear the consequences of the application of PRC law in Hong Kong. In a reversal of what might be feared in Hong Kong, the Guangdong authorities have already announced an intent to incorporate a number of Hong Kong ordinances into the Shenzhen legal regime. These primarily concern economic legislation, but also include civil service rules. In the long run, mergers of Hong Kong and Shenzhen SEZ, and Macao and Zhuhai SEZ, are not inconceivable.

GUANXI TRADING

There is a difference between PRC trade law on the books and in operation. This difference is most evident in the practice known as "trading through the back door." Such practices constitute a return to the venerable *guanxi* system of private "relationships." The *guanxi* system breeds corruption, inefficiency and illegal behavior. Some instructive examples of trading through the back door are given by Walter Keats, writing in *The China Business Review:*

> How does *guanxi* manifest itself today in China trade? It can be seen in high officials who pass the word to favor certain vendors with whom they have a special "relationship." It reveals itself in the way some overseas Chinese agents represent Chinese units that are perfectly capable of dealing with foreign companies on their own—simply because the agent has a "relationship" with one of the Chinese officials. It can be seen in the willingness of officials in Guangdong Province to permit the import of

agricultural material in violation of Chinese quarantine restrictions because of their "relationship" with the vendor or vendor's agent....

Sometimes the price asked in exchange for buying your product or service is sponsoring an official's child to attend college overseas.

* * *

All too often, the abuses are even more blatant. A financial official may delay approval of a contract or letter-of-credit until he or she is invited to join a delegation going overseas. Or a visiting delegation may demand that each of its members receive a percentage of the value of a contract in U.S. dollars. And worst of all for China, certain projects receive approval or foreign exchange allocations based on who knows whom, not the true merits of the project. Jan.—Feb.1988 at p. 30.

Guanxi trading practices, combined with the cumbersome bureaucracy the Chinese have been cultivating for generations, create major problems for trade law. They challenge the very idea of a rule of Chinese law governing trade relations. Much of the progress represented by the FECL and China's accession to the CISG could be undermined if *guanxi,* not law, prevails.

FOREIGN INVESTMENT OPTIONS

The foreign investment climate in the People's Republic of China changed dramatically after the

Cultural Revolution. The country moved from a position of outright hostility and suspicion of foreign investors to open embracement of their capital, talent and technology. If anything, this embracement actually increased after Tiananmen Square in 1989 as the government tried to cut special deals for new investors and attempted to persuade existing firms to return their expatriate staffs to the country. Many such persons, especially from the Beijing area, took refuge in Hong Kong and managed their PRC investments at long distance while awaiting events in China. Slowly and discreetly most have returned.

Since 1989, some new foreign investments and loans have been delayed, cancelled or made prohibitively expensive. Political and economic stability has always been a basic premise upon which most China investment is undertaken. With this premise in doubt after Tiananmen Square, the investment climate was initially perceived by foreigners as risky. Nevertheless, while North American and European investment in China at first declined or plateaued, capital and technology imports from Hong Kong, South Korea, Taiwan, and Singapore (the Four Dragons) increased. Since South Korea and Taiwan are not officially recognized by the PRC, much of this trade and investment is channeled through Hong Kong companies. From China's perspective, the Four Dragons of East Asia represent an increasingly desirable alternative for foreign investment resources, an alternative which brings with it far less criticism of domestic policies.

Time has also brought North Americans, Europeans and Japanese actively back into the Chinese market. Early in 1992, for example, General Motors announced a new joint venture to make pickup trucks in the PRC.

The embracement by the People's Republic of foreign investors is mirrored in the progression of laws, regulations and treaties on foreign direct investment since the Cultural Revolution. For example, State Council regulations adopted in 1986 (known as the "22 Articles"), favor "export" and "technologically advanced" enterprises with reduced land use fees, more independence from the State, the right to hire and fire at will, lower labor and utility costs, and less taxation. Many existing investments have been certified by local authorities as qualifying for such benefits. Indeed, cities and provinces have competed for foreign investment in offering these types of incentives. They also compete among themselves in enacting liberal investment regulations. Guangdong Province and the Shenzhen SEZ adjacent to Hong Kong have attracted the most foreign investment using these techniques. However, in a harbinger of the changing investment climate after Tiananmen Square, Shanghai has issued new regulations which subject foreign enterprises to more government controls over price, transport, labor, supplies and sales. The main thrust of these regulations is to remove the preferential treatment once accorded foreign investment and subject it to "equal treatment" with domestic enterprises.

China has created three basic foreign direct investment options. These are equity joint ventures, contractual joint ventures and wholly-owned subsidiaries. Each investment option is discussed below along with its governing law and implementing regulations.

EQUITY JOINT VENTURES

The first major step taken by the Chinese to open their economy to foreign investors was the passage of joint venture legislation in 1979. The Law on Joint Ventures Using Chinese and Foreign Investment (JVL) allows joint ventures, known as "equity joint ventures," to be established between foreign corporations and Chinese enterprises. The JVL is accompanied by its own income tax law and a number of implementing regulations. Equity joint ventures must be approved by the Ministry of Foreign Economic Relations and Trade (MOFERT). Prior to 1988, MOFERT increasingly delegated this power to local government organizations. Such delegation was part of the general trend toward decentralization of economic controls in China, a trend recently reversed as the government's central planners attempt to get a stronger grip on foreign investment decisions.

The most distinguishing features of Chinese law on equity joint ventures are as follows:

- 10 to 30–year terms
- profit and risk sharing proportionate to share capital

• limited access to sales in the Chinese market

• arbitration of labor disputes

• nonnegotiable shareholdings

• regulated debt-equity ratios

• flexibility in terms of types of capital contributions (technology included)—25 percent foreign capital minimum

• priority to Chinese sources of materials

• foreign currency account must be balanced, including remission of profits

• foreigners could not (prior to 1990) serve as chairs of boards of directors

• 33 percent maximum tax rate

Amendments to the Joint Ventures Law were adopted in 1990 which reduced the differences between it and the Contractual Joint Ventures Law. No "nationalization" may take place. But any "requisition ... when the public interest requires" is subject to a duty to pay "appropriate compensation." One suspects that the difference between "nationalization" and "requisition" may be lost on foreign partners to PRC joint ventures. Foreigners may now serve as chairs of the board of directors. Joint ventures may run beyond their original term with special permission, and may bank at any approved foreign exchange institution.

Equity joint ventures, as the oldest form of foreign investment in the PRC, have the longest track record. Partly because of the early adoption of the

JVL and the legal security it created, equity joint ventures have become the most popular Chinese investment vehicle of multinational corporations. Thousands of well known firms have agreed to equity ventures in the PRC. Thus one can find the label "Made in The People's Republic of China" on such diverse products as Camel cigarettes, Nike shoes, Kodak film, Otis elevators, Jeep trucks, Xerox copiers, Singer sewing machines and Heinz baby foods.

Within the limits of the JVL and its implementing regulations, and taking into consideration the model contracts the Chinese have developed, the terms of these joint ventures are negotiable. The regulated nature of joint venture investments in China often requires that local government representatives be brought into the negotiations. Although various central investment authorities will be involved, local officials typically hold important keys to approval of the venture, and most critically, its successful operation in the future. They will, for example, heavily influence such variables as taxation, labor supply, utilities, land use permits and the like. The equity joint venture bargain thus determines much of its future viability. But, as many foreign investors have discovered, reaching agreement is just the beginning of an equity venture in the PRC. The Chinese often perceive that the agreement merely provides a framework within which negotiations are ongoing. Foreign investors tend to be less flexible and are more likely to want to stick to the terms of the deal and accompanying government representations. These differing perspectives frequently produce disputes.

In addition, the PRC is simply a difficult place to invest. The abruptness of the change in China's investment outlook and laws since the Cultural Revolution has left some uneven edges. Governmental interference with joint ventures is common, quality control problems endemic, the necessary infrastructure, managerial talent, skilled labor and hard currency absent, and so on. Repatriating profits (if there are any) is an art form. A severe government credit squeeze in 1988 and 1989, combined with rising inflation and corruption, was particularly painful to many joint ventures. Government insistence since 1989 upon adding a Communist Party member responsible for Party organization and loyalty to the management team at joint ventures has increased the discomfort level of foreign investors. When these general "environmental" difficulties are combined with differing contract perspectives, it is not surprising that serious disruptions can occur.

One of the most publicized disruptions was that of the American Motors Corporation (now owned by Chrysler) "model" equity joint venture in Beijing. It is representative of the problems encountered by many other investors in the People's Republic of China. This excerpt appeared in a 1986 edition of the *Shanghai World Economic Herald:*

> The original contract called for the Chinese and American sides to jointly design a new jeep

using only Chinese components. However, according to the *Beijing Review,* 'after several months of work by Chinese and American engineers ... it was found that the vehicle designed was defective in such areas as its exhaust system, noise, visibility, and speed, none of which could match international standards.... AMC suggested that the idea of joint design be postponed.... The Chinese, however, took AMC's suggestions as a symbol of the Americans' unwillingness to cooperate on a jointly designed vehicle and ... of AMC's desire to control China's market.' Ultimately, the Chinese agreed to build AMC's XJ model series, including the Cherokee jeep, using imported components—but clearly in a suspicion-marred environment that foreshadowed the more serious troubles that arose later.

* * *

In mid–1985 the Beijing International Trust and Investment Corporation—an arm of the Beijing city government—reportedly loaned the venture $8.5 million to buy equipment for a new Cherokee jeep assembly line and to import kits. At that time, AMC chipped in an additional $6 million for the assembly line. But recent indications are that the loan was made under the assumption that the vehicles could be sold to end-users in China for foreign exchange. Since December 1985, these end-users have proven unwilling or unable to buy the vehicles with foreign exchange—chiefly because foreign exchange allocations to enterprises have been slashed across the board, but perhaps also because a 60 percent duty on imported parts makes the Beijing price considerably higher than the North American price. During the first part of 1986, local authorities were unwilling to renew foreign exchange allocations or loans to the venture, since the venture's expected foreign exchange earnings were not forthcoming.

This forced a major showdown in which AMC allowed its grievances to leak into American newspapers and, according to numerous reports, threatened to pull out of the venture. The gesture aroused enough high-level concern in China to guarantee the venture renewed foreign exchange for kit purchases, at least for the time being. According to Chinese press reports, the central government has offered $2 million for jeeps already assembled, in addition to an unspecified amount for further kit imports. But the venture's Cherokee jeep production will almost certainly fall well short of the earlier 4,000 unit target.

* * *

The Chinese argue that AMC should also take some responsibility for maintaining the venture's foreign exchange flow. And a number of foreign observers point out that AMC's initial cash contribution—$8 million—was very small in relation to its goal of building an export-quality jeep in China. The corporation has apparently agreed to increase equipment supplies to the joint venture as part of the settlement of the foreign exchange dispute. Reproduced in *The China Business Review* (July–August 1986).

Despite these obstacles, foreign firms continue to invest in the PRC in record numbers. Surprisingly, many of these investments (even after Tiananmen) are *not* covered by political risk insurance against expropriation, civil unrest and other such contingencies. United States' investors, for example, have channeled billions into uninsured Chinese equity joint ventures. This response may have more to do with evaluations of China's market potential than its investment laws. Nevertheless, the sustained, substantial effort on the part of PRC lawmakers to improve the legal environment within which equity joint ventures function is impressive.

WHOLLY-OWNED SUBSIDIARIES

Joint ventures with foreign investors are often found in developing countries like the PRC. Such joint ventures were reasonably common in Eastern Europe before the Iron Curtain came down, and were permitted in the former Soviet Union. There is a sense therefore in which China's 1979 equity joint venture law was merely catching up to world trends. The 1986 law allowing wholly foreign-owned enterprises (WFOEs) is another matter. With this law, China leaped ahead of other socialist countries and many developing nations as well. WFOEs are indicative of just how open and embracing the country can be to foreign investment.

Beginning in 1980, wholly-owned enterprises were allowed in a few preferential economic zones, such as the Shenzhen near Hong Kong. Most WFOEs are still small companies established in Shenzhen by Hong Kong Chinese. Success with this experiment led, in 1983, to the designation of a number of coastal cities where wholly foreign-owned enterprises could be established. The first wholly-owned enterprise outside a SEZ was that of 3M in Shanghai. For 3M in China, the need to balance foreign exchange receipts, uncertainty over applicable tax law, and labor relations proved troublesome. From the Chinese perspective, however, the march forward was not to be denied. In 1986, a general law was passed permitting WFOEs *anywhere* in the PRC. By 1990, however, only about 1,500 such enterprises had been approved.

The Law on Wholly Foreign–Owned Enterprises and its implementing regulations (particularly those issued in 1990) create the most restrictive of all of the PRC's foreign investment rules. These rules reflect caution and concern about total foreign ownership of enterprises located in China. The main legal features of the law on WFOEs are as follows:

- foreigners may serve as chairs of boards of directors

• mandatory use of advanced technology and equipment *or* exportation of nearly all products

• protection of investment, profits and other rights "under Chinese law"

• expropriation in "special circumstances," with "commensurate compensation"

• "for the record" submission of production and operational plans to the government—noninterference is to be the rule

• Chinese tax and financial supervision, 50 percent maximum tax

• Chinese insurance required

• priority to local sourcing if terms are competitive with international market

• foreign exchange account must be balanced

• mandatory trade union facilities

• general supervision by approving authorities

To some extent, the restrictive terms of Chinese law on WFOEs have deterred multinational foreign investors. In general, however, their preference for equity joint ventures is primarily based upon a desire to have a Chinese partner to escort them through the bureaucratic and political maze that foreign investors encounter. If the investment climate in China improves and investor satisfaction increases, the historic decision to allow wholly foreign-owned enterprises may yet bring the substantial payoff in capital, technology and export earnings its creators envisioned.

CONTRACTUAL JOINT VENTURES

Hong Kong, overseas Chinese and other foreign investors have often preferred "contractual joint ventures." Historically, this has been a less regulated form of doing business in China. Thousands of such enterprises (many of them hotel investments) have been established since the Cultural Revolution. Because there are no equity shares, contractual joint ventures resemble partnership agreements. Prior to 1988 a principal attraction of such agreements was the *absence* of a basic law governing them. Even after the adoption in 1988 of a contractual joint venture law, flexibility is still their chief attraction.

The 1988 Law on Chinese–Foreign Contractual Joint Ventures (CJV), and its implementing regulations, were promulgated after years of experience with cooperative enterprise agreements. Viewed together with the 1986 General Principles of Civil Law, the most notable features of the law on CJVs are as follows:

- any split of profits may be chosen
- limited liability is available to CJVs qualifying as legal persons under the Civil Law
- protection of the rights and interests of the CJV and its parties "according to the law"
- noninterference with operational and managerial decisions
- trade unions required

• balance in foreign exchange receipts required, subject to state assistance

• no minimum percentage of foreign capital

• foreigners may serve as chairs of boards of directors

• no limit on duration of contractual agreement

Contractual joint ventures are the principal form of small business investment in the PRC. Until 1986, they easily outnumbered equity joint ventures. The scheduled return of sovereignty over Hong Kong and Macao by the end of the century has caused Chinese investors from those cities to want to be on friendly terms with the mainland. The most common means for such investments is the CJV.

TECHNOLOGY TRANSFERS

Major changes have been undertaken in the licensing and intellectual property law of the People's Republic of China since the Cultural Revolution. These changes reflect China's desire to create a modern economy by importing technology and by fostering its development. According to a July 1987 report issued by central authorities in Beijing, the importation of technology augments China's modernization program in four ways: (1) by decreasing the gap on product quality and standards between China and the developed world; (2) by helping to promote the technological upgrading of Chinese enterprises; (3) by enhancing the ability of Chinese enterprises to independently develop their own new products and technology; and (4) by improving enterprise management.

China's desire to modernize its economy through technological imports is most evident in PRC patent and licensing law. A host of technology import regulations authorizing license agreements with foreign sources has been enacted. These regulations are not a blank check permitting technology importation at any cost. Rather, they are carefully constructed rules intended to promote technology transfers to China under acceptable terms and conditions.

Despite the adoption of major PRC patent, trademark, copyright and technology transfer laws and their implementing regulations, a dark shadow hangs over much of Chinese intellectual property practice. Counterfeiting of goods and unlicensed use of technology is approaching epidemic proportions. Computer software is perhaps the most recently prominent victim. The official remedies discussed below, however diligently applied, seem inadequate to the task of dealing with this problem. Partly, one suspects, there are cultural forces at work. To copy another's work is traditionally a compliment in China. Partly also, the economics of development fuel piracy in the PRC. It is simply much less expensive to "borrow" from foreigners and (increasingly) domestic entities whatever can be reverse-engineered and imitated. Even

"Beijing Jeeps" are reportedly being knocked off by a large number of township enterprises. There are no quick solutions to an environment that is fundamentally hostile to intellectual property. In this area, Chinese law will take a long time to mature.

As in many developing countries, there is a fear in China of paying excessive royalties for potentially redundant, outdated or inappropriate technology under oppressive contract terms. Likewise, there is a fear of standardized licensing contracts created by attorneys of foreign licensors. The principal objective of China's technology import regulations is to insure that such contracts do not contain restrictive clauses and to increase the bargaining power of Chinese licensees. Although pure licensing agreements are reasonably common, many technology transfers take place in the context of equity or contractual joint venture investments.

The 1985 Regulations for the Administration of Technology Import Contracts and 1988 implementing provisions (Regulations), are the most important example of China's modern approach to licensing agreements. Similar regulations exist in some of China's economic development zones and coastal cities, notably Shenzhen, Xiamen and Guangzhou (Canton), which compete for technology transfers. The Regulations govern patent, trademark, know-how and technical service contracts with foreigners. They also apply to technology transfers in connection with foreign investment. Once the parties have reached agreement, all such contracts must be examined and approved by government authorities before implementation. Since 1988, in a welcome reform, any technology transfer contract not disapproved within 60 days of filing is deemed approved. Most Chinese licensing agreements are essentially installment sales. This is achieved by limiting the licensing agreement to a maximum of 10 years followed by the absence of restraints on the licensee's use of the technology after expiration of the agreement. The result is truly a technology transfer.

The Regulations stipulate that the imported technology must be "advanced," "appropriate" and "necessary" to modernization of China's industrial base. To this end, a feasibility study (which can be conducted by foreign experts) precedes the contract. The licensing agreement must contain certain terms, such as a guarantee by the supplier that the technology is "complete, free of error, effective and can achieve the objectives stipulated in the contract." This is an important representation and probably the most common source of lawsuits and arbitrations initiated by the Chinese in the technology transfer area.

Certain terms cannot appear in the agreement. These include restraints on the Chinese recipient's ability to choose the sources of relevant raw materials, spare parts or equipment. Such restraints are generally called "tying arrangements." However, the Chinese licensee can choose to take such supplies from the foreign licensor. In that case, the supplies must be offered at competitive international prices, itemized in the contract and are subject to special approvals. The Regulations also prohibit contract terms that are harmful to the public interest, that violate China's sovereignty, or that are unclear, unequal or unreasonable. In general, these regulations are designed to promote economic modernization in China while protecting it from foreign exploitation.

In other areas, either by law or practice, greater flexibility has been shown. For example, there is no legally stipulated maximum royalty payment. Royalties of 2 to 5 percent of net sales value have been routinely approved. Higher royalties get close scrutiny by the examining authorities. Given China's shortage of foreign exchange, barter and countertrade are often substituted for cash royalties. The Regulations prohibit unreasonable restraints upon the Chinese recipient's domestic or export sales. Nevertheless, as a matter of practice, contract terms which effectively eliminate sales competition with the foreign licensor's products have often been permitted.

Once approved and executed, PRC technology transfer contracts are subject to ongoing regulatory approvals. The contract will often stipulate that certification of the delivery of the technology and its integration into the existing Chinese facility is required before payment to the licensor is allowed. This can get complicated because most technology importation is done by central or regional trading companies, not the end user. These trading companies often lack sufficient knowledge of the application of the technology by a factory hundreds or thousands of miles from their offices. Yet they are the ones who typically must make the necessary certifications.

The level of Chinese sophistication about licensing agreements is increasing. They have developed model patent and knowhow licensing contracts with which they frequently initiate negotiations. In their negotiations, and in the administration of their technology transfer law, the Chinese have so far successfully walked a fine line between providing sufficient incentives to bring foreign licensors into a bargain and discouraging them altogether.

PATENTS

For many years the PRC followed standard socialist practice in connection with inventions. Patents were not available. Instead, Chinese inventors were given awards of money, certificates of meritorious service, housing benefits or other privileges by the State. Although many other contributing factors could be cited, these incentives were insufficient to produce a bounty of inventions in Maoist China. In contrast, since inventors' rights were formally recognized in the 1986 Civil Law, China has exported a small amount of technology under its new patent regime.

China is trying to promote internal technological development and foreign licensing by granting patents. The 1984 Patent Law, which coexists with the traditional domestic awards system, is administered by the Chinese Patent Bureau. When the Law became effective in 1985, many patent applications were filed with roughly one-third of the initial filings by foreigners. The issuance of Chinese patents has been painstakingly slow as the authorities cautiously create their patent system. Nevertheless, by 1990, over 50,000 patents had been granted with more than 90 percent of them to Chinese applicants.

The Patent Law allows inventions, utility models and exterior designs to be patented. Inventions and utility models must be new, original and practical. The newness of an invention is measured against world-wide publication or other prior knowledge. To be original, the invention must have substantial distinguishing features constituting a marked improvement over the prior art. The practicality of an invention is tested by its manufacture or other utilization to "produce positive results." Exclusive rights to exploit patented inventions are granted for 15 years.

Chinese enterprises generally own the patents on the inventions of their employees. The employee may benefit from a right to increased compensation. However, individual Chinese citizens may obtain patents for their "spare-time" inventions, which in fact have accounted for the large majority of PRC domestic patent applications. In the end, all patents become the people's property upon expiration of their 15 year terms. Moreover, the Chinese want patent holders to help them modernize and develop their country. To avoid the possibility of foreign patent owners "sitting on" their inventions, compulsory licensing with "appropriate compensatory fees" is authorized after three years of nonuse. Domestically held patents of "great significance" are subject to compulsory licensing at any time.

The 1984 Patent Law provides that certain items cannot be patented. These most notably include pharmaceuticals, purely scientific discoveries, food flavorings and products, chemicals (e.g., pesticides), nuclear and atomic energy discoveries, disease treating methods, and animal and plant species. However, process patents are available in some of these categories, including chemical, microbiological and pharmaceutical processes. "Integrally related" computer software is apparently patentable. The adoption of a patent system is symbolic of China's commitment to technological advancement. For the most part, the PRC's patent law is similar to that found in developed nations. There are, however, some distinctive features which reflect developing world perspectives. The ban on pharmaceutical patents, for example, is a common third-world viewpoint. The health of its people should not be subject to a legal monopoly. Another example is the general authorization of compulsory licensing. China's patents are to be applied to its needs and thereby contribute to the development of the country.

TRADEMARKS

Until relatively recently, many products of the People's Republic bore no trademarks. As China's economy has become increasingly subject to market forces, the utility of trademarks as indicators of source and quality, as well as marketing vehicles, has been recognized. Hence, trademarks are now commonly found on a wide range of domestic and imported products.

China's first trademark regulations were adopted as early as 1950, and were substantially expanded in 1963. A revised Trademark Law was passed in 1982 and detailed implementing rules were issued in 1983 and 1988. China's 1982 Trademark Law, like the 1984 Patent Law, is mostly in the mainstream of world law. Except for a few socialist features, and the failure to cover service marks, and the "first to file" rule, it could be transplanted to many other nations. The Chinese Trademark Office now receives hundreds of thousands of domestic and foreign trademark applications annually. In 1989, China acceded to the Madrid Convention on the International Registration of Trademarks.

The 1982 Trademark Law establishes exclusive rights for trademark registrants on a "first to file" rather than the more common "first to use" basis. The first to file approach tolerates trademark speculation, but is tempered for foreigners by China's accession to the Paris Convention on Intellectual Property. The Convention provides for a six months grace period (measured from the date of home country filings) during which foreign trademark applicants obtain priority over other applicants for the same mark. In addition, the 1988 implementing rules allow anyone to apply for cancellation of "improperly registered" marks. Under the Paris Convention, this could provide holders of trademarks that are well known or "famous" in the PRC with a remedy against speculative registration of their marks by others. For these purposes, a mark's reputation in Hong Kong may be used to prove that it is well known in China.

The 1982 law indicates that trademarks are words and figures that "impel producers to guarantee the quality of goods." Trademark rights are derived solely through the registration process. To be registered, a trademark must have easily distinguishable characteristics. Trademarks employing common symbols or the names of goods cannot ordinarily be registered. However, because China has joined the Paris Convention, "famous" trademarks may be registered. For example, VITASOY combines the generic terms vitamin and soybean. Its registration was initially rejected but allowed on appeal as a "famous" mark.

Trademarks descriptive of the quality, raw materials, functions, uses, weight, quantity or other characteristics of goods cannot be registered. Registration of SHARP for knives was denied on this basis. Trademarks that contain exaggerated claims, and deceptive marks, will be rejected. State names, flags, and emblems cannot be registered. In addition, racially discriminatory trademarks and those that "harm socialist morality or have other bad influence" are unregisterable. It is unclear how the latter criteria is applied. Trademark holders and licensors are responsible for controlling the quality of goods bearing their marks. Quality control failures can result in cancellation by the government of a trademark registration. Such registrations are granted for ten years, and are routinely renewed.

The PRC's commitment to principled enforcement of its trademark law is evident. Dai Yifei of the China Trademark Agency has illustrated an opposition proceeding in which foreign and domestic trademark interests were at stake:

> Let me take the trademark of DONALD DUCK first, which is a world famous design mark owned by the Walt Disney Company of the United States. In June 1986, . . . the trademark CHU BAO & DEVICE applied by No. 2 Plastic Factory of Hanyang County in Hubei Province, China was published. The duck holding a plate in the trademark of CHU BAO & DEVICE looked very similar to DONALD DUCK. Our Agency received, in the last but one day of the deadline, the instruction for an opposition. . . . However, we had two major difficulties: One was

that the company only had the registration in the PRC of its word mark DONALD DUCK, the other was that even the registered word mark DONALD DUCK was not registered in the category of the goods which was used by the opposed trademark. First of all, we made an analysis concerning the review standards adopted internationally, that is to say, when making the judgment whether these two trademarks were identical or similar, it was necessary to make a comparison of their connotation ... besides their appearances and pronunciation. So far as the connotation was concerned, it was no doubt that the trademark DONALD DUCK equals DONALD DUCK design. Furthermore, we cited the clauses in the Paris Convention, of which the PRC has been the member since 1985, regarding the protection of famous trademarks.... For example, if someone applied for registration for the trademark COCA–COLA in the PRC covering goods which are not registered by The Coca–Cola Company, then that sort of application would certainly not be granted.... Through all our efforts, the opposition was a success with the result that the applicant had amended its design part of the trademark. Reproduced in R. Folsom and J. Minan, (eds.), *Law in the People's Republic of China: Commentary, Readings and Materials* (1989) at p. 790.

As this example indicates, China's government does not officially encourage trademark piracy as a means of economic development. Changes in the definition of infringement found in the 1988 Trademark Rules specifically permit remedies against almost any activity injuring the exclusive trademark rights of another person. Nevertheless, trademark piracy frequently occurs in the People's Republic. Indeed, late in 1989, the State Council issued a circular ordering all ministries and local governments to crack down on counterfeiting of goods and unauthorized use of trademarks.

Infringement remedies under China's Trademark Law include criminal prosecutions against passing-off, private actions for damages or lost profits, and administrative sanctions. The latter is most commonly pursued, often at the instigation of foreigners who wish to avoid the stigma of litigation, and can be reasonably effective. Zhao Xiuying has illustrated the use of administrative remedies in several case studies, including the following PEPSI–COLA example:

> A world famous soft-drink PEPSI–COLA of Pepsico Inc. bearing the trademark PEPSICO Three–Field Device is now very popular in China. Under these circumstances, several soft-drinks bearing trademarks very much similar to the PEPSICO Three–Field Device appeared in several provinces during the recent two years. Pepsico entrusted us to handle these cases and sent us labels used on the infringing products. The infringing trademarks not only closely imitated the shape but also the color of the PEPSICO Three–Field Device. We sent warning letters to

> the infringing factories as ususal. Up to now, a case that happened in Sichuan Province has been successfully concluded. Another case that occurred in Hainan Province ended not very satisfactorily because the label is still bearing some resemblance to the PEPSICO Three–Field Device after amendment by the infringer. Therefore we are still negotiating with the infringer. For other Pepsico cases, we are doing our utmost to strive for a complete stop of infringement. Id. at pp. 805–806.

Trademark authorities can order the removal of offending logos, cancellation of registrations, payment of administrative fines and injunctive relief. These important state remedies were recently and rapidly applied to Shenzhen infringers of IBM trademarks. An administrative remedy not expressly permitted in the Trademark Law is seizure of the infringing goods. Since trademark violations are said to be sweeping China (over 60,000 violations were officially reported between 1983 and 1986), amendment or liberal interpretation of the Trademark Law to allow this result is needed.

COPYRIGHTS

Copyright law was the last area of intellectual property to undergo major reform after the Cultural Revolution. Party and government concerns over the control of information and communications delayed progress. Traditionally, authored works have been the property of the State, which pays stipulated fees for writings. It was not until 1986 that the Civil Law recognized the right of authorship of citizens and legal persons. The Civil Law also provides for authors' rights to sign, publish and be paid for their works "in accordance with law." Civil copyright infringement actions for compensatory and injunctive relief are authorized. Plagiarism is specifically cited in the Civil Law as an example of copyright infringement.

China's Copyright Law was finally adopted late in 1990, with an effective date of June 1, 1991. Its promulgation did not coincide with PRC accession to the Berne or Universal Copyright Conventions, although either may follow. This means at present that works by foreigners first published outside the PRC cannot be copyrighted. Most foreign copyrighted materials will fall into this category. A range of creative works are covered under the Copyright Law: literature, music, drama, choreography, art, films, engineering and product designs, and maps. Notably absent are works of applied art, databases and directories, sculpture and architectural designs. Most Chinese copyrights are valid for the life of the author plus 50 years and include (in perpetuity) the "moral right" to protect the integrity of the work. Compulsory licensing may occur with commercial performances, musical works and radio and television broadcasts.

The Copyright Law adopted in 1990 appears more political than earlier drafts. It specifies that the Law is to encourage works "beneficial to socialist spiritual civilization" and to promote "the development and prosperity of socialist culture." Furthermore, no copyrights may be exercised in violation of the PRC Constitution, laws or public interest. This provision is remarkably open-ended and threatens the credibility of the entire law.

The 1990 Copyright Law does not offer much hope for piracy victims. Indeed, it allows free use of copyrighted works for personal study, research and "enjoyment." The free translation of copyrighted foreign works, such as college coursebooks, for teaching and research purposes is also permitted. The draft law originally excluded computer software from copyright protection. Given the rather high level of software piracy in the PRC, this constituted a major omission. However, a 1989 Memorandum of Understanding between the U.S. and China undertaken to avoid American trade law sanctions promised inclusion of software. The new law and its implementing regulations fulfill this promise, but whether effective protection of software in the PRC will actually emerge remains to be seen. One concern is that the PRC authorizes royalty free reproductions of software for noncommercial purposes such as classroom teaching, scientific research and carrying out the official duties of state agencies.

The United States Trade Representative is skeptical of the PRC's commitment to intellectual property rights. In 1991 she commenced a special investigation into the adequacy of China's computer software and other intellectual property regulations. This was done under the "Special 301" provisions of the Trade Act of 1974 as amended in 1988. See 19 U.S.C. § 2422. Absent satisfaction through negotiations, the U.S. threatened massive retaliatory trade sanctions blocking Chinese exports to America. Early in 1992, a last minute agreement was reached on significant reform of China's copyright, patent and trade secret laws. In the copyright area, China has agreed to join the Berne Convention and the Geneva Convention on Phonograms, to extend protection to existing as well as new works, and to treat computer programs as literary works protected for 50 years. Accession to the Berne Convention will remove the barrier to Chinese copyright protection of works by most foreigners, including U.S. citizens, first published outside the PRC. Regarding patents, China has promised full protection for pharmaceuticals and agricultural chemicals with a 20-year patent term. It has also promised a substantial waiver of the risk of compulsory licensing for all U.S. holders of Chinese patents, including a ban on such licensing if the U.S. holder does not manufacture the product in the PRC. This promise does not appear to apply to European or Japanese owners of Chinese patents. Trade secrets will be protected by legislation against unauthorized use or disclosure, including that by third parties.

The People's Republic of China has now covered all of the major fields in intellectual property law. The task in the next decade will be refinement and application of these new legal regimes.

CHAPTER X

HONG KONG

From the Chinese perspective, the People's Republic is not a whole nation. Three critical areas are missing: Hong Kong, Macao and Taiwan. Only after these missing parts are reunited with the People's Republic will China be whole again.

Hong Kong was acquired from the Manchus by Great Britain during the nineteenth century. The island of Hong Kong was ceded in perpetuity after the Opium War of 1839–42. Kowloon on the mainland and Stonecutter's Island were acquired in perpetuity under the 1860 Convention of Peking. In 1898, the Manchus leased to Great Britain the "New Territories" for ninety-nine years. This lease covers approximately 350 square miles, numerous islands and a large body of sea. It encompasses 92 percent of the area of modern Hong Kong. China has always considered these acquisitions the product of "unequal treaties" obtained during periods of weakness. From the Chinese perspective, they were forced to submit to these losses of territory in order to further British trading interests.

Over the years, China (including the PRC) settled into a reasonably comfortable acceptance of the benefits of Hong Kong under British rule as a trading center linking it to the West in many profitable ways. For example, the PRC presently earns large sums of hard currency through Hong Kong for its exports. Hong Kong also has served as an important center for training mainland Chinese in marketplace skills—banking, commercial transactions, shipping, and the like. And it is through Hong Kong that large quantities of foreign investment capital and technology have entered the PRC, particularly coastal and southern China, since 1976. The Hong Kong business community has financed or operated industries located in the PRC now employing over two million people. At the same time, however, Hong Kong has increasingly exported the values and ideology of capitalism to the PRC. This "spiritual pollution" worries China's orthodox leadership, and there is ample evidence of its fallout in adjacent Guangdong province.

A colonial atmosphere has surrounded the Hong Kong legal system. Trials and judicial appeals are for the most part conducted in English with Cantonese translators. Many of the solicitors and barristers teaching or practicing law and sitting on the bench in Hong Kong have been expatriates from Britain, New Zealand, Canada and Australia. Limited deference has been given to customary Chinese law and significant numbers of ethnic Chinese in the legal profession are a recent phenomenon. Translation of Hong Kong's statutes into Chinese has just recently been undertaken, but will eventually result in equally authentic English and Chinese texts.

Macao is a Portuguese overseas territory located on a mainland peninsula of the PRC slightly west of Hong Kong. It also includes two adjacent islands in the South China Sea. During a period of weakness, China ceded Macao in perpetuity by treaty to Portugal in 1887 after decades of open Portuguese claims of sovereignty. Unsuccessful attempts were made periodically by Holland and Britain to capture Macao. Modern Macao has about 500,000 inhabitants; the vast majority are ethnic Chinese. Following installation of a left-wing government in Portugal in 1974, the Portuguese offered to return Macao to the PRC. The Chinese refused to negotiate any change in status for Macao at that time. However, after establishment of formal diplomatic ties between the PRC and Portugal in 1979, it was agreed that Macao was Chinese territory under temporary Portuguese administration and that it would be returned to the PRC at an appropriate time.

The Governor of Macao is appointed by Portugal and its Legislative Assembly consists of seventeen members, six of whom are directly elected. The remaining legislators are either appointed by the governor or selected by local economic interest groups. Municipal affairs are handled by the *Leal Senado* (Loyal Senate). Macao is perhaps best known for its gambling casinos. Like Hong Kong, but on a much smaller scale, Macao services considerable trade with the PRC.

THE RETURN OF CHINESE SOVEREIGNTY

The prospect of the New Territories' lease terminating in 1997 led Britain and the People's Republic of China to begin negotiations on the future of Hong Kong. British Prime Minister Margaret Thatcher and the Chinese leader Deng Xiaoping met in September of 1982 for this purpose. Formal negotiations continued through twenty-two rounds with the government of Hong Kong participating as a member of the British delegation. The goal of both sides in these negotiations was to create a system that would maintain the stability and prosperity of Hong Kong. On December 19, 1984 British Prime Minister Thatcher and Chinese Premier Zhao Ziyang formally signed the Sino–British Joint Declaration on the Question of Hong Kong. It was ratified by both sides in 1985. The Declaration covers Hong Kong Island, Kowloon, Stonecutter's Island as well as the New Territories. It envisions the return of sovereignty over *all* of these areas (including those ceded in perpetuity) to the People's Republic on July 1, 1997. The more than five million inhabitants of Hong Kong in 1984, many of them refugees from the mainland, had no material input into the terms of the Declaration. They were presented with a *fait accompli.*

Under the Sino–British Declaration, Hong Kong will be a "special administrative region" of the PRC "with a high degree of autonomy." While the degree of the autonomy planned for Hong Kong is much debated, it will clearly be more than that enjoyed by the various autonomous regions of the People's Republic. Indeed, the Chinese are taking great pains to avoid analogies to the terms and operational realities of Tibet's "autonomy." Hong Kong will be the PRC's first attempt at its "one country, two systems" policy. This policy is premised upon the idea that the communist political and economic system of the PRC can coexist with a democratic and capitalistic system in Hong Kong. The policy is ultimately targeted at Taiwan. In March of 1987, the "one country, two systems" policy was extended to Macao when Portugal agreed to return control over it to the PRC on December 20, 1999. Except for special arrangements concerning the rights of ethnic Chinese who are also Portuguese citizens (dual nationals), Macao will become a special administrative region under conditions substantially the same as those for Hong Kong. Mismanagement of the reversion of Hong Kong and Macao to the PRC will complicate immensely any hope of reunifying Taiwan with the mainland.

The Declaration reached in 1984 between China and Britain on the return of Hong Kong promised significant autonomy for the Hong Kong Special Administrative Region (HKSAR). Most importantly, it provided a list of "policies" that the PRC agreed to incorporate into a "Basic Law" for the HKSAR and to maintain for fifty years after 1997. These policies provide that the HKSAR will have "independent" executive, legislative and judicial power. How this independence is to be achieved is less certain. The legislature is to be elected, although the exact method and degree of such elections were not specified in the 1984 Declaration. The legislature is to have the power to create HKSAR law, but foreign affairs and defense matters are reserved to the central people's government (the PRC). The chief executive is to be appointed by Beijing first on the basis of local consultations, and later by elections. This executive will appoint the principal officials in the HKSAR government. The 1984 Declaration specifies that the HKSAR courts are to be independent and possess a power of final adjudication, but their relationship to Chinese legal institutions is unclear in the Declaration. Furthermore, the PRC's policy that "the laws currently in force in Hong Kong will remain basically unchanged" for fifty years after 1997 is proclaimed.

Visitors to Hong Kong immediately sense its love of capitalism and freedom. The 1984 Declaration specifies that the law of the Hong Kong Region is to insure individual rights and freedoms concerning speech, press, assembly, association, travel, movement, academic research, private property, ownership of enterprises, inheritance and foreign investment. The Chinese declared that the Region will be able to issue its own travel documents for entry into and exit from Hong Kong and its free port and separate customs territorial status will be preserved. It is PRC policy that the Hong Kong dollar will remain a freely convertible currency and that the HKSAR will develop its own international trade and cultural relations under the name "Hong Kong, China." The Chinese declared, rather remarkably, that the central people's government will not levy taxes against the HKSAR. The Region is to have its own system of taxation. In addition, Annex I to the Declaration provides that the "socialist system" and "socialist policies" of the PRC will not be practiced in the Region for fifty years after 1997. Hong Kong's "capitalist system and lifestyle" are to be preserved during the 50–year period.

The Chinese declared that all of these policies would be "stipulated" in the Basic Law of the HKSAR. The 1984 Declaration anticipated that the PRC would create this law. In other words, Hong Kong's future became critically dependent upon a quasi-constitutional document essentially drafted in Beijing. Thus, China's first opportunity to make good on its Declaration with Britain and make believers out of the residents of Hong Kong was the drafting of this law.

THE BASIC LAW AND THE FUTURE OF HONG KONG

The Basic Law Drafting Committee was appointed by and hence responsible to the National People's Congress of the PRC rather than any Hong Kong or British body. Of its fifty-nine members, thirty-six were from China and twenty-three from Hong Kong, the latter mostly representing big business and groups sympathetic to Beijing. Many of the uncertainties contained in the 1984 Declaration surrounding the governance of the HKSAR became even more pronounced as the Basic Law moved through its draft stages to final adoption in 1990 by the National People's Congress. The first draft of the Basic Law for the Hong Kong Special Administrative Region was released by the PRC for review and comment in the Spring of 1988. This draft posed many difficult legal issues. For example, the supremacy of the Basic Law in the event of conflicts with the PRC Constitution was unclear. The power to interpret the Basic Law seemed to be unevenly split between the NPC Standing Committee and the HKSAR courts. The independence of the HKSAR judiciary was in doubt and the civil liberties of the people were less than concretely established.

The review and comment period generated considerable dialogue between Britain and China, in Hong Kong and throughout the world community. China evidenced some, but not great, flexibility on the major issues provoked by its draft Basic Law for the HKSAR. One major issue was the promise of elections to Hong Kong's Legislative Council. Democratic governance has never been a strong part of British rule over Hong Kong. Traditionally, the Governor of Hong Kong (who is appointed by the Crown) appoints many members of the Hong Kong legislature. The remaining members are either civil service officials, or elected by functional constituencies (e.g., professional and business bodies) or electoral colleges. The Governor appoints Hong Kong's judges and executive officers. The Governor's staff drafts Hong Kong's laws and its budget. The legislature obligingly approves most (if not virtually all) submissions of the Governor. In addition, much of Hong Kong's government is conducted in secrecy. Professor Peter Wesley–Smith provocatively describes the colonial constitution of Hong Kong as entailing "the four nots:" no self-government, no democracy, no representative legislature and no government responsible to an elected legislature. See P. Wesley–Smith and A. Chen (eds.), *The Basic Law and Hong Kong's Future,* Chapter 1 (1989). Nevertheless, there presently is a substantial degree of benign liberty in Hong Kong—the freedom from oppression by government.

In 1984, the British government made general representations that direct elections were expected for 1988 in Hong Kong. These representations were made in order to secure ratification of the Joint Declaration by the British Parliament. By 1986, however, the PRC had declared that direct elections in 1988 were not in order and the British acquiesced to this position. The draft Basic Law released for comment in 1988 provided that only one-fourth of the legislators would be elected directly. Needless to say, the local populace was concerned that China should more fully honor its commitment to an elected legislature. The revised draft of the Basic Law adopted by the Standing Committee of the National People's Congress in 1989 increased the number of elected representatives to one-half by the third term of the operation of the HKSAR legislature. The revised 1989 draft also indicated that the "ultimate aim" is the selection of all Legislative Council members through general election.

The final 1990 text of the Basic Law provides for one-third of the HKSAR legislators to be elected directly in its first term of operation (1995–1999). Initially, one-sixth of the membership of the Legislative Council will be selected by a "grand electoral college," the composition of which is left vague. By the third term, this method will be eliminated in favor of one-half direct elections and one-half functional constituency representatives. In a move aimed at the growing acquisition of foreign passports by Hong Kong residents, the final text of the Basic Law limits the number of HKSAR legislators with a "right of abode" (residency) abroad to 20 percent. Similarly, neither the chief executive, the chief justice nor any of the principal executive officers of the HKSAR may have a right of abode abroad. Many perceive that these rules will simply add to the exodus from Hong Kong and diminish the talent available for governance after 1997.

The first elections to the Legislative Council of Hong Kong (under British rule) were held in September of 1991. Only half of the people eligible to vote registered to vote, and of these only 39 percent actually went to the polls. Eighteen of the sixty Legislative Council seats were at stake. Fifteen went to the group most openly critical of the PRC, the United Democrats and their allies. Three independents were also elected, while none of the candidates backed by the PRC were chosen.

Arguably, the autonomy of the HKSAR will actually be better protected by the legal safeguards under the Basic Law than at present under British rule. However, the reality of the future governance of the HKSAR legitimately creates great concern. When the PRC appoints the chief executive of the HKSAR in 1997, this person will largely succeed to the British Governor's broad powers with relatively few (though more than at present) checks and balances. It seems unlikely that the HKSAR legislature as initially constituted, even with its impeachment power and a very circumscribed ability to override the chief executive's rejection of legislation, will serve as an effective counterweight to the chief executive appointed by Beijing. Whether more democratic governance through a fully elected legislature, and an elected chief executive, will emerge in the HKSAR is an open question. Equally uncertain is the viability of the Basic Law's provision for individual lawsuits against executive branch actions, a right just recently secured for PRC citizens under its law. The crushing of the Democracy Movement in 1989 and the intimidation of people on the mainland makes it hard to be optimistic on these questions.

Another controversial issue during the drafting period of the Basic Law was the power of the British between 1984 and 1997 to alter the "laws *currently* (emphasis added) in force." These are the laws that the PRC in the 1984 Declaration pledged to maintain "basically unchanged" for fifty years after 1997. This was a transitional question with long-term implications. For example, controls over the media were increased in Hong Kong under a 1986 criminal law. This law can be construed to require publishers of "false" news to prove their own innocence. Censorship of books and films under this law reportedly increased when PRC sensibilities were offended. Assuming this 1986 law is in force in 1997, it will be part of the legal legacy of Hong Kong because the final text of the Basic Law indicates that the law of Hong Kong in 1997 (not 1984) is that which must "remain basically unchanged." This commits the PRC to all legal changes implemented by the British between 1984 and 1997 and explains Chinese sensitivity to current Hong Kong legal developments.

The Basic Law specifies which types of Hong Kong law will be maintained after the return of sovereignty. These include the "common law, rules of equity, ordinances, subordinate legislation and customary law." However, these laws are to be maintained only if they are consistent with the

Basic Law and are not subsequently amended by the HKSAR legislature. The Standing Committee of the National People's Congress will draw up a list of all invalid existing Hong Kong laws in 1997.

The most controversial legal development facing the PRC and the British is the Hong Kong "Bill of Rights Ordinance" adopted in 1991 in reaction to the massacre at Tiananmen Square and the continued repression of the 1989 Democracy Movement. Great effort has been spent on convincing the PRC that this Bill of Rights Ordinance does not create a law superior to or inconsistent with the Basic Law such that it might be invalidated in 1997 by the Standing Committee of the NPC. The British have also emphasized that the Bill of Rights Ordinance can be amended or repealed in the future by the HKSAR legislature, although this arguably might be a breach of the 1984 Declaration and the Basic Law.

The Bill of Rights Ordinance was enacted both in English and Chinese, and applies only to actions of the Hong Kong government, public authorities or their agents. It relies heavily on the International Covenant on Civil and Political Rights. This Covenant, although not adopted by the PRC, is specifically referenced in the final text of the Basic Law as part of the legal heritage of Hong Kong that will be continued for fifty years. It seeks to preserve the following individual rights: life, liberty, security, free movement, equality before courts, fair and public hearings, free thought, conscience and religion, free expression, peaceful assembly and association, a ban on torture and slavery as well as protection of minority rights. All preexisting Hong Kong legislation must now be construed by the Hong Kong courts in a manner consistent with the Bill of Rights Ordinance. If this is not possible, the legislation is invalidated to the extent of the inconsistency. This has already happened in several instances as the Hong Kong judiciary proceeds to develop a body of Bill of Rights case law. Many Hong Kong residents hope that this jurisprudence will be well entrenched before 1997.

The Basic Law allocates control over Hong Kong's defense, foreign and emergency security affairs to the PRC. In the period since Tiananmen Square, the Chinese, the British and all of Hong Kong have focused on the possibility of a declaration of emergency powers or martial law in the HKSAR. By amendment added in late 1989, the Basic Law vests the power to declare a HKSAR state of emergency in the Standing Committee of the National People's Congress when "turmoil" beyond local control within the Region "endangers national unification or national security." In such an emergency, the central people's government (PRC) can decree the applicability of relevant Chinese laws to the HKSAR. The Basic Law further provides for the replacement of British troops with PRC military forces. These forces are not supposed to "interfere with the local affairs of the Region." However, the HKSAR government may request their assistance in maintaining public order. The specter of PRC troops in the streets of Hong Kong after 1997 is frightening its people. Martial law, Chinese style, is the ultimate disaster scenario.

A broad economic and civil autonomy for the HKSAR is contained in the Basic Law. However, the HKSAR legislature can only adopt laws consistent with the Basic Law. All HKSAR legislation must be reported to the Standing Committee of the National People's Congress. No doubt all of this legislation will be reviewed by that body, but the Standing Committee's veto powers over HKSAR legislation are limited by the Basic Law. The Standing Committee has a veto power over any act not consistent with the Basic Law concerning affairs which are the responsibility of the central people's government (PRC) or which affect the relationship between it and Hong Kong. Similarly, through a mandatory referral procedure from HKSAR courts, the Standing Committee is empowered to decide in limited cases questions of the consistency with the Basic Law of prior and subsequent Hong Kong laws. This litigation review power only covers issues of defense, foreign affairs, security emergencies and other central government responsibilities under the Basic Law as well as relationships between the Region and central authorities.

The Standing Committee's legislative veto and litigation review powers do not apply if the law in question falls within the autonomy of the HKSAR as delineated in the Basic Law. In other words, the Standing Committee may act only within the sphere of authority granted to the central people's government (PRC) by the Basic Law. However, it appears that the Standing Committee gets to decide the jurisdictional limits of its powers such as what constitutes HKSAR security emergencies, foreign affairs or defense.

The involvement of the Standing Committee of the NPC in the legislative and judicial processes of the HKSAR amounts to a mortgaging of fifty years of Hong Kong's legal future to an institution not known for refined, balanced reviews of complex legal questions. However, the Basic Law (by way of instruction to the Standing Committee) conveys the final power of judicial interpretation over issues falling within the autonomy of the HKSAR to the Region's Court of Final Appeal. This new five-judge court will replace the Privy Council in 1997 as Hong Kong's ultimate judicial forum. Since the economic and civil autonomy contained in the Basic Law is broad and subject to exclusive HKSAR control (absent a triggering of the Standing Committee's limited review powers), this is an important judicial power. The central government's control in this respect will theoretically be limited to indirect influence over judicial appointments made by the chief executive.

In September of 1991, Britain and China decided that only one judge on the Court of Final Appeal will be a "foreigner". Many in Hong Kong had expected that at least two judges would be "foreigners" in order to insure independent judicial power. Presently, the vast majority of Hong Kong judges sitting on its highest courts are expatriates. The Hong Kong Legislative Council, with its newly elected members, was so angry with this result that it overwhelmingly adopted a motion asking both governments for reconsideration of their decision. This is not likely to occur. It is hoped, of course, that nothing resembling Party review of judicial decisions will be transplanted from the PRC to Hong Kong. Thus, considerable burden and hope for a meaningful reality to the principles of economic and civil autonomy is likely to fall upon the judiciary of the HKSAR.

An overwhelming sense of insecurity exists in Hong Kong today. Its robust economy has suffered. The real estate and stock markets have been particularly hard hit. Money from the PRC is pouring into Hong Kong to insure that the bottom does not fall out of its economy. Several major banks have been rescued in this way and minority PRC shareholdings have been acquired in Cathay Pacific Airways and Hong Kong Telecommunications, two companies that are prominent locally. Beijing is also said to secretly control the Federation of Trade Unions, an umbrella labor group. In order to make up for private sector unemployment and maintain stability, the Hong Kong government is prepared to spend on massive public infrastructure projects through 1997. Such projects include, after difficult negotiations with the PRC, a new airport. In these negotiations, the PRC basically obtained British assurances that public expenditures will not be excessive and that substantial budgetary funds will be available to the HKSAR government in 1997.

Beijing has also begun to more openly increase its involvement in Hong Kong's affairs. Since 1985, the Hong Kong branch of *Xinhua*, the New China News Agency, has set up ten departments to monitor and coordinate with different sectors in Hong Kong. These include administration, research, propaganda, foreign affairs, economics, culture, education, arts, sports and social affairs. It is through the increased activities of *Xinhua*, an informal but official agent of the PRC, that Beijing has established a virtual shadow government. This increases Beijing's control apparatus in preparation for the return of Hong Kong in 1997.

The British Parliament has adopted the Nationality (Hong Kong) Act of 1990. It gives the option of British citizenship to approximately 2,500,000 Hong Kong subjects, including a right of entry into the United Kingdom. This right of entry had been previously denied. In a sign of things to come, the PRC has publicly rejected the Act and announced its intention to refuse to honor passports issued under it. The PRC Nationality Act of 1981 treats nearly all persons of Chinese descent as PRC citizens. One exception is for those Chinese who have established "genuine links" with other nations, such as by "permanent" settlement there. Furthermore, the PRC has limited (through the Basic Law) the opportunity for people who remain in Hong Kong but hold a right of abode (residency) in a foreign country to occupy key civil service, judiciary, Legislative Council and Executive Council positions in the HKSAR. In the face of all this, wealthier Hong Kong persons are establishing residency elsewhere in the world, especially Vancouver. Their sons and daughters are often sent overseas for education. A brain drain is painfully in progress and people and capital are generally in exodus, although this seems more true for the Chinese and British than the Japanese and Americans located in Hong Kong. Some 62,000 persons emigrated in 1990.

Hong Kong's lawyers, who have witnessed the mortgaging of the future of HKSAR law, are part of the exodus. Many of the territory's solicitors and barristers intend to leave. For example, a recent Hong Kong Bar Association President who is an ethnic Chinese plans to exit. He nevertheless hopes for significant increases in the number of Chinese law graduates to replace the departures of attorneys and judges. His greatest fear is that PRC-trained people's lawyers will be called upon to fill the gap created by the exodus. A second law school has been established in Hong Kong to increase the number of attorneys and "localization" has led to appointments of Chinese judges, prosecutors and government attorneys. Such efforts are dwarfed, however, by the continuing erosion of confidence in Hong Kong's future. This erosion has been greatly accelerated by the suppression of China's 1989 Democracy Movement and the renewal of the Party's dictatorial leadership. Hong Kong lawyers wonder whether to believe any of the protections and promises contained in the Basic Law of the HKSAR.

Many people of Hong Kong do not have the option of leaving. They must accept the realities of 1997. Their greatest assurances of a future consonant with the 1984 Joint Declaration and the 1990 Basic Law may be the desire of the PRC to regain sovereignty over Taiwan and to continue to receive a steady stream of bounty from Hong Kong. For all the people of Hong Kong and Macao, the credibility of the Chinese legal system is not an academic question. It is something upon which their future and the lives of their children will turn.

*

INDEX

References are to Pages

†